"The problem of Māori underachievement is endemic because we allow it, falsely label it, blame the culture and students, and believe it is intractable. Russell Bishop shows that we already know how to truly improve the learning lives of Māori (and thence all other students), such that their culture is not left at the gate. His anger, insights, and hope imbue this book, from the 3 case schools, the model of learning and instruction, and his lifetime evidence of the major impacts of his program. He shows that it only takes 2 years for every school in NZ to truly make a difference IF we want to and commit to Bishop's fundamental premises and ideas. It can be done, it has been done, it should be done."
Emeritus Professor John Hattie
University of Melbourne.

"Russell Bishop takes readers on a realistic journey into the intriguing world of educational leadership that explains the twists and turns, and ultimate rewards derived from culturally responsive practice. This latest navigation toward a north-east destination reiterates the pivotal place of Te Ao Māori ..."
Angus Macfarlane
Professor, Te Rū Rangahau/Māori Research Lab, University of Canterbury

"Implementation of evidence-based pedagogy with fidelity, underpinned by quality teacher-learner relationships, is a winning formula. Russell Bishop has combined decades of research into a compelling rationale for leaders to follow, to unlock the potential of every student. Developing quality relationships with learners, using evidence-based pedagogy, in-class coaching and formative assessment practices are the keys to success. He has provided a clear, evidence-based rationale for school leaders to follow that creates success in learning for Māori and success in learning for all students. The most compelling reason to follow his research is that it works."
Dr. Cherie Taylor-Patel
National President New Zealand Principals' Federation | Ngā Tumuaki o Aotearoa

"Any educational scholars writing on culturally responsive relationship-based pedagogy, especially across the Pacific, are indebted to Russell Bishop for his conceptual and theoretical work. If you are seeking ways to support schools to be faithful to their students' wellbeing and learning through ensuring teacher's fidelity of practice, you will find this work a treasure trove. This book should be a staple for every teacher education program."

Lester-Irabinna Rigney
Professor of Education, University of South Australia

"In *Leading to the North-East*, Russell Bishop provides educators with a clear pathway for schools to become more successful in delivering better outcomes for all students, by focusing on what he knows to have delivered for Māori students in Aotearoa. Through concrete case studies of schools with whom Bishop and his colleagues have worked for many years, this book offers educational leaders insights into the daily work needed to make schooling valuable for everyone. The path we are invited to join is one leading to an education in which academic success does not come at the cost of marginalising a culture that does not fit the colonial dictates of schooling. On the contrary, Bishop shows us that by establishing secure, culturally respectful pedagogical relationships in the face-to-face daily interactions between teachers and students, schools who support that work with fidelity can succeed where so many before have failed. This work is of major significance for educators globally, especially in the many lands still struggling to move beyond our colonial past."

Assoc Prof James G Ladwig
The University of Newcastle, Australia

Leading to the North-East:

Ensuring the fidelity of relationship-based learning

Leading to the North-East:
Ensuring the fidelity of relationship-based learning

Russell Bishop

NZCER PRESS

NZCER PRESS
Te Pakokori
Level 4, 10 Brandon St,
Wellington

www.nzcer.org.nz

© Russell Bishop, 2023

ISBN 978-1-99-004088-7

No part of the publication may be copied, stored, or communicated in any
form by any means (paper or digital), including recording or storing in an
electronic retrieval system, without the written permission of the publisher.
Education institutions that hold a current licence with Copyright
Licensing New Zealand may copy from this book in strict accordance with
the terms of the CLNZ Licence.

A catalogue record for this book is available from the National Library of
New Zealand.

Designed by Smartwork Creative

Dedication

This book is dedicated to my wife Rowan,
our children, Mathew, James, Stephanie and Sam,
and their children, our mokopuna, who, after all,
are why we do this work.

Oscar, Stella, Senan, Ayden, Ruby, Finn, and
Florence.

Contents

Acknowledgements	xi
Preface	xvii

Chapter 1 Teaching and Leading to the North-East? — **1**
- Introduction — 1
- We found four major problems that were limiting our improving learning outcomes — 3
- The impact of the lack of a means of ensuring implementation fidelity within schools — 5
- North-East schools show the way forward — 6
- This picture shows a further problem — 10
- Expanding the model further: Leading to the North-East — 11
- The need for institutional support — 13
- How do North-East leaders ensure a North-East pedagogy and its support systems are embedded in their schools? — 15

Chapter 2 What caused the literacy crisis? — **18**
- Introduction — 18
- The problem of implementation fidelity — 19
- Summary: Addressing the lottery effect — 42

Chapter 3 GPILSEO: A model for reform — **47**
- Introduction — 47
- Solutions: The need for schools to become responsive North-East learning institutions — 48
- A model for school transformation into North-East learning institutions — 50
- Using GPILSEO for quality assurance purposes — 58

Chapter 4 Goal-setting and commencing the transformation into a North-East school — **61**
- Introduction — 61
- 1. The first part of a goal-setting exercise is to identify the current pattern of relationships and interactions in the school — 63
- 2. What do North-East goals look like? A SMART analysis — 70
- 3. The need for objectives and a strategic plan — 77
- 4. Goal setting also requires of school principals that they lead the de-cluttering of their school — 78
- Summary: The main purposes of goal setting — 79

Chapter 5 Pedagogy: The North-East Leaders of Learning Profile — **82**
- Introduction — 82
- The North-East Leaders of Learning Profile — 83
- Summary — 105

Chapter 6 The need for support systems — **107**
- Introduction — 107
- Infrastructure and leadership — 108

The teaching process used in North-East schools	115
The role of outside experts	128
Conclusion	133

Chapter 7 Spread and evidence — **135**

Introduction	135
Evidence	142
The need for effective data management systems	143

Chapter 8 Ownership — **145**

Evidence that the school is taking ownership	146
What does it mean to take ownership of a reform process?	149

Chapter 9 Introduction to the case studies and Case Study 1: Sylvia Park School — **152**

The leaders' achievements can be seen in terms of the GPILSEO model	153
An advance organiser to guide your reading	155
Case Study 1 Sylvia Park School	156
Pedagogy	161
Leadership	165
Spread: Including all staff and parents in the learning process	167
Evidence	172
Ownership	175

Chapter 10 Te Kura Tuatahi o Papaioea – Central Normal School — **178**

Introduction	178
Achievement patterns	179
The need for goal setting	182
Pedagogy	183
Infrastructure	187
Summary	195

Chapter 11 Kerikeri High School — **197**

Introduction	197
Achievement patterns	198
Goal setting	203
Pedagogy: Introducing the discursive classroom	204
Summary	223

Chapter 12 The benefits of North-East schools — **224**

Introduction	225
The benefits of North-East schools	226
The messages from this book	235
So, all things considered, what is a North-East leader?	238

References — **241**

Index — **244**

Acknowledgements

Once again I am indebted to all those students, their families, community leaders, teachers, school leaders, and principals who have taken part in my research work over the past 30 years. I am sure they will forgive me if I don't mention them all by name, but as you can imagine, there are actually thousands of people to whom I owe a debt of gratitude. I am grateful for their insights and understandings of what makes North-East schools work. I can't say "thanks" enough because it is their example that is going to inspire others to follow in their footsteps to improve the lives of our children.

Deserving of my gratitude are all the people who worked in the Te Kotahitanga project from 2003 to 2013. Special mention goes to Mere Berryman, who put in many long hours working with me to develop and implement the project. Mere became Director in 2012 when I retired from that position. We were ably supported by our kaumātua kuia Rangiwhakaehu Walker and Mate Reweti and koroua, Morehu Ngatoko and Koroneihana Cooper, the research team and the professional developers—a great bunch of people. All of these people made a significant contribution to making that project the success it was.

I would like to acknowledge a number of people who have read an earlier iteration of this book. Their comments were very useful in galvanising me to produce a far better version of my thoughts about leadership.

I sent a rough copy of my draft to Nina Hood of the Education Hub because I have long been an admirer of her ability to "see the wood for the trees". Her feedback on my first draft enabled me to align the text with my own approach to teaching and learning as set out in this book. I am very grateful for her time and attention to the detail in my book as I am always impressed by her work in the Education Hub.

John Hattie read the draft and said that by the end of the first two chapters he was depressed. I took this to heart. I did not want to be responsible for turning one of our best educational researchers into a depressed wreck. So if you think this book is depressing now, you should have seen it before John gave me his take on it. It is a far more hopeful document now. I am also grateful for his meta-analyses that are so useful to those of us seeking out what makes a difference for our children's learning.

Michael Fullan gave me the benefit of his long-term experience and musings in a way that enabled me to internationalise the book somewhat. He did so by alerting me to the common issues we face in our deliberations about what makes a difference for those students currently marginalised from the benefits that education has to offer.

Cherie Taylor-Patel also read the draft text and wrote me an enthusiastic endorsement. I have always enjoyed my collegial interactions with Cherie and I am looking forward to working with her and her organisation again in the future. I spoke at their conference in 2022 and I am grateful for the feedback I received following my presentation. Engaging in this form of dialogic interaction with colleagues of her standing has meant that what this book contains is that much better.

Michele Morrison, the kaiwhakahaere of the New Zealand Educational Leadership Conference held in Hamilton in 2022, read the final draft of the book. I am very grateful to her for her insightful comments and her supporting my final "sign-off" of the manuscript. Michele is an expert in leadership theory and practice, having been a deputy principal of a large secondary school and latterly a senior lecturer in Leadership Studies at Waikato University. I am extremely grateful to Michele and all those other conference organisers who provided me with opportunities to try out the ideas in this book prior to publication.

I am also grateful to my friend and neighbour Yvonne Godfrey who talked me into pulling out some of the main messages in the text to highlight them. A great idea from a great speaker and author. Yvonne has also been a wonderful helper when I have been lost in the detail and needed someone to help me see "the wood for the trees".

I am always grateful to Bruce Wilson for his long-term friendship and assistance to me throughout the years, from when we first started teaching together in Porirua to his support and mentoring me in my later efforts to become a credible academic.

Like Sesame Street, I want to thank the words tikanga, rangatira, whānau, kaupapa, tautoko, koha, and akoako among others because they made it possible for this book to be understood in terms of some of the key concepts in te reo Māori. It makes more sense in Māori somehow because these generic concepts have been tried and proven over generations. Many is the time someone has asked me to explain what a concept means in English and it has proven to be clearer in te reo Māori.

I am very grateful to the three principals who gave me their time, energy, and support for my attempts to relay their stories to others. The three are Barbara Ala'alatoa, past principal, Sylvia Park Primary School; Regan Orr, principal, Te Kura Tuatahi o Papaioea – Central Normal School, Palmerston North; and my long-term colleague and friend, Elizabeth Forgie, past principal, Kerikeri High School. These leaders are shining lights in our attempts to identify how to get your school to the North-East and keep it there!

I am grateful to David Ellis of NZCER Press for his encouragement and support over the many years I have been publishing books with him and NZCER. He has always been very professional in the support he has provided for my work.

I had never set out to make this book accessible for an international audience. I had always meant it to be for New Zealanders because we have an opportunity to create another "world first" in our country. We have been world leaders in many social endeavours in the past. North-East school principals can lead the next revolution that will put New Zealand on the world map again because the issues addressed in this book are at crisis point in many other countries as well.

I am also grateful to my fellow author, Dominic O'Sullivan, for the first iteration of the GPILSEO model as it appeared in the Ngā Pae o Te Māramatanga publication, *Effective Leadership for Educational Reform.* The second iteration of the model appeared in *Scaling Up: Addressing the Politics of Disparity,* published by NZCER Press, where the model was developed further. I am grateful to Dominic for continuing with the project and to Mere Berryman who joined us for this later iteration. In this book, I have developed the model further and have applied it as a means of explaining how North-East leaders can support their staff to become North-East leaders and teachers.

There were two large reports on the state of literacy in New Zealand that were essential for me to complete this book. Stuart McNaughton provided an excellent overview of the literacy conditions here in his 2020 report on the state of literacy learning in New Zealand. His experience and clarity of expression led me to understand the need for implementation fidelity as a solution we can all easily access. And of course, I drew on the 2022 review by Taylor Hughson and Nina Hood and I have loads of respect for their calling it for what it is—a crisis.

James Ladwig was a collaborator in Te Kotahitanga. He took the large sets of data we had accumulated and made sense of them for us. The resulting patterns allowed me to reflect upon the impact of the project and refine the model into Teaching and Leading to the North-East.

Alison Arrow helped me to confirm that you really can't conflate Māori learning experiences with those of non-Māori.

Dr Jennie Watts pointed me in the direction of Te Kura o Papaioea. Thanks for that Jennie.

My friend and colleague Laurayne Tafa introduced me to her friend and Sylvia Park School principal, Barbara Ala'alatoa. Many thanks for this my friend. I have also been greatly enriched by meeting and working with these great educational leaders. I met Elizabeth Forgie and her late husband, Alan, over 20 years ago. I stand in admiration of their outstanding leadership and dedication to the people of Northland. Nō reira, moe mai ra e te Rangatira. We miss Alan, but know that his great work will continue to impact positively on the lives of young people for many years to come.

I wish to acknowledge my colleagues at Cognition Education who have the unenviable task of turning my theories and suggestions into practical PLD programmes for schools. This is no easy task as I well know and I am very grateful to past PLD leaders, Mary Sinclair, Shaun Hawthorne, and latterly Jenna Crowley, for leading their team's implementation of 'Relationships First' with fidelity. Lindsey Connor provided me with very useful feedback on this book. Arran Hamilton asked me to read two of his books prior to publication. This latter activity was very productive for my own theorising about what is needed in North-East schools. Lastly, I wish to acknowledge Mary Sinclair and Terry Bates, two outstanding New Zealand educators whose foresight and perseverance has kept me on the pathway to the North-East. Mihi ana ki a koutou.

I will always acknowledge the many people I have worked with in the New Zealand Ministry of Education. They provided me with funding and support for research and development projects, including the highly successful Te Kotahitanga. We developed this project as an iterative, Hegelian dialectic. I know, I know. This means that we had an original idea (a thesis), and as we ran into problems (an antithesis) we had to revise what we were doing and develop a new solution (a synthesis). In this way, we made progress that saw Māori students' achievement grow in ways not seen before. I will always be grateful for their support and wonder what our schools would have been like if we had been able to continue to develop Te Kotahitanga in this manner. In many ways, Teaching and Leading to the North-East is the further development of the basic ideas that underpin Te Kotahitanga, the notion that relationships are fundamental to all we do in education. And of course, I am always grateful to my family members who taught me this lesson all those years ago.

I am very grateful to all those people whose ideas I have used and perhaps not acknowledged. All I can say is that I wanted this book to be readily accessible to school leaders and I didn't want it to be full of references. My aim in writing this book was to support our children becoming successful learners by supporting their teachers and their leaders in turn. So someone had to miss out and my apologies if you see something you have said or written and I have not acknowledged you.

Lastly, I wish to acknowledge my primary editor, my wife, Rowan. Like Ted Glynn, who was one of the supervisors of my PhD and co-authored my second book, she gave me a bag of full stops for Christmas to make my sentences shorter. Not only that though, she spent hours poring over my attempts to have my ideas make sense to readers. Rowan has made a very valuable contribution to this book and if you think it makes sense, then much of the thanks for this needs to go to her.

I realise that this acknowledgement section is very long, but that just goes to show how many people it takes to develop such a project. Or of course, it could also just be that I am getting old and therefore know lots of people.

Preface

I had always intended following up my earlier book, *Teaching to the North-East* (Bishop, 2019), with a book about the support North-East teachers needed from their schools' leaders so that they could sustain their North-East teaching practices. For one reason or another, I had managed to put off the starting date, but I was galvanised into action when I was asked to address the New Zealand Literacy Association's annual conference in 2020. Not being that well versed in the current state of literacy in New Zealand at that time, I went to the literature on the area and reviewed a number of recently published research reports into the state of literacy learning in New Zealand.[1]

What I found was shocking. Despite their having been at school for over 10 years, 35% of 15-year-olds in New Zealand schools struggle with the basic functions of literacy and numeracy. In other words, despite the best efforts of our education system, only 65% of our primary and secondary students have a basic proficiency in reading, writing, and maths. Further, this situation has been getting worse since about 2009. It was made worse by the pandemic, but the trend was well in place over a decade ago.

What really upset me was that, once again, young Māori people are over-represented in this negative figure to an alarming extent. Yet, literacy skills and knowledge are crucial for young Māori people being able to take part in te ao Māori, New Zealand society, and in the wider world. The downstream effects on themselves and their families of not being able to take part in these settings are egregious and catastrophic, and unless there is something done about it, this situation will impact upon them for their lifetimes.

I was intrigued to find out what had caused this problem because, although I am in no way an expert on literacy, it seemed to me that, in

---

1   I focused on reports by the Education Hub (Hughson & Hood, 2022), The Office of the Chief Scientific Advisor to the Prime Minister (McNaughton, 2020), and Lifting Literacy Aotearoa from their website. I also investigated the Massey Early Literacy Project (Chapman et al., 2018) and the Better Start Literacy project from Canterbury University (Gillon et al., 2019).

many ways, literacy is actually an indicator of the wider field of educational disparities in New Zealand that I have been working on for decades. By this I mean that it is indicative of what is happening in the wider schooling scene—what is happening in literacy is happening in most other curriculum areas as well.

Teaching to the North-East

In contrast, in what I have come to call North-East schools, Māori and other marginalised students don't experience the common pattern of educational disparities in New Zealand schools. This is where marginalisation from the benefits of education is based upon students' membership of ethnic, religious, or other such groups. Māori and other students who are currently marginalised from the benefits of education are culturally safe in North-East schools. In these schools, they learn with North-East teachers, who are supported by North-East leaders to successfully improve their learning within a whanau context.

Marginalised students include the children of refugees, migrants, faith-based groups, gendered groups, and students now being referred to as the neurodiverse. Although the lived experience of Māori students is often markedly different from these other students—often referred to as children of "diversity"—they do have something in common: they are marginalised educationally by what they bring to learning settings being seen as deficiencies rather than these qualities being seen as positive attributes that can be built upon to promote their learning.

North-East teachers enable all previously marginalised students to become successful learners because they are supported by their leaders to put the theory that relationships are fundamental to learning into practice. In *Teaching to the North-East* (Bishop, 2019), I identified how the theory of relationships being fundamental to teachers being able to do their job as teachers developed out of my own experiences as a teacher in Porirua, and my later doctoral study into how researchers could undertake research with Māori people (Bishop, 1995).

The extrapolation of this theory into classrooms was later tested in classroom settings in the large-scale education reform programme known as Te Kotahitanga, which ran in some 50 New Zealand secondary schools from 2003 to 2013. During this time we were able to gather a large data-set of information from observations of teachers who were being supported to implement this theory about the centrality of relationships in their classrooms. This evidence showed that teachers whose Māori students made the most gains in achievement were those who were able to create extended family-like, whānau, contexts for learning in their classrooms which then enabled them to use those pedagogic interactions we know make a difference for Māori and all students' learning.

These teachers were those who were located in what I have come to call the "North-East". This doesn't mean that we all have to move to Gisborne to receive effective teaching for our children. The North-East is a figurative position on a scatter plot that shows where effective teachers of Māori and other marginalised students are located. What North-East teachers do was the subject of my previous book on this topic, *Teaching to the North-East* (Bishop, 2019). How teachers are supported by their schools' leaders to become and remain North-East teachers is the subject of this book.

Leading to the North-East is how North-East principals and team leaders support teachers to become and remain North-East teachers. North-East leaders ensure that North-East teachers are able to implement the North-East, relationship-based pedagogy detailed in *Teaching to the North-East,* with fidelity. Ensuring the fidelity of relationship-based teaching practices is fundamental to North-East leadership practices.

Fidelity has two main meanings. The first is "faithfulness in relationships". The second is "the degree of exactness with which something is reproduced". In this book, I will mostly be using fidelity in this second sense of "implementation", meaning that teaching practices ensure outcomes as intended by the original developers. This places the focus of the book on the means that North-East leaders use to ensure that both their own and North-East teachers' practices are consistently those that we know are most effective for realising Māori and other marginalised learners' potential in ways that are culturally sustaining.

In te reo Māori, the word for fidelity is tikanga which is the right way to do things, in hui or equally in classrooms and schools, so as to ensure that the processes and the outcomes of our hospitality (relational contexts for learning) and deliberations (dialogic interactions) are as we intend. There is also a strong expectation in this term that the mana and tapu of all participants is acknowledged and enhanced, not diminished.

So, fidelity in this book means the right way, the tika way, to ensure the implementation of a relationship-based pedagogy that research has shown to be effective for realising Māori peoples' aspirations for the education of their children. In this way, school leaders and teachers are able to realise their responsibility to be "faithful" to their students' wellbeing and learning through their professional fidelity of practice.

It is vital that teachers are supported to sustain North-East teaching practices with fidelity so that all students are enabled to realise their potential. Hence, the need for this book. *Leading to the North-East* provides school leaders with a model for transforming their schools into a North-East learning institution. A North-East learning institution is a culturally safe place where Māori and other marginalised students become successful learners on their own terms. North-East leaders don't allow Māori and other children of diversity to be marginalised from the benefits that education has to offer because of who they are and what they bring with them to school being seen as deficiencies.

What is also important is that North-East schools do not have frustrated, angry, and upset teachers whose only recourse is to leave the profession. North-East teachers are sound, committed professionals, who know how to realise Māori and other marginalised learners' full potential. They do so because they are supported by North-East leaders who enable their professional fidelity of practice.

Where to start? The role of the principal

"Where to start?" is a common question. I believe the answer is in the wero laid down by Elizabeth Forgie, the recently retired principal of Kerikeri High School, when she explained that unless the principal is leading the transformation needed to ensure the desired gains in Māori student achievement, nothing will happen. I could not agree more. There are three case studies later in this book that focus on the understandings and actions of the principals, for it is they who initiate the changes and above all who take on the responsibility for the necessary transformations their school must go through to realise improvements in Māori students' schooling experiences. I have intertwined their stories with my own notions of *Teaching to the North-East* and *Leading to the North-East* in ways that illustrate how school leaders have addressed the literacy crisis and the wider pattern of educational disparities.

What is spectacular about these three North-East leaders and their schools is that, once their principals and senior leaders had identified the transformation that was necessary, it only took them 2 years to raise Māori students' educational achievements to match that of their non-Māori peers. What is more, they did so in ways that ensured that Māori students were able to succeed as Māori—not having to leave who they are at the school gate. Further, the transformations they made to improve educational outcomes for Māori students were also of immense value to other students who are currently being marginalised from the benefits that education has to offer.

Of course, there are other Leaders of Learning, including all senior and middle-level leaders and all the teachers in the school who have important roles to play in the transformation of the schools.[2] However, unless the agenda for change is set by the principal, unless they take on the challenge offered in this book to cease accepting that educational disparities can be based on ethnicity and not on the realisation of a child's potential, nothing will change.

Like no other time in history, there is a tremendous amount of support currently being provided for this agenda by Māori and non-Māori leaders, politicians of all persuasions, Ministry of Education officials, other school leaders in Kāhui Ako, school teachers, parents, families, and community leaders. But the power to take up the challenges identified in this book to ensure Māori students are able to achieve on par with their non-Māori peers, to succeed as Māori and for those other marginalised students to also realise their potential in the same ways as Māori students are enabled to do, remains with school principals and

---

2   Due to the multiplicity of descriptors that schools use for their leaders, I have decided for the sake of clarity to talk about three levels of leadership: principals, team leaders, and teachers. Of course, large schools are far more complex than this, but the leadership roles I will be using are firstly the "principal" for those who have leadership roles for the whole school. Secondly, I will use the term "team leader" for those who have leadership roles for their part of the school. They provide learning opportunities for teachers in their teams. "Teachers" are those who have responsibility for learning in classroom or learning spaces. All levels of "Leaders of Learning" may interact with parents and families.

other leaders. They are really the only people in our society who can do so at this time.

This book is divided into 12 chapters.

Chapter 1 is an introduction to the book.

Chapter 2 examines the causes of the "literacy crisis" as an indicator of the educational disparities that are impacting upon Māori students' learning.

Chapter 3 details those dimensions of schooling that school leaders need to address in order for them to create a school in which approaches to literacy, numeracy, and other learning areas can be addressed.

Chapter 4 commences by detailing the seven dimensions of the GPILSEO model and what they look like when implemented by aspiring North-East principals. This chapter then deals with *goal setting*, that essential part of the transformation process that focuses the actions of all teachers, team leaders, and principals towards addressing those crises in education that continue to plague our people and our society

Chapter 5 is about the need for school leaders to lead the implementation of a relationship-based *pedagogy* as the main agent for realising the goals of North-East schools.

Chapter 6 introduces the support systems that school principals need to implement in their schools so as to ensure that teachers are able to learn about, use, and sustain the use of the relationship-based pedagogy.

Chapter 7 details how the process of transforming the school into a North-East learning institution can be *spread* to include all teachers, leaders, parents, families, and community leaders into learning partnerships in ways that will add value to Māori students' learning outcomes.

Chapter 8 demonstrates what it means to take *ownership* of the problems and solutions by strategically planning for the realisation of the school's goals, resourcing the transformation in ways that signal its significance and self-reviewing how well the school is progressing towards realising its goals.

Chapters 9 to 11 contain the stories of three North-East leaders, and their schools.

Chapter 12, the final chapter, seeks to make sense of what I am proposing as an education reform process that is long overdue, but one that can be achieved in a very short time.

Perhaps the main message of this book is that educational leaders have the responsibility to transform our schools in ways that makes a difference for Māori and other marginalised students and need to do with urgency. It will be they who are remembered for the transformation that is possible in our society by their schools becoming successful North-East learning institutions. Unless school principals and other leaders grasp this challenge, they will instead be remembered for the lost opportunities and the lost lives. In this book, along with its companion volume, *Teaching to the North-East*, I have set out a model for change, for transformation, and have identified a specific time-frame for it to happen within. It can be done! It has already been done by some whom I describe as North-East leaders. It is now necessary to follow their lead and transform our schools into successful North-East learning institutions.

Russell Bishop
Wānaka, 2023.

Chapter 1
Teaching and Leading to the North-East?

Introduction

When looking for the cause of the literacy crisis, I initially considered that perhaps it was a matter of the literacy learning approach currently being used by most schools that was at fault. There has been a lot of publicity recently about the problems caused by the most commonly used "balanced" approach to literacy learning and suggestions that a more "structured" approach would be far more effective. "Balanced" literacy is the most commonly-used literacy learning approach in New Zealand schools. It is an approach that developed in the 1990s as a compromise between the earlier whole language approach and more structured approaches to literacy learning. In this approach, teachers are encouraged to meet students' learning needs where they are encouraged to use word analogies and pictures or context to identify words. "Balanced" literacy instruction is focused on shared reading (e.g., the teacher reads aloud to students and asks questions about the text), guided reading (e.g., students read texts at their current ability level and discuss them with the teacher in homogeneous groups), and independent reading (e.g., students self-select books to read on their own). Although phonics, decoding, and spelling may be taught in word study lessons, the skills typically are not emphasised and rarely taught systematically.

"Structured" literacy is explicit, systematic teaching that focuses on phonological awareness, word recognition, phonics and decoding, spelling, and syntax at the sentence and paragraph levels. "Structured" literacy is deeply rooted in the sounds from which our spoken language is composed (phonemes) and systematically introduces the letters or letter combinations (graphemes) that correspond with each phoneme.[3]

The suggestion that shifting from that most commonly used "balanced" to a "structured" approach seemed to be supported by John Hattie's (2009) meta-analyses of literacy approaches which identified that the earlier "whole language" approaches have a very limited impact on student learning. An effect size of .06 to be exact, whereas "structured" literacy approaches have a medium effect size of 0.7. The best I could find for a "balanced" approach was 0.33 by Graham et al., (2017). These data from a series of meta-analyses indicate that the balanced approach has very limited impact on improving student learning whereas the "structured" approach has a very useful effect. (Note that anything below an effect size of .4 shows little if any teacher effect.) Hence it would seem that schools' shifting literacy learning approaches would be a logical move.

Also supportive of this suggestion is the great deal of interest and excitement about the gains that are currently being made for Māori students when schools introduce the more explicit, "structured" approach to literacy learning. I share this excitement. Having been on the trail of a means of improving Māori student achievement for over 30 years now, I am always looking for outcomes such as this. However, these are decisions for school leaders and I wonder if it is simply a matter of replacing one means of teaching literacy with another or is there something else that school leaders need to consider?

The main problem with this idea of transforming the teaching approach being used in the school is that I have been here before, and it is not the simple matter that it seems to be on the surface. In the early stages of the Te Kotahitanga project in the early 2000s, which similarly focused on improving the pedagogy being used by their teachers,

---

3   https://www.liftingliteracyaotearoa.org.nz/support/balanced-vs-structured-literacy

we saw many gains being made in Māori student achievement at the outset of the project. We were very excited and were convinced that all we needed to do was to spread this new pedagogy far and wide in order to address the educational disparities facing Māori students. There was a great deal of excitement and enthusiasm about the intervention. However, we failed to realise the impact of our working with "the keen and the interested". Part of the reason for their enthusiasm was that it involved our providing a very select group of teachers with a new and interesting journey into the Māori world. Sometimes it was a bit uncomfortable, but we made sure that they were well supported in the spirit of manaakitanga. In other words, they were a highly selected group—in the education reform literature they are called "early adopters"—and what they can do and achieve is often not replicable with "late adopters".

We found the importance of this difference when we began to spread the pedagogy to other staff members in the project schools, and later to other schools. Because of the different responses to the intervention from the different "adopters", we began to realise that something more than just changing specific teaching approaches was necessary. This is not in any way to belittle the impact and effectiveness of the need for changing literacy learning approaches, or even revitalising the current approach for that matter, for these are a crucial foundation for improvements in Māori student achievement being possible. Instead, we began to find a number of problems were having a major impact upon our attempts to improve Māori students' educational outcomes that needed to be addressed as part of the implementation of the project.

We found four major problems that were limiting our improving learning outcomes

The first problem was the tendency for many teachers to blame the children rather than look to their own practice if and when the new pedagogic approach did not work. This problem was so limiting that, unless we developed a systemic means of supporting teachers to see the impact of what they were doing in terms of their own in-class teaching and learning relationships and interactions, their resorting to deficit explanations about why their efforts were not being rewarded thwarted our best efforts.

The second problem we faced when designing the Te Kotahitanga project was the need to overcome the monocultural nature and socio-economic status (SES) focus of the dominant transmission mode to teaching. These transmission approaches to pedagogy had been developed with children of the majority culture in mind, and focused on their learning needs in ways that matched their prior knowledge and learning and the aspirations of their parents and communities. In this way, the teachers using the dominant pedagogy were leaving Māori students out of the "success" picture and were also marginalising other learners who came to school with different skills and knowledge. Our attempts to address this dominant pedagogy were thwarted by many schools having difficulties providing the necessary support systems for teachers to enable them to learn how to use a more effective, responsive pedagogy, and the removal of funding for these support systems before they had had sufficient time to become embedded in the schools.

The third problem was that our attempts to move teachers to be responsive to the learning needs of Māori students were thwarted by most of them not implementing the pedagogy as it had been designed, that is, with fidelity. They got the idea that changing the way they related to Māori students was necessary, but they did not fully accept the idea that this was only a means to an end, not an end in itself. By this I mean that improving relationships for learning actually enables teachers to use those pedagogic interactions we know make a difference for student learning, but most teachers did not make this move to use these effective interactions. Hence, Māori student achievement did not progress to the extent it did in those schools where the pedagogy was implemented with fidelity, that is, *as it had been intended or designed*.

The fourth problem was that funding the intervention was a problem in itself and it also had an impact upon all of the other three problems as well. As part of the project, we had introduced support systems into the schools to enable teachers to implement the pedagogy in the way we knew made a difference for Māori students' learning. However, these support systems and the people to lead them, were funded from outside of the schools' usual allocations for staffing and general purposes. The problem was that, when the external finance provided by the Ministry of Education ceased at the end of the first 3 years, the schools were expected to take over funding these positions to sustain the support systems. However, most didn't. This meant that the implementation of the pedagogy was no longer being supported in the way it was designed, with consequent negative impacts on student outcomes.

On the other hand, a few schools did take on the ownership of the project by re-allocating funds and staffing they already had—but which were being used for different purposes—to resource the support systems in ways that were necessary to maintain the fidelity of the implementation of the pedagogic intervention. These schools saw Māori students' attendance, engagement with learning, retention and achievement in a number of areas—including cultural sustainability— continue to improve. One of these schools features later in this book.

Overall, the impact of these four problems—deficit explanations, the dominance of the monocultural transmission approach, the lack of using effective teaching interactions, and the confusion over the need for ongoing resourcing of the support systems—meant that teachers were left to vary the ways that they implemented the pedagogy we had developed. The pedagogy was a relationship-based approach that we had shown, when it was implemented as designed, supported Māori students to become successful learners in ways that also supported their communities' aspirations for cultural sustainability. This problem of our not being able to ensure the consistent implementation of the pedagogy with fidelity meant the eventual demise of the project in most schools.

The impact of the lack of a means of ensuring implementation fidelity within schools

Turning back to the recent reports on the literacy crisis, it was clear that, among other pedagogic problems, a similar process of modification of teaching practices has occurred over time in the field of literacy learning. This dilution of the fidelity of the implementation of the approach most commonly used—the "balanced" approach—in association with changes taking place in the wider society such as the growth in the use of social media, screens, and reduced reading for pleasure, has had a gradual and cumulative negative impact on literacy learning. This means that the current pattern of literacy learning across most schools and, most importantly, within schools, is one of variability of teaching practices. That is, in most settings across the whole time students are at school, they may receive what we know are effective literacy learning practices, but it seems that it is more than likely that they won't. So, it is clear that to improve the current, most commonly used literacy teaching approach, this variability of practice needs to be rectified—a tall order, given the current level of support that is provided to teachers.

What this also means is that, just as we found in Te Kotahitanga schools, if schools don't provide in-school support systems, run by knowledgeable leaders, to support teachers to maintain the implementation fidelity of their literacy learning approaches, dilution and modification will occur. And problematically, this will happen in whatever literacy learning approach is used, no matter how effective it is at the outset. By this I mean that just as the commonly used "balanced" approach has been modified over time and its effectiveness diluted, so too will any replacement approach suffer the same fate over time simply because it is too difficult for any teachers, working on their own, to maintain the implementation fidelity of literacy learning or indeed any learning approaches, in ways we know realise intended outcomes.

In contrast, we also know that by schools providing systemic support for staff, teachers can be included in what John Hattie[4] calls "collective efficacy"; that is, all staff engaging in collaborative decision making and problem solving about the impact of their teaching practices on students' performance. Of course, this does not happen by chance; it is important that schools' leaders provide formalised support systems to ensure this occurs and outcomes are as they should be.

North-East schools show the way forward

Therefore, it is not sufficient just to change the literacy learning approach, even though the need for this may be indicated or even desired. What I am arguing is that to effectively solve the literacy learning crisis *in the long term*, schools' leaders need to take ownership of problems facing implementation of the pedagogy used in their school by providing effective support systems for teachers so that they become what I have come to call North-East teachers.

North-East teachers are those who are located in a figurative "North-East". It is the upper right position on a graph; a scatter-plot (see Figure 1.1). This graph is made up of a simple cross-hatch of two lines or

---

4   https://visible-learning.org/2018/03/collective-teacher-efficacy-hattie/

continua. The horizontal line identifies, from low at the left to high at the right of this continuum, how well teachers are able to implement "caring and learning relationships", or whanaungatanga—an extended family-like context for learning in their classrooms. The vertical line shows, from low at the bottom to high at the top, how well teachers make use of "effective pedagogies" that we know make a difference for students' learning. It is the positive interaction between these two variables that creates the conditions within which Māori students are able to become successful learners.[5]

Figure 1.1 Teacher positioning

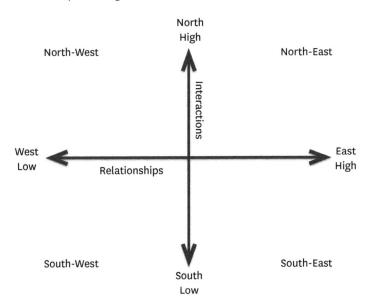

---

5   It is important to emphasise at this point that in this setting, the terms "relationships" and "interactions" have very specific meanings and should not be confused with everyday meanings of the words. In this context, "relationships" means the relational rights and responsibilities that one would expect to find in an extended family, a whānau. In this case, a classroom, or a school for that matter, established as a metaphoric whānau, would see teachers rejecting deficit explanations for Māori students' educational performances, caring for their learning in a culturally responsive manner, demonstrating having high expectations for their learning, knowing what the students need to learn and how best to ensure this happens. Similarly, "interactions" are those that research has shown to be those that make the most difference for learners. These interactions include building on learners' prior knowledge, using formative assessment feedback and feedforward, using co-construction processes, and power-sharing strategies.

The combination of these two variables, relationships and interactions, creates four quadrants where teachers can be located by identifying how well they are implementing them in their classrooms. I have used compass points as an easy way of labelling these quadrants. The four quadrants, going counter-clockwise, are the North-West, the South-West, the South-East and the North-East.

This now gives us a picture of where teachers can be located in relation to their students. As can be seen in Figure 1.2 below, their location impacts on their pedagogy.

- In the North-West, teachers exhibit low levels of observable caring and learning relationships and high levels of effective pedagogies.
- In the South-West, teachers exhibit low levels of caring and learning relationships and low levels of effective pedagogies.
- In the South-East, teachers exhibit high levels of observable caring and learning relationships, and low levels of effective pedagogies.
- In the North-East, teachers exhibit high levels of observable caring and learning relationships and high levels of effective pedagogies.

Figure 1.2 Teachers can be positioned in one of four locations.

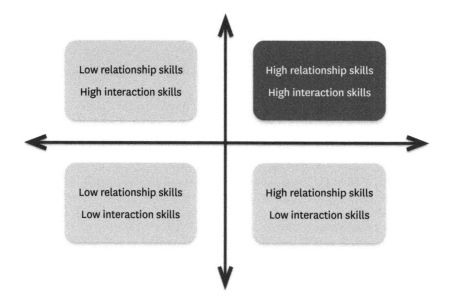

What is really useful about this picture is that it identifies where the most effective teachers of Māori students are located. The numerous Māori students we spoke to over the years were quite adamant that of the four possible locations for teachers, it was only those teachers located in the North-East who were able to effectively support their learning. These were the teachers who were able to establish whānau relationships, include Māori students in these contexts, and then use learning interactions in ways that ensures that their students made progress as learners. One student summed up what the rest were saying:

> [Our teacher is] dedicated to what we do in our class; she knows what to do. I think it's just her passion that she likes to see kids achieve instead of failing; feels cool that we've got someone who's gonna help us get through school.[6]

However, a major problem developed

Hence the main aim of the Te Kotahitanga project was to support teachers to move from the South-West, where most had been positioned prior to the intervention, to the North-East. However, Figure 1.3 shows that the majority of teachers in the Te Kotahitanga programme moved not to the North-East, but to the South-East.[7] In Figure 1.3 below, Figure 1.2 is superimposed on a scatter plot of observation data from Te Kotahitanga schools. This observation data (shown as dots) consists of 3500 observations from 1,263 teachers in 31 schools at different times of the day and week, and places. The data is also drawn from all curriculum areas. Superimposing these data on one another shows that the majority of observations (the dots) are located in the South-East.

---

6   Students, School 2, 2007.

7   A further feature of the scatterplot is there very few plots in the North-West, that is the upper left quadrant. That means that it is very difficult to use those pedagogic interactions that we know make a difference for student learning when teachers are not able to create a whānau-like context for learning.

Diagram 1.3: Most teachers moved to the South-East, not the North-East

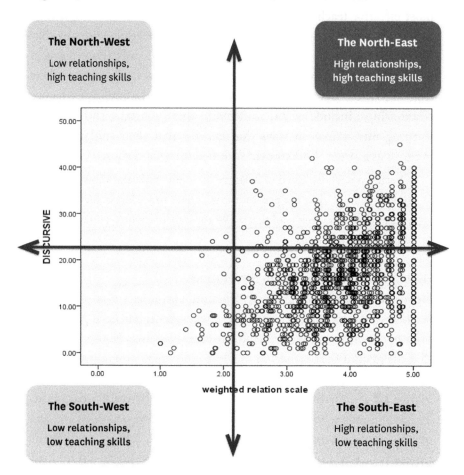

This picture shows a further problem

It looks like the message about the need to improve relationships got through to the teachers, so they moved their practice along the horizontal axis. However, the message about needing to improve their teaching practices did not. So most did not move up the vertical axis.

I see this again and again. Numerous reform initiatives, now focusing on the need to improve relationships, tend to see this as sufficient, not as part of a process. This is probably due to the lingering effect of behaviourism on education that suggests that improving behaviour will lead to learning, despite teachers continuing to use the same teaching practices that caused the behavioural problems in the first place. It could also be due to teachers being happy once students' behaviours improve as a result of improving relationships; learning taking a back seat to the need for peace and reduced confrontation. Or it could just be that teachers are led to believe that improving relationships is sufficient, and somehow learning will improve as a result. Sadly, this is not the case. Changing contexts for learning is clearly necessary by teachers rejecting deficit explanations of Māori student performance and improving Māori students' feelings of self-worth and identity, but this is not sufficient in itself to bring about changes in learning outcomes. Learning is not something "caught" in a conducive environment. It is something "taught" in a culturally responsive context.

Clearly, what is needed is a means of ensuring that teachers are able to implement the Teaching to the North-East model with fidelity; that is, in ways developed by research that identified the most effective actions by teachers. By this I mean that they needed to move their practice to the North-East, especially in terms of the interactions they develop with their students. And the best way for teachers to do so is for them to use feedback from their students' performance to critically reflect on the impact their teaching practices are having on Māori students' progress.

In order for teachers to be able to undertake this reflection, they need to learn and use a means of monitoring students' learning in two specific ways. The first action they need to learn is how to use evidence of student performance on task assessments to identify next teaching steps. The second is the need for teachers to learn how to monitor how well students are learning "how to learn"; that is, how well their students are learning to become self-regulating and self-determining learners, not remaining reliant upon the teacher.

Expanding the model further: Leading to the North-East

The pedagogic model developed as part of the Te Kotahitanga project needed to be expanded to include a means where teachers could interrogate evidence of student progress on task assessments to identify next teaching steps. Secondly, it needed to include a means where teachers could interrogate evidence of student performance in targeted skills and knowledge (such as goal setting skills, use of evidence, taking leadership roles, among others) to monitor how well they were learning those skills that would enable them to become self-regulating and self-determining learners. In this expanded model, this evidence is used as feedback from students on how well the learning processes that make up the relationships and interactions are impacting upon students' learning. This feedback on impact then enables teachers to modify their teaching practices appropriately to sustain learning gains being made by all of their students.

We also know from John Hattie's meta-analyses that this process of monitoring the impact of their teaching practices on student outcomes is best taken collaboratively with other teachers, and preferably led by a "knowledgeable other". But more on that latter condition later in this book. In this way, just as teachers are seeking to move students to be self-directed learners, the model also needed a means of moving teachers from being participants in collaborative learning conversations to their being able to apply their knowledge to new situations on their own. This involves moving from "inter-actions" to "intra-actions", meaning that once teachers learn these skills in collaboration with others, they should embed them in their own practice. Then they can use them on a daily basis in their classrooms as a means of responding to feedback from their students.

Hence the initial model was expanded to provide teachers with a means of using formative approaches for both "task learning" and also for "process" and "self-regulation" purposes. This revised model is shown in Figure 1.4 below. The original movement to the North-East, by the combination of high levels of observable caring and learning relationships and high levels of effective pedagogies, is enhanced by the provision of a means of monitoring the impact of teaching practices on the performance of all learners, be they students, teachers, or leaders. In this way, teachers are able to modify their practices in ways that are responsive to students' and other learners' learning needs and progress.

Figure 1.4. Teaching to the North-East

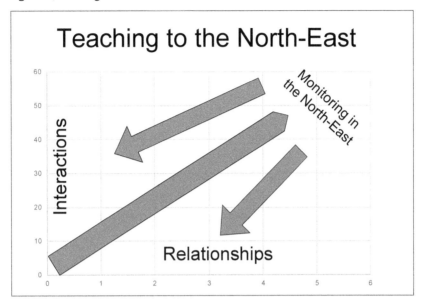

What does the profile of an effective Leader of Learning look like now?

This further iteration of the profile of an effective Leader of Learning includes the following.

1. A means of creating an extended family-like, whānau, context for learning to create the conditions wherein all students (and teachers and leaders) are able to become successful learners on their own terms.

2. A means of interacting with learners within this context in ways that allows the use of those teaching principles and practices that we know make a difference for learning.

3. A means of monitoring learners' progress and the impact of teaching practices on task and process learning and modifying teaching practices responsively.

This model is detailed in Chapter 5.

The need for institutional support

However, earlier research in the US by Richard Elmore identified that teachers are unlikely to develop and especially sustain new teaching strategies on their own (Elmore et al., 1996, p. 7; 2004). He identified that the key to improving teaching practice is *teacher action supported by responsive structural reform*, with the emphasis being on *responsive*. By this he meant that schools that succeeded in changing practice in a sustainable manner, are those "that start with the practice and modify school structures to accommodate to it" (Elmore, 2004, p. 4) rather than the other way round.

This understanding meant that in addition to a model of effective pedagogy, we needed to provide responsive structures to ensure these effective teaching practices are sustained. In order to address this need, in the Te Kotahitanga project we developed some systems to support teachers to learn about the profile of an effective teacher of Māori students and to apply their learning both in their classrooms and elsewhere when interrogating evidence of student performance. The first support system following on from an explicit explanation of the profile consisted of a series of observations and feedback sessions to induct teachers into the teaching process. The latter was a structured meeting, termed a co-construction meeting where teachers were supported by a learning coach (a facilitator) to collectively interrogate evidence of student progress to determine their next teaching steps.

However, for a variety of reasons, these important institutional support mechanisms were the first thing to be abandoned once the external funding for the programme was reduced or eliminated. This meant that one of the most useful learning processes, formative assessment (the one activity that most teachers find very difficult to implement), was abandoned. We found that where the necessary institutional support to embed this knowledge in teaching practice was missing, or abandoned, teachers tended to revert to more traditional teaching practices that have proven to be harmful to Māori students and other marginalised students on a number of levels. That is, they moved to the South-East, not the North-East, or even more problematically, if they had managed to reach the North-East, they were not able to remain there on their own.

This meant that the revised pedagogic model that included a means of interrogating the impact of teaching practices on student performance to ensure teachers' movement to the North-East was found to be insufficient. Don't get me wrong. It was important that the pedagogic model be extended to include this reflective practice. However, learning about how to implement such a process is difficult and requires multiple opportunities to *embed* these processes in everyday teaching practice. It was clear that it is one thing to reach the North-East, but it is another thing to remain there. Teachers need consistent systemic support embedded within the school for them to, in turn, learn how to implement and embed North-East teaching practices in their classrooms.

How do North-East leaders ensure a North-East pedagogy and its support systems are embedded in their schools?

The answer to this question is really in two parts. As Elizabeth Forgie explained, they had the "will" but not the "way". Te Kotahitanga provided them with the "way" but we did not have to provide them with the "will". They already had that.

As Elizabeth explained, the "way" came from outside of her school just as it might today with Cognition Education's Relationships First programme or other such effective research-based approaches. What is crucial, however, is that those principals who have become North-East leaders ensure that neither they nor their team leaders or teachers, modify, dilute, or abandon the pedagogy itself or the support systems that are necessary to ensure the pedagogy is implemented with fidelity in their schools. As will be detailed in the following chapters, they embed the support systems; that is, the schools' infrastructure, its' North-East leadership practices, the inclusion of parents, families and community leaders,[8] and the provision of evidence-based decision-making processes. North-East leaders "don't let go" of the means of realising their goals. North-East leaders take ownership of the "way". They plan, resource strategically, and constantly review the progress

---

8   It might appear strange to include parents, families, and community leaders as one of the support systems of a school, but research into what constitutes effective learning partnerships demonstrates that where parents and families are involved in formative deliberations about their children's learning, they are able to add value to what schools provide. Further, as will be seen, where community leaders are involved in student, teacher, and school leaders' learning, they can also add value to what is offered by the school and indeed can also take a leadership role in goal setting, strategic planning, curriculum content, leadership practices, what constitutes evidence of progress and learning, and indeed ownership of the resourcing and reviewing of the processes of learning.

their school is making towards realising their goals. They don't have to come up with the solutions themselves, but once they have them, they stick with them. To Elizabeth Forgie, they "stick to their knitting". What is clear is that those leaders who have done so have seen wonderful gains in achievement for Māori and other marginalised students in their schools.

The second part to the question is "How does this happen? What does it mean to have *the will?*".

There are a number of attributes that North-East principals have in common that contribute to their having "the will" to make a difference for Māori and other marginalised students in their schools. These include being determined, courageous, believers in social justice, committed, and dedicated.

The principals featured in the case studies later in this book all demonstrate these characteristics. Indeed, two of them commenced the transformation of their schools into North-East learning institutions nearly 20 years ago and, what is more important, they kept going with what made the difference. They did not abandon the means of realising their goals when the going got rough, in the face of competing demands for scarce resources or under the deluge of initiatives that school leaders are expected to respond to or incorporate in their schools. The third case study principal will almost certainly follow in their footsteps.

However, the most important characteristic that North-East leaders have is their refusal to accept differences in outcomes based on ethnicity, group membership, or beliefs. Their not accepting disparities being determined in this way means that they understand the necessity to be primarily outcomes- and performance-focused. They continually question how their school, its systems and pedagogy is performing for Māori and other marginalised students. Their focus is continually on how well support systems are performing, not just on if the institutions are running, but rather on their impact on improving student learning. Just as teachers interrogate the impact of their teaching practices on students' learning, North-East leaders interrogate how well the school's support systems are supporting teacher and student learning in ways that ensure they are being implemented with the fidelity necessary to ensure intended outcomes. This is how they see their goals being realised.

In the following chapters, I will be detailing "the way" that North-East leaders realise their goals. Of course, this is important, but probably far more important is that North-East leaders also either have or develop "the will" to make the difference we so desperately need.

But first we need to return to what is happening in the literacy landscape in our country as an example of the sorts of issues that North-East leaders address successfully.

Chapter 2
What caused the literacy crisis?

You are right about the teacher variability issues. It is one of the key pieces of the puzzle in my opinion and something we're not often addressing in NZ (or at times acknowledging). The PISA data shows that while we have high between-school variability we have even higher within-school variability, which speaks to the different educational opportunities different students within the same school are receiving—definitely an area for concern.

Dr Nina Hood, Founder, The Education Hub, 16 June 2022
(personal communication)

Introduction

There is no debate about Māori culture having been characterised by high levels of oral literacy for centuries. What is not generally well known is that Māori people have also been part of the written literacy world since the 19th century, when arguably, Māori people were among some of the most literate cultures in the world. Hence, nowadays, for many Māori to be denied a place in this world and for many young Māori people to be functionally illiterate and innumerate is totally unacceptable. These problems impact on themselves, their families, educability, health challenges, frequency of hospitalisations, employability, lifetime earning potential, potential to be incarcerated, and longevity—in other words, health, wealth, and identity.

Illiterate adults are four times more likely to be in low-paying jobs (and some of these people don't make enough to feed their families), 2.7 times more likely to be convicted of a criminal offence, and three times more likely to die before age 60 (Hamilton et al., 2022, p. 35). For Māori, other impacts include incarceration (50% of male prison inmates are Māori; 75% of female prison inmates are Māori); higher unemployment than the rest of the population and, when employed, more likely to be in lower-skill jobs; lower life expectancy in the order of nearly 8 years difference to their non-Māori peers; more frequent hospitalisations for childhood and "lifestyle" medical issues (increasingly we are seeing the return of diseases once thought to have been eradicated); and generally low levels of participation in the benefits that modern societies have to offer their citizens.

The critical (and growing) importance of literacy is well illustrated by a recent OECD estimate that the basic qualification needed for an individual to enter into the modern economy is a level 2 qualification. Literacy is one of the most basic standards for a learner to gain such a qualification; in fact, it is a co-requisite for awarding the NCEA level 2 certification. It is therefore not hard to see what impact low levels of literacy have upon further learning and life chances of our young people.

The problem of implementation fidelity

One of the most pressing issues that affects Māori students being able to be successful literacy learners is the variability of the literacy practices used by their teachers. That is, teachers' use of literacy learning approaches varies from those who implement the approaches with fidelity, as it was intended so as to realise the outcomes expected, to those teachers who don't use them this way. What needs to be emphasised at this point is that most teaching and learning approaches, and especially those for the teaching of literacy, need to be implemented as they were intended, as they were developed.

A recent PISA study found that teaching variability was a major issue and is to be found between schools and even between classes in the same school. This means that, in the same school, some children may be being taught in ways we know ensure they will learn to read and write effectively, but it is just as likely that children may be in a class where they are not being taught in ways we know work. In Stuart McNaughton's (2020) comprehensive review of the state of literacy learning in New Zealand, he identified that almost every literacy action implemented by teachers during the whole time that children are at school is at some—if not most—time, in breach of the means or protocols designed for the effective realisation of the intended or expected outcomes of the intervention or teaching practice. This variability of practice means that we are not seeing acceptable outcomes because most literacy learning practices being used are not being implemented in ways that work.

The impact of this persistent pattern of the variable implementation of literacy teaching means that going to school for a Māori child is actually a lottery. They may be fortunate to be assessed well at each transition point in their schooling, and have these data interrogated by a well-educated teacher who is being collaboratively supported by leaders and other teachers to identify the students' learning needs, and their next learning steps and be provided with an appropriate learning programme within a responsive pedagogy. They may be fortunate to have this occur within a culturally responsive learning context with school policies, processes, and institutions oriented to support this formative approach in ways that are responsive and inclusive of their parents' and communities' expectations and aspirations. However, it is more likely that this will not happen, or if it does happen once or twice, chances are that it probably will not ever happen again.

This unsatisfactory set of circumstances is made more problematic for the Māori learner because the pattern of learning to read, then reading to learn, is sequential, the latter parts building on the former. Where this does not happen, children fall by the wayside, feel unwelcome, and head into a downward spiral of disillusionment and despair, and what makes matters worse is they get blamed for their declining performance.

Literacy learning approaches—and most others from other curriculum areas—need to be implemented as they were originally designed. That is, with fidelity to the original research because they were designed using an evidence base to produce similar results. What has happened, over time, is that literacy providers have taken their "eye off the ball" of the necessity for what is called "implementation fidelity" or, in Māori terms, "tikanga". Implementation fidelity is the degree to which an intervention is implemented *as intended* so that expected outcomes are realised. This means that, from the original development of any literacy approach, any further implementation of the strategy needs to be done in the same manner as the original. Clearly, there is a right way to implement these approaches and a wrong way.

The Māori word for this process of implementation fidelity is tikanga. Tika means the right way or the correct way to do something. Māori people are very staunch on the implementation of tikanga. At every Māori event, there are institutionalised means of ensuring that tikanga is being observed, so that the outcome of the hui has the best chance of being as expected. This concept provides us with an excellent metaphor for institutional practices that seek to improve Māori student learning outcomes. In this way, it is signalling the need for the widespread use of institutionalised means of addressing this tendency towards the lack of implementation fidelity.

There is no doubt that the lack of implementation fidelity over time has impacted severely on the efficacy of the "balanced" approach to literacy learning to the extent that its continued use for Māori students has to be questioned. Principals must lead a radical reformation and restitution of its means of implementation like that which happened at Sylvia Park School detailed in Chapter 9.

In effect, what has happened over time is that the tikanga or the implementation fidelity of the "balanced" approach to literacy learning has been eroded. Teachers have been able to modify and change the "balanced" approach in ways they determined themselves. This variability in teaching practices has been caused by a range of problems that I identified in the introduction to the book and which I am going to detail below.

My concern for those who are advocating for the need for "structured" approaches to replace the "balanced" approach is that the causes of teaching variability still exist in our schools and, unless they are addressed, they can also potentially impact upon "structured" literacy approaches as well. By this, I mean that, if those issues that created the conditions within which the variability in practice currently seen in the "balanced" approach were able to occur are not attended to, either as part of the design or the implementation of the literacy learning approach, fidelity will be compromised, with negative consequences for children's learning.

As I identified in the introduction to this book, we found when implementing Te Kotahitanga that there were a number of problems that impacted on the long-term fidelity of the implementation of the pedagogic intervention that was central to the project. These problems meant that, despite our best efforts, many teachers and schools involved in the project were not able to realise the outcomes that could be expected. These problems included the tendency for teachers to resort to deficit explanations for the declining performance of Māori students, current pedagogies being monocultural and socio-economic status focused, the limited use of those interactions we know are most effective for improving Māori and other marginalised students' learning, and the impact of resourcing issues on the sustainability of the projects' positive outcomes.

We found these problems in our research into what was limiting Māori students from being successful learners *20 years ago*. What the investigations into the current situation facing literacy learning in New Zealand by Stuart McNaughton, Taylor Hughson, and Nina Hood identify is that dismayingly, these problems still remain in our schools. On the other hand, in those schools where they have been addressed, Māori and other marginalised students have been able to realise their potential as successful learners on their own cultural terms. Three of these schools feature in this book. However, most schools have not been able to successfully address these problems and, as a result, we have a "literacy crisis" in our country and Māori and other marginalised students continue to be unable to access the benefits that education has to offer. These problems are now detailed below.

1. The tendency to resort to deficit explanations

The first factor that has impacted upon current literacy learning practices being implemented with fidelity over time is the tendency of teachers to resort to deficit explanations for Māori students' performance when the expected outcomes do not occur. You might expect that teachers would look at what is happening in their classrooms, and specifically at what and how they are teaching, if Māori students are not making expected progress with literacy learning. However, there is a strong tendency among teachers to blame the children instead of examining their own practice for declining performance. This means that the implementation of the literacy learning approach is not under scrutiny; instead, they focus on the children's supposed "deficiencies". Why this occurs is a complex matter, yet the solution is quite simple.

As I explained in the preface, when we commenced the Te Kotahitanga project, we began by asking all those involved with Māori students' learning to talk to us about their understandings as to why Māori students were struggling at school. We spoke to a sample of Māori students, those parenting these students, their schools' principals, and a sample of their teachers. All interviewees were from a range of secondary schools: single sex to co-ed, rural to urban, large to small.

What we found was very illuminating. All the groups, except the teachers,[9] identified that the main impact on Māori students' learning was the relationships that existed in the classrooms, within the schools, and with those outside the school. Māori students in particular identified that the relationships they had with most of their teachers were toxic and negative; these heavily impacting on their opportunities to become successful learners. They also told us about their being randomly "targeted" by teachers outside of their classrooms, identified as "troublemakers" when they spoke out, given easy work, and not expected to be able to cope with the work other students were doing. Above all, they told us about mainstream classrooms and schools being culturally unsafe for them as Māori.

Sadly, those parenting the students also recalled their experiences of schooling were very similar and they were very upset at the intergenerational continuation of these negative relationships. They spoke of their aspirations to be involved in their children's learning, but they were unaware of ways that they could participate and contribute. Their own negative experiences made them very hesitant to approach their children's schools and this, combined with schools' ongoing tendency to blame their children for their poor performance, cemented the divide.

---

9   Using an analysis of unit ideas, we identified that 80% of what the students talked about drew on the discourse of "relationships" to identify various factors that impacted upon Māori students' achievement outcomes. These figures were 63% for those parenting the students, 49% for the principals, and 29% for teachers.

In contrast, the majority of the teachers we spoke to identified that the factor that had most impact upon Māori students' learning performance was the students themselves, and most of these impacts were negative because of the deficiencies that Māori students arrived at school with. The teachers were mostly frustrated and felt they were not able to really help Māori students to become successful learners because of the overwhelming problems they presented when they came to school.

When we asked these groups about what solutions they could suggest, most interviewees in the students, parenting, or principals' group were able to offer numerous, comprehensive suggestions about the sorts of relationships and interactions that would improve learning. Again, in contrast, most of the teachers were not able to offer any really realistic solutions. Some did mention pedagogic relationships needing to be improved, but the vast majority were bewildered by what they saw as the multiple deficiencies of Māori learners. Most were frustrated and angry, but bereft of any effective solutions, essentially resigned to what they saw as being inevitable. Among the teachers we interviewed, there was a palpable degree of acceptance that the existing patterns of disparities was a reality and there was very little they could do about it. They were mostly at pains to assure us that they would like to do something about it, but the problems that Māori students either presented with or caused overpowered their abilities to make a difference for Māori students' learning.

To understand why this happens, a leading educational psychologist, Jerome Bruner (1996), explains that most teaching occurs, progress is evaluated, and practices are modified as *a direct reflection of the beliefs and assumptions the teacher holds about the learner.* In other words, teachers' actions are driven by the mental images or understandings that they have of those for whose learning they are responsible. This means that learning interactions are driven by these explanations, and where teachers "see" Māori students as having deficiencies, their levels of caring and expectations for their learning are different than for other children. Most problematically, there develops an acceptance among teachers that disparate outcomes are inevitable and "normal". As a result, the relationships developed are mostly negative and unproductive, and result in less effort, less engagement, frequent absenteeism, and troublesome behaviour by students—all dealt with by behaviour modification approaches instead of pedagogic.

This acceptance of educational disparities based on ethnicity has seen the lowering of Māori student outcomes in literacy learning outcomes. It is a manifestation of over a century of deficit and racist explanations that have become embedded in the dominant discourse in New Zealand. Basically, this discourse says that Māori are just not as capable as non-Māori and there is really nothing that anyone can do about it. This mode of thinking came to New Zealand with the early settlers and their government. It was reinforced through the news media, communication systems, and educational practices over the years and has become a self-fulfilling prophesy. "Māori are inferior" was the original mantra of the colonisers, and they "proved" it by their treatment of Māori. Removal of the Māori economic base, and marginalisation from full participation in the new nation's political and cultural systems including education, meant that Māori peoples' lack of success "proved" the original hypothesis; resulting in the victims of oppression being blamed for their inability to prosper under such an onslaught. This "deficit" thesis has become so embedded in the majority discourse that even seemingly caring and well-meaning educators accept this explanation when faced with apparently immutable disparities instead of looking at their own practice, at their own pedagogy and systems for example.

These deficit explanations spill over into the teachers' and school leaders' relationships with parents and families. When children and parents from different cultural groups than those of the teachers are seen as having deficiencies, what they do to bring to learning relationships is ignored or unappreciated. It is certainly not included to the extent that teachers can build upon it to expand their students' learning or as a means of including parents and families to support their children's learning.

Such is the dominance of the deficit discourse and the related acceptance of disparities being along ethnic lines, that many principals either find themselves accepting this situation as being inevitable, and/or are frustrated in their attempts to address the issue of educational disparities. It appears that while many principals identify that improved learning relationships are necessary to improve Māori students' learning, they are not able to act on these understandings partly because of the dominance of the use of the deficit discourse among teachers to explain Māori students' performance. A further contributing factor to this frustration appears to be the lack of effective support systems in their schools to ensure teachers are able to challenge these assumptions that just lead to frustration and build more effective formative and responsive approaches to improving learning.

In a recent conversation with Barbara Ala'alatoa of Sylvia Park School, she was clear that accepting or being bewildered by disparities in achievement along ethnic lines was totally unacceptable and that it was to be corrected without delay. She knew the answer was firstly with the pedagogy that needed to be deployed and secondly, the support systems needed in her school to ensure the pedagogy was implemented with the fidelity needed to ensure expected outcomes. Importantly, she knew the details of the pedagogy that was being employed in all the classrooms in her school. She knew what outcomes were to be expected and what she needed to do to ensure all students were being successful learners in her school. She understood that it was her responsibility to have this knowledge and to support learning across the school by ensuring her teachers were well supported to challenge deficit notions about student learning. She also knew of the need to support teachers to learn what they needed to do to ensure student learning. She was clear that it was her role and responsibility to be the principal "Leader of Learning" at the school. To her, that is what "principal" means. As will be seen later in this book, the results of literacy practices at her school, where within 2 years Māori students realised parity with non-Māori students, is testimony to this understanding, this different discourse.

Therefore it is more than just understanding that relationships are central to learning. It is understanding that deficit explanations about Māori student performance cannot be tolerated. It is this refusal to accept disparities being along ethnic lines that identifies a North-East leader like Barbara Ala'alatoa.

However, it is important that we do not reverse the situation and resort to blaming teachers or school leaders for Māori student performance. That is a very unproductive activity. Instead, implementing in-school support systems to enable teachers to challenge deficit explanations, interrogate the impact of their teaching practice on students' performance, and the fidelity of the implementation of their teaching practices is far more productive for all concerned. Such an approach has been shown to engage teachers and school leaders in improving Māori and other marginalised students' learning very effectively.

2. The dominance of a monocultural and socio-economic status focus of the most commonly used pedagogies

A second main issue we faced when designing the Te Kotahitanga project was the need to overcome the monocultural nature of the dominant transmission mode of teaching. These transmission approaches to pedagogy had originally been developed with children of the majority culture in mind and focused on their learning needs in ways that matched their prior knowledges and learning and the aspirations of their parents and communities. Māori students told us that they found these approaches to teaching to be difficult to understand, boring, and very poor when it came to them learning how to be successful learners. Most often they voted with their feet when these approaches were those most often used in their classrooms.

Stuart McNaughton (2020) identified in his report on the state of literacy in New Zealand that a similar problem impacted upon the effective, long-term implementation of literacy learning approaches with fidelity. He found that the most commonly used approach, a "balanced" approach, tends to be essentially monocultural and more suited to children who come from the same culture and socio-economic status background as do the majority of their teachers. Hence the potential for variability in effectiveness was actually built into the literacy learning approach itself.

We often hear about how we once had one of the most effective means of teaching reading and writing some decades ago—in fact, we hear about how we were world leaders in the field. However, I wonder if it was all that great for Māori students. My suspicion is that it was not, but rather it suited those students more culturally similar to their teachers, mostly non-Māori people, until recently when the teaching force has become more multicultural.

In Stuart McNaughton's terms, the "balanced" literacy approach appears to suit those students who have the "cultural capital" necessary to make satisfactory progress at school; those literacy skills that were gained in homes more attuned to the expectations of schools. Just as we found in schools prior to the Te Kotahitanga intervention, the recent literacy reports all emphasised how schools placed a lot of importance on students being prepared for their arrival at school or ECE centres; any child who was not well prepared in the ways expected by the teachers being left behind early on. The problem with these expectations is that, if the child does not arrive with the expected skills and knowledge, it will affect the rest of their time at school. Hughson and Hood (2022, p. 15) identify that "[t]he problem with this progression is that if children don't get into this process at the outset, teaching and curriculum expectations are such that learners will continue to be left behind by their not being able to participate in ways expected."

The need for children to be "literacy ready" on their arrival at school privileges children from homes where reading is prioritised, where books are prominent, and where language is English and articulated often. These homes prepare children for integration with the expectations and pedagogies used by the majority of the teachers who either came from these homes themselves or who now have developed them for their own children. Children who do not come from this type of home are seen as being deficient, requiring remediation and catch-up programmes, but in reality they never "catch up" because that is not what is needed. Being seen as having deficiencies and having one's own understandings and experiences sidelined or ignored has seriously negative effects on children's willingness to participate in learning activities. Many observers of Māori students in mainstream schools comment on how "the lights" go out of Māori students' eyes in a very short time after their arrival at school.

In short, the current reality is that the transition to school, for instance, is strongly impacted by the school-related literacy and oral language skills that children have on entry and the expectations and pedagogic practices they find at school. In other words, there is currently a strong emphasis on the need for children to be ready for what the school is about to provide, and this emphasis is reinforced by teachers' expectations about what students need to be successful learners, rather than teachers being able to be responsive to students' ways of making sense of the world.

An increasing number of families are culturally different from those that most teachers come from and in which they raise their own children. These families have different ways of making sense of and interacting with others in the world. They need teachers to be inclusive of and responsive to their ways of knowing and of developing knowledge. Yet, many teachers do not have any understanding that these differences exist, let alone knowledge of the differences, and they most often see these differences as deficiencies.

The lack of effective means for teachers being responsive to children of diverse backgrounds within current literacy pedagogic approaches is exactly what we found in the early stages of Te Kotahitanga. Put simply, the potential for teachers to be able to respond to these differences in cultural backgrounds is continuing to limit the realisation of goals for improving the educational outcomes for Māori students. However, again, I need to emphasise that I am not blaming teachers for this situation, rather the limited nature of support systems in schools to enable them to learn how to become culturally responsive North-East teachers.

This lack of a responsive pedagogy means that socio-economic status and membership of an ethnic group remain very strong predictors of literacy learning. It is also why the relationship of socio-economic status and ethnicity to learning outcomes is essentially uninterrupted by schools, despite there being good evidence from a number of studies[10] that this is quite possible and, indeed, given the changing demographic of most schools, entirely necessary (McNaughton, 2020, p. 12).

Stuart McNaughton describes this as a lack of "diversity awareness". I would prefer to call it a lack of cultural responsiveness. Whatever the case, it is the lack of teacher preparedness and abilities to use an alternative pedagogy that is responsive to the learning needs of the children in ways that engage with their individual, culturally determined prior skills and knowledge. The ability to be responsive to, rather than prescriptive towards, what diverse students bring to their schooling experiences is an increasingly important skill needed for teachers to respond to an increasingly diverse student population.

---

10 These include studies by Christine Rubie-Davies, Helen Timperley, Stuart McNaughton, and Gail Gillon among others.

However, teachers are not going to learn this on their own, or, if they do, they will learn different approaches individually. What is needed is a consistent and responsive pedagogic approach being used across all classrooms by all teachers to provide Māori students with a common learning experience. This means that school leaders need to determine an effective pedagogy and then develop and implement systems to support teachers to learn about and how to implement that pedagogy with fidelity; that is, in ways that we know are effective over time. I still hear about school leaders who are proud that their teachers teach in the ways that they know are best or that are reflective of their personalities. The problem is that this has not led to successful learning outcomes for Māori students. It has led to chaos and the current literacy crisis by encouraging variability in teaching practices with variable outcomes which are then in turn rationalised by the use of deficit explanations.

These concerns about the lack of cultural responsiveness are increasingly being voiced by Māori parents, families, and community leaders. They are not only concerned about their children not achieving at the same levels as their non-Māori peers, they are also concerned about the tendency of the New Zealand education system to assimilate students into the dominant culture's way of making sense of the world. Māori people are concerned by the use of pedagogies that dismiss what Māori students bring to school with them as being deficiencies needing remediation. Māori people voice their concern that their children should not have to give up who they are in order to become successful learners. They are calling for Māori students to be successful "as Māori".

North-East schools are responsive to this call to affirm the identity of Māori students in ways that have been sought after by their families for generations, but never realised. Compared to the explicit teaching of Māori values that happens in traditional schooling practices, North-East schooling enables Māori students to bring their own understandings to learning conversations that incorporate Māori values and tikanga into the pedagogy. North-East educators do so by creating a context for learning constituted in terms of manaakitanga, tiakitanga, wairuatanga, and tautoko ki ngā tamariki. The caring and relationship-based whānau context created by *culturally competent* classroom teachers in these schools has major impacts on the reduction of deficit explanations for Māori student performance, increases visible caring for Māori students as learners, and raises teachers' expectations for their learning.

Further, the relationship-based, culturally responsive pedagogy common to North-East classrooms enables Māori students to learn as Māori, to be successful learners, to stand tall and proud of their identity as Māori, and take their rightful place alongside other successful learners. In effect, implementing culturally responsive pedagogies ensures both successful outcomes for Māori students *and* cultural sustainability.

In this way, North-East schools are responsive to Māori peoples' aspirations for mana motuhake, for tino rangatiratanga, that is self-determination by implementing the *North-East Leaders of Learning Profile* which is a relationship-based, culturally responsive pedagogy that is detailed in *Teaching to the North-East.* Culturally responsive pedagogies used in North-East classrooms enable the prior knowledge of students to be legitimated within collaborative, co-construction activities in classrooms that are facilitated by the use of power-sharing strategies. Further, formative assessment approaches that enable Māori students to feedback to teachers what sense they are making of the learning tasks before them also enables them to develop the skills of being self-regulating and self-determining learners because these skills are fundamental to these learning processes. It is leaders in North-East schools, led by the principals, who make it possible for this pedagogy to be embedded within the school.

North-East school leaders, in orientating pedagogic approaches to realise goals of cultural sustainability, build on what their students bring to school with them, and include their students' parents and families into schooling practices. Many research studies over many years have shown the benefits when schools and parental aspirations and understandings match and the positive impact this relationship has on improving students' outcomes. This match is relatively easy to attain when the schools' parents are culturally similar to those of the teachers, but schools that can move beyond this and include parents and families of diversity into supporting their children's learning often see their students making gains in learning beyond that which the schools can achieve on their own.

Do "structured" literacy approaches have the potential to address the tendency for pedagogies to be monocultural and socio-economic status focused?

The answer to this question is yes, but ... By this, I mean that not all "structured" literacy approaches have the potential to address this issue. Some have not had this built into their design and, as a result, have not seen Māori students' learning accelerate to match that of their non-Māori peers. However, one approach has. It is called the Better Start Literacy Approach (BSLA) and, currently, the Ministry of Education is providing schools with funds to support its implementation. The development of this approach was led by Gail Gillon and Angus Macfarlane at Canterbury University and it is proving to be excellent for accelerating literacy learning and reducing disparities between Māori and non-Māori students.

BSLA was built from the concern "that children who enter school with lower levels of oral language are at risk for persistent literacy difficulties, particularly when they are from impoverished backgrounds" (Gillon et al., 2019, p. 2). This early gap tends to persist or expand over time, with consequent ongoing inequities in future educational success, health, economic participation, and outcomes. From this concern, the Canterbury University team developed a study that aimed "to investigate the feasibility of a teacher-led intervention designed to accelerate phonological awareness, letter knowledge, and vocabulary knowledge for 5–6-year-old children with lower oral language ability and who are living in communities that create multiple challenges to successful learning" (Gillon et al., 2019, p. 5).[11] The investigators asked if such an intervention could accelerate children's foundational literacy skill learning compared to the "regular literacy curriculum ... to an extent that can be transferred to the reading and writing processes" (Gillon et al., 2019, p. 2).

---

11 The original intervention study focused on 141 children (mean age of 5 years, 4 months) from 10 schools who entered school with lower levels of progress and oral language ability. These children lived in Christchurch and were born around the time of the earthquakes that impacted severely on the lower socioeconomic areas of Christchurch, the area where many of the children lived and went to school.

Of significance to the concern about monocultural and socio-economic status focused pedagogy is that the research team also asked if teachers, setting this intervention within a culturally responsive framework, "would advantage or disadvantage any particular cultural group and do boys and girls respond to the teaching in similar ways?" (Gillon et al., 2019, p. 6). To do so, they included common Māori words and concepts from the Māori world through:

> [the] teaching materials, children's readers, and quality children's stories books associated with BSLA. In addition, teachers are supported to engage with the *Hikairo Schema Primary* (Rātima et al, 2020) to advance their personal cultural competence and confidence in supporting young learners and their whānau. A further unique aspect of this literacy teaching approach is its inclusion of all children, including those with complex communication needs, through the adaptation of assessment, teaching materials and teaching supports to ensure every child is acquiring the critical foundational skills necessary for reading and writing success … (Macfarlane A., 2022, personal communication)

The BSLA website also identifies that whānau engagement is a critical component of early literacy success and includes information workshops and weekly newsletters to parents for the purpose of "strengths-based reporting". They have also found that "Over 90% of participants in the whānau workshops led by BSLA teachers indicated that their workshop experience was positive, and that they now understand how to support their child's oral language and early literacy development …" (Macfarlane, 2022, personal communication).

The outcomes of this responsive approach are accelerated learning gains of the target students to the extent that there were no or negligible differences between Māori and non-Māori children's achievement gains. "Achievement gaps evident at school entry between Māori and Non-Māori have significantly closed after just 10 weeks of BSLA teaching. This is the first time we have seen literacy data indicating that our teachers are successfully reducing educational inequities during children's first year at school" (Macfarlane, A., 2022, personal communication).

It is clear that the BSLA approach to "structured" literacy has the potential to address the tendency for past approaches to literacy learning to be monocultural because it does not rely upon students arriving at school with the "cultural capital" that is necessary for the "balanced" approach to be effective. Instead, it provides teachers with a means of responding to the cultural understandings that Māori students bring to school with them. It does so by providing teachers with a means of creating a whānau context for learning in their classrooms and interacting with Māori students within this context in ways that ensure their cultural understandings can be built upon. It also follows that any attempt to resurrect the "balanced" approach would need to meet the same criteria.

A further feature of the BSLA approach is that it tends to mitigate the tendency of the "balanced" literacy approach to privilege the children of the dominant culture in New Zealand, in that it is far more responsive to the need to have foundational understandings explicitly taught to each child. The problem of schools not implementing the "balanced" approach with fidelity, coupled with the "social promotion" policy, is that children who have not acquired the fundamental foundation skills necessary for success with reading and writing are passed on to the next level, not recycled to ensure these skills are acquired as happens in BSLA.

3. The limited use made of those dialogic interactions we know make the most difference for Māori students' learning

In Te Kotahitanga, we found that our attempts to move teachers to the North-East were thwarted by most of them moving to the South-East instead. As I detailed in Chapter 1, the North-East is characterised by teachers being able to develop *high* levels of learning relationships which enables them to use *high* levels of effective interactions. Whereas, while teachers in the South-East were able to develop *high* levels of learning relationships, they were only using low levels of effective interactions. Māori students identified for us that it was only teachers in the North-East who were able to effectively support their becoming successful learners, not the South-East.

The main impact of teachers being located within the South-East and not in the North-East is that South-East teachers do not generally use those teaching interactions we know make a difference for Māori students' learning. Māori students knew this. However, they told us that it was much better being in these classrooms than in those in the South-West (low levels of caring and learning relationships and low levels of effective interactions) that had been most common when we had commenced Te Kotahitanga. This was because they were cared for in South-East classrooms. However, they also knew that they didn't learn much there; despite their improved attendance and their willingness to learn improving.

Teachers being positioned in the South-East meant that the most common teaching interactions remained transmission with behavioural feedback. Whereas North-East teachers use very effective interaction strategies that draw upon students' prior knowledge and create opportunities for students to provide feedback on how well they are learning. They are also able to provide feedback and feed-forward to their students and co-construct learning with them through the use of power-sharing approaches. Being located in the North-East also allows teachers to monitor how well their students are performing in both task and process learning and modify their own approaches accordingly. In this way, further enhancing their students' learning those skills associated with learning how to learn. South-East teachers are unable to engage in these activities.

Again, Stuart McNaughton (2020) identifies one of the main problems facing literacy learning is the "the lack of cycles of formative assessment followed by effective teaching practices that are necessary to intervene in literacy differentials" (p. 12). I would add the lack of culturally responsive approaches that includes Māori students' culturally generated prior knowledge in ways that effectively engage them in co-constructing learning in "learning conversations" that facilitate learning and learning how to learn.

A recent survey in 2020 by the Education Hub's developer, Nina Hood, identified that most teachers reported that the most difficult practice they were expected to use was that of formative assessment; that is, the interrogation of the evidence of student performance in relation to their teaching practice. This is an amazing outcome given the focus that has been on formative assessment for decades now. I would suggest that this problem is caused by there not being effective support systems established within schools where teachers can learn how to undertake this practice of investigating the impact of their teaching practices on student performance in collaboration with others.

In North-East schools, teachers gain proficiency with the use of formative assessment procedures and culturally responsive approaches in concert with others and are not left on their own to solve what, to them, seem insurmountable problems. Further, as will be detailed in Chapter 6, North-East team meetings, established with the purpose of collaborative decision making and problem solving, that are led by a North-East leader who is well-versed in what is needed to implement the literacy learning approach with fidelity, ensure that consideration or what constitutes effective practice is prioritised and "red herrings" like deficit explanations are not considered.

Of course, the use of data of student and teacher performance also presupposes that schools have an adequate means of gathering evidence of students' performance and teachers' practice in relation to each other. This process also needs to be easily usable and understandable so that patterns of achievement and progress are readily identifiable.

This process of institutionalising formative assessment practices and the use of culturally responsive approaches to learning also addresses the tendency for teachers to modify and dilute the literacy learning approach, to introduce different texts, and reduce the time necessary for comprehensive implementation. The reason is that formative, responsive approaches will inform the teacher of the need to focus on what has been shown to work if they see students' performance falling off. This is especially so when examining the evidence of student performance is undertaken collaboratively with others. So, no matter the literacy learning approach chosen, there is a need for dialogic, interactive strategies to become part of the approach. In this way, the implementation fidelity of the literacy learning approach is assured. And, finally, as detailed in Chapter 6, the principal needs to be aware of what is happening in all team meetings so as to ensure that the strategic means identified as being necessary to realise the school's specific equity and cultural sustainability goals are being implemented with fidelity.

The problem of the explicit nature of "structured" literacy approaches becoming an end in themselves

A further problem may arise in schools that implement "structured" literacy approaches if school leaders do not provide support systems to enable teachers to maintain their focus on formative, responsive approaches to learning. Without support, teachers tend to abandon the need to interrogate the relationship between what is being taught and what is being learnt. I have seen this disjunction occur in a number of settings and my concern is that, because "structured" literacy approaches require explicit teaching of its key dimensions, including phonological awareness, letter recognition, and blended sounds to be undertaken in a systematic, consistent manner, teachers may see this as being sufficient. However, problems arise if instruction ceases at this point in the process.

The designers of most "structured" literacy approaches are very aware of the needs for literacy teaching to move beyond the explicit teaching part of the process so as to extend literacy learning into a wider world of literacy. This includes students investigating the communicative function of texts, specific disciplinary attributes and the reasons why authors create texts with a purpose.[12] However, not all teachers will be aware of this need and, unless there are appropriate in-school supports to ensure the ongoing use of formative assessment in a responsive manner, "structured" literacy approaches could become prescriptive instead of responsive in terms of its basic pedagogy.

As I said before, responsive pedagogies include the use of formative assessment practices that assist teachers to modify their practices in response to the impact of their teaching on students' learning. To see teachers revert to traditional transmission pedagogies given the harm these approaches have already done to our children is unacceptable and would fly in the face of the evidence of the effectiveness of responsive pedagogies. Clearly, explicit teaching has its place, but unless teachers have a way of receiving feedback from students about their performance

---

12 This latter area of literacy learning in commonly referred as "critical literacy" at the heart of which is understanding the relationship between language and power. It involves readers identifying how texts position them by their analysing issues of inclusion, benefits, representation, legitimation, and accountability (see Bishop & Glynn, 1999).

by means of a responsive pedagogy, they will not necessarily know what progress learners are making. Explicit transmission of knowledge does not necessarily mean that students receive it.

Encouragingly, Regan Orr, the principal of Te Kura Tuatahi o Papaioea – Central Normal School—who is a very staunch proponent of a "structured" literacy approach being used in his and other schools—is very clear that part of the explicit pedagogic approach to teaching is an interactive "task-oriented" feedback loop that provides teachers with a means of identifying the impact of their teaching on learners' progress. Further, he was clear that his school's approach to "structured" literacy was "seamlessly integrated with the wider Assessment for Learning (formative) approaches used throughout the school (R. Orr, personal communication, 2022). A recipe for success indeed and one that needs to be duplicated in other settings.[13]

4. The problems caused by confusion over resourcing

The fourth problem we found when implementing Te Kotahitanga was associated with resourcing. In hindsight, this problem probably did the most damage because it made it very difficult to address the other three problems. By this I mean that, as an integral part of the project, we had introduced support systems into the schools to support teachers to implement the pedagogy in the way we knew made a difference for Māori students' learning. These support systems included: in-class observations to gather evidence of teaching practice in relation to student performance; feedback and feed-forward sessions with teachers to support them to implement the profile of an effective teacher; and team meetings designed so that teachers could collaboratively interrogate evidence of student performance so they could determine their next teaching steps.

These support systems and the people to lead them were funded from outside of the schools' usual allocations for staffing and general purposes. The problem was that the external finance provided by the Ministry of Education ceased at the end of the first 3 years. At that time, the schools were expected to take over funding the leadership

---

13 How this can be achieved is explained later in Chapter 6 when the Hattie/Marzano teaching process is detailed.

positions so that the support systems could remain in use. However, most schools didn't.

This meant that the support systems in the school that were necessary to ensure teachers were able to implement the Te Kotahitanga project with the fidelity needed to realise the outcomes that we knew were possible, were abandoned because they could not be led by a trained facilitator/coach any longer.

So, this raises the question of what happens when the funding to support teachers to implement BSLA, for instance, finishes? Currently, BSLA comes with initial funding support from the Ministry of Education for its implementation by staff from Canterbury University and outside literacy coaches. This external funding is "soft money" that is extra to the schools' current funding allocations. There is an expectation that, once the teachers in a school have been supported to implement an approach, the school will take over the task of repeating the implementation with new teachers and maintaining the implementation fidelity with existing teachers from their own resources.

In my experience, the provision of funding from external agencies such as the New Zealand Ministry of Education is meant to be "seeding funding"; that is, funding to get the project off the ground and up and running by using external experts, for example. However, the disjunction between the intentions of the provider, and the use made of this funding by the receivers, the schools, creates a mismatch in expectations and understandings about the purpose and importance of the funding that is very difficult to reconcile. My experience when attempting to transform schools by initially using "soft money", then expecting schools to re-prioritise their existing funding to continue to implement the programme, has been spectacularly unsuccessful. Even in the face of evidence that Te Kotahitanga ensured achievement gains for Māori students, for a variety of reasons, most schools could not reprioritise their resourcing so as to continue to provide the support necessary to maintain the programme. This led to the consequent dilution of both the programme and its benefits to Māori students.

What this means is that any intervention needs to contain a means of ensuring that schools take ownership of the solutions provided and engage in a strategic re-allocation and re-alignment of the staffing and funding resources *that already exist in schools*. This transformation of staffing resources is necessary to ensure that the support systems that ensure the pedagogy is implemented with fidelity, are themselves implemented with fidelity. North-East leaders need to lead the implementation of these support systems. They need to develop the skills and knowledge necessary to run these systems. North-East leaders therefore need to be "grown" in their own schools so that ownership of the intervention moves from the external experts in ways that ensure ongoing fidelity of its implementation.

Schools that have been transformed into North-East schools have been spectacularly successful in maintaining both implementation fidelity and outcomes because they see solving these structural, funding issues as being part of their strategy for realising their goals for equity and cultural sustainability.

A further funding problem

There is a further funding problem that also affected Te Kotahitanga. When we were asked what it would take to expand the Te Kotahitanga project to many more schools in the country, we replied that it would cost more than the schools currently had by way of professional learning and development (PLD) funding. This was one of the reasons why the Ministry of Education's officials chose to cease funding the project completely. They felt it was too expensive to take to scale.

The BSLA approach faces the same problem. For example, Gail Gillon and her colleagues explained in their 2019 paper that when they developed the BSLA approach:

> "... teachers' participation is pre-intervention workshops, on-line learning modules as well as the support they received through the 10-week intervention period, appeared adequate to ensure the integrity of the instruction. However, the support (on average 12h over 10 weeks) was much greater than that typically received in supporting the early literacy development of children in their first year at school. (Gillon et al., 2019, p. 207)

Therefore, what is necessary to ensure the fidelity of implementation is greater than what is usually provided. In other words, what is "normal" is immediately inadequate.

So, an excellent programme that has been proven to accelerate literacy learning of Māori and other marginalised students to match non-Māori students will not necessarily be successful when it is placed within the normal parameters of an ordinary school. Unless the Ministry of Education is able to fund all New Zealand primary schools—and there are almost 2,000 of them—to implement the intervention with the level of support necessary, I doubt that this will be the case. Gail Gillon and her colleagues are aware of this problem and suggest that increased funding from that currently provided could be important for "increased teacher support to promote early literacy development within disadvantaged communities" (p. 208).

Schools may well use the increased funding they will receive from the new equity funding system that is due to replace the decile funding model. However, there will be much competition for this extra funding. So, unless this need is seen as a priority or some other re-prioritisation of existing resourcing occurs, an excellent programme is being released for use in settings where there is no guarantee that sufficient funding will be available to ensure its continued fidelity of implementation.

It becomes a lottery effect again for students as to which schools will provide the necessary funding. Some will. My experience tells me that most won't. This means that schools' leaders need a model that ensures they know how to take ownership of the intervention. This means principals will need to ensure they have a means of developing and staffing support systems by re-allocating funding to ensure ongoing fidelity of the approach. Unless attended to, this is a recipe for the replication of the pattern of teaching variability that will impact on the "structured" approach to literacy learning to the detriment of our children once again. What will be frustrating for the designers of this approach is that such issues are outside of their control yet will have a major impact upon its efficacy.

I hope I am wrong, and that the wonderful work done at Canterbury University to develop and trial BSLA is not wasted like so many other excellent interventions have been in the past. But I suspect that putting innovations into schools that have not undergone the transformation into being North-East learning institutions will see the benefits of this and other similar interventions diluted and modified so as to not realise their potential for our children. To my consternation, I have heard anecdotal evidence that this dilution of implementation fidelity is happening in some schools already where "structured" literacy approaches have been introduced recently.

Summary: Addressing the lottery effect

Realising North-East goals of equity and cultural sustainability means that literacy learning approaches need to have a means of ensuring implementation fidelity so that when the approach is expanded beyond its initial setting, the outcomes will continue to be as expected.

In this chapter, I have considered the causes of the literacy crisis that are potentially within the control of teachers, team leaders, and principals. Of course, there are other factors that impact upon literacy, but instead of expressing concerns about the impact of societal changes, we need to concentrate on doing what we can with fidelity and integrity. This means that, once we have included Māori and other marginalised students into being successful literacy learners, we can support them to become critical observers of what is happening in the wider world. In other words, literacy is a major means of providing young people with the tools to understand, respond to, and participate effectively in the world we live in. To be denied this tool is to be denied a major means of interacting with the wider world with agency.

My central thesis is that the most commonly used, "balanced" approach to literacy learning has declined in usefulness over a number of years because teaching practices have been enabled to vary from how they were originally designed and implemented. The diminution of the fidelity of these practices has come about for three reasons. The first is the lack of an effective pedagogic framework of those educational principles we know are necessary to realise equity and cultural sustainability goals. The second is the lack of a means of ensuring schools can develop in-school support systems to ensure implementation of the pedagogy with fidelity over time. The third reason is school leaders not taking "ownership" of the intervention being provided in ways that ensures the implementation of specific literacy learning approaches, or any other learning areas, with fidelity.

I appreciate that there may well be other factors outside of schools such as the changing provisions of Initial Teacher Education (ITE) institutions, and wider societal changes that will also impact upon literacy learning. However, what I am concerned with here is the major differences we can achieve by reforming and transforming our schools.

I realise that some advocates of the alternative "structured" approach argue that the "balanced" approach was never much use for literacy learning because of inherent problems with its initial design. They may well be right, and their solution of shifting literacy learning approaches may well be necessary. However, it is important that school leaders understand that not all "structured" literacy approaches have been designed in ways that realise North-East goals for equity and cultural sustainability. Only some have and these are the ones to be identified during school leaders' process of due diligence.

Whatever the case, there remains in our schools a number of issues that advocates of any approaches to literacy learning need to address if their specific approach is to be successful in realising North-East schooling goals of Māori students succeeding on par with their non-Māori peers and doing so "as Māori".

In this chapter, I have detailed the impact of a number of these problems. I detailed how they had initially impacted on the implementation of the Te Kotahitanga project. I then detailed how these same issues have created problems for the current most commonly used approach to literacy learning, the "balanced" approach. I then identified how they could also impact upon newer "structured" literacy approaches if these problems were not addressed either in the initial design of the approach or within its implementation.

These problems include the tendency for many teachers to blame the children rather than look to the impact of their own teaching practices on students' performance if and when the new pedagogic approach does not work. The second was the overwhelming dominance of the monocultural nature and socio-economic status focus of the most common modes of teaching. The third problem was the limited use made of those pedagogic interactions we know make the most difference for Māori student learning. The fourth was of limited changes in resourcing the support systems needed to ensure the pedagogic framework is implemented with fidelity. These problems meant the key to making a difference, the pedagogy, was not implemented with the fidelity necessary for expected outcomes to be realised. All of these pedagogic issues were exacerbated by the lack of sufficient in-school support systems.

Leading to the North-East: Ensuring the fidelity of relationship-based learning

This situation was made worse by the lack of a means whereby schools could take ownership of the solutions provided by the intervention by way of their leaders re-prioritising the resourcing of the intervention.

If these problems are addressed at the design stage, then well and good, and I have indicated in the text how the BSLA approach, for example, has made good in-roads into these design parameters and seen North-East goals being realised. However, what still remains is

Figure 2.1: A summary picture of the problems that need to be addressed by North-East schools

Main concern about current literacy learning practices is the variability of implementation.	
This means there is a lack of implementation fidelity or tikanga of teaching practices so that outcomes vary between schools and classrooms within schools.	
This lack of implementation fidelity has been caused by:	These problems are exacerbated by:
• the tendency among teachers to blame students for limited performance rather than scrutinise their own practice	• the lack of in-school support systems to enable teachers to challenge deficit explanations and interrogate the impact of their teaching practice on students' performance and the fidelity of the implementation of their teaching practices
• the monocultural and socio-economic status bias of current pedagogy	• the lack of in-school support systems to assist teachers to implement and use a relationship-based pedagogy that is culturally responsive and sustaining, dialogically interactive and formative-focused with fidelity in the long term
• the limited use of those interactions we know make a difference for students' learning	• the lack of in-school support systems that ensure teachers are able to implement a relationship-based pedagogy that is culturally responsive and sustaining, dialogically interactive and formative-focused with fidelity in the long term
• the problem of resourcing the intervention in the long term.	• the lack of an in-school means whereby schools can take ownership of the solutions provided by strategic planning, re-prioritising existing staffing and funding resources and self-reviewing progress made so as to ensure the support systems identified above are implemented with fidelity .
	Note: Support systems include the provision of infrastructure, the tasks of leadership, a means of including parents and community leaders, and the use made of evidence. These systems are detailed later in Chapters 6 and 7.

the problem of schools ensuring fidelity when they take on the task of implementing the approach themselves; that is, the necessity for a means of supporting teachers to implement the specific approach to literacy learning in schools in ways that ensure outcomes are as expected.

The process of addressing these problems

These problems mean that aspiring North-East principals need to lead the transformation of their school into being a North-East learning institution. This means that the school needs to become a whānau, a supportive collective wherein teachers are able to provide an education for Māori students in ways we know will realise North-East goals of equity, cultural sustainability, and benefit to others.

Principals lead the transformation of their school into North-East learning institutions by leading the following interventions:

- The first is a strategic refocusing of the school so as to reorient all of the actions of all involved in the school to realising the North-East goals of equity, cultural sustainability, and benefit to others.

- The second important action will be the introduction of a relationship-based pedagogy that is culturally responsive and sustaining, dialogically interactive, and formative-focused. Such a pedagogy provides an effective alternative to the dominance of traditional, monocultural, prescriptive pedagogies that blame students and their families for their declining performance and progress. This alternative pedagogy also rejects the acceptance of educational disparities being based on students' membership of ethnic groups. It promotes the importance of teachers interrogating the inextricable relationship between teaching practices and student outcomes. Specific literacy learning approaches can then be implemented within this pattern of pedagogic principles in ways that ensure their implementation with fidelity in the long-term.

- The third action is the development and implementation of a number of in-school support systems. These systems provide teachers with an effective means of implementing the relationship-based pedagogy with fidelity over time, adds value to students' learning, and ensures there is an evidence base for decision making and problem solving.

- Finally, there is the need for school leaders to take ownership and responsibility for solving the problems of disparity and cultural marginalisation by planning, re-prioritising staffing and funding resources, and self-reviewing their practices to demonstrate the importance and means of realising their school's goals for equity and cultural sustainability.

In effect, what is needed is a model that commences with the establishment of goals that focus all the actions of those involved in the school toward the realisation of the goals. Secondly, a relationship-based pedagogy is needed that is responsive to the learning needs of all the students and other learners in a way that realises the school's goals. Thirdly, support systems needs to be implemented to ensure that the pedagogy is implemented with fidelity over time, value is added to students' learning, and an evidence base is provided for decision making and problem solving. Finally, ownership by the principal and other leaders is vital so that the support systems are resourced and implemented in ways that ensure the pedagogy will realise the goals of the school.

This model is developed in the next chapter and detailed in the chapters to follow.

Chapter 3
GPILSEO: A model for reform

Introduction

In Chapter 2, I detailed how the lack of an effective means of ensuring literacy approaches are implemented with fidelity in most schools has meant that, over time, strategies have been gradually modified and recommended procedures or activities omitted. This lack of implementation fidelity has had a major impact upon the expected learning outcomes of many children in our schools, especially Māori.

I suggested that addressing this matter of implementation fidelity is not simply a matter of changing the literacy approach. There may be immediate gains with the introduction of a new approach that will be very pleasing to see, but it is the long-term outcomes that we are really concerned about. For expected gains to be realised in the long term, schools need a means of avoiding the drop-off in fidelity that has afflicted most schools' attempts to implement the "balanced" literacy approach. In order to do so, schools need support systems that ensure an effective pedagogy is used and the implementation fidelity or tikanga of literacy practices is embedded in the school. Just as on any marae, schools need an institutionalised means of interacting effectively; that is, a "pedagogy" and a means of ensuring tikanga is observed—a means of ensuring that literacy practices are implemented with fidelity.

Solutions: The need for schools to become responsive North-East learning institutions

The New Zealand Ministry of Education released a new literacy and numeracy strategy in 2022 to guide needed improvements,[14] the aim of which is:

> to help them deliver consistent and high-quality teaching and learning experiences to ākonga. This requires us to get the balance right between what is 'tight' and 'loose' in the system … Reducing the element of chance by offering more clarity and system stewardship is a key step towards ensuring kaiako, teachers, and leaders can confidently provide ākonga with the teaching and learning they need. (p. 2)

To achieve these goals, the new Literacy, Communications and Maths Strategy is organised around five interconnected focus areas. These include:

- clear expectations for teaching and learning to guide effective practice
- capability supports along the career pathway to develop effective teachers who can meet the needs of diverse groups of learners
- educationally powerful connections between learners, families, iwi, communities, and education settings to enhance learning
- a system of learning supports to respond to the needs of learners
- and system-wide evaluation to support a "system that learns".

These are sound suggestions as to *what* school leaders need to do to support the implementation of the new strategy. However, it is not clear just *how* school principals and other leaders can respond to this strategy and embed the practices with fidelity for long-term sustainability. There is talk about a "common code of practice" being introduced

---

14 Cabinet Paper material. Proactive release. Minister & portfolio Hon Jan Tinetti, Associate Minister of Education. *Strategies for Literacy and Mathematics & Statistics, and for Te Reo Matatini and Pāngarau.* Date considered 13 December 2021. Date of release 28 March 2022. https://assets.education.govt.nz/public/Documents/our-work/information-releases/Issue-Specific-release-School-Building-Performance/Literacy-and-Mathematics/Strategies-for-te-reo-matatini-and-pangarau-literacy-and-mathematics.pdf

which makes good sense when you consider the negative impact of deficit theorising, monocultural pedagogies, and the variability in teaching practice in the immediate and longer term. The strategy also identifies some of the structural transformations that are needed to ensure that literacy and other teaching strategies are implemented with fidelity beyond the initial support offered when new approaches are being implemented. However, what is missing is the specifics of what the transformations look like in practice. Hence this book.

What this book explores is an intervention model that is led by the school's principal, that engages the school's team leaders to support teachers in ways that ensure they can effectively implement literacy and other learning approaches with fidelity in collaboration with others. The model also identifies the means that leaders use to support teachers so that they can support their students' learning in ways that reinforce and embed the approach, not modify or dilute it. Without this intervention, teachers will modify or even abandon effective approaches once support is removed. I am not advocating a surveillance approach. In contrast, I am advocating the implementation of an institutionalised means whereby teachers can be supported to collaboratively interrogate the impact of their teaching practices on student performance, modify their practices responsively, and, in this way, realise their school's goals for equity and cultural sustainability.

What I am suggesting is that perhaps the solution to the literacy crisis does not lie in the field of literacy or in arguments between the advocates of the various approaches to teaching literacy. What I am trying to say is that adherents of the "structured" literacy approaches are just as likely to fall down the same rabbit hole that the "balanced" literacy approach has been down for some time now. I think there are some wonderful ideas in both approaches. What I am trying to provide is a means of ensuring success for whichever approach is being used or chosen. My contention is that the long-term, successful implementation of literacy approaches with fidelity (and teaching in all other curriculum areas for that matter), lies in the pedagogy used and the "within-school" support systems provided by principals and activated by leaders.

It is necessary to acknowledge that developing and implementing effective support systems to ensure ongoing sustainability and fidelity of implementation of the literacy approach and the pedagogy chosen will have a huge impact upon a school. It will involve changing the structure and purposes of meetings, the role and tasks of senior and middle-level leaders, how evidence of teaching practice and student performance is gathered and how it is used, and who is included in learning processes in the school and in what ways they are included. It will involve a culture change in many schools away from the notion that teachers are the best determiners of what constitutes effective pedagogy to a more collaborative and responsive approach based on evidence of student performance in relation to teaching practice. This means the de-privatising of classrooms with all that entails. And perhaps above all it will involve principals in leading the reprioritising of how staffing is allocated and used and how funding is spent so as to realise the school's goals.

Crucial to the ongoing success of any intervention is the fidelity or the tikanga of its implementation. If schools do not have a means of ensuring the tikanga of implementation, teachers modifying or diluting the processes of the intervention will overwhelm the benefits of any innovation. However, instead of blaming teachers for this variability in practice, North-East leaders provide them with effective support systems to ensure they maintain effective North-East teaching practices. What is of further significance is that the equitable achievement gains in literacy, made through the implementation of North-East teaching and leadership practices, are also mirrored in other areas of learning.

A model for school transformation into North-East learning institutions

In this chapter, I will detail those dimensions of schooling that school leaders need to address in order for them to create a school in which literacy approaches—and other similar approaches to numeracy and learning in other curriculum areas, for example—can be addressed. To do so I have used the GPILSEO model that we developed as part of the Te Kotahitanga project over a decade ago to identify those actions school principals and other leaders need to undertake to support their teachers to move to the North-East and remain there.

As I explained in the introduction, our initial focus when developing the Te Kotahitanga project had been on changing classroom relationships and interactions in order to improve Māori students' achievement. We were delighted to see gains being made in Māori student achievement measured across a number of indicators, from Māori students' schooling experiences, to classroom engagement, through to improvements in national, external examinations. However, we began to notice that, gradually, as the initial impetus, funding, and external support for the project were withdrawn at the end of the project's initial 3-year implementation period, three trends began to develop. The first was that the pedagogy that was central to the successful improvements in Māori students' achievement began to be diluted and modified to the extent that, in only a short period of time, what was happening in many classrooms was unrecognisable as what we knew were the crucial components of the successful pedagogy. The second impact was that many teachers began to move away from being able to use the pedagogy entirely, leaving those who did as an enclave within the school. A third outcome was that only half of the schools continued to maintain the programme within their schools in any form at all.

Some schools did maintain the impetus on their own, re-prioritising their own funding to support the coaches, but most went back to the way they had been teaching and supporting teachers prior to the project's initiation. We also saw Māori student achievement outcomes reverting to those prior to the intervention, that is, lower than that of their non-Māori peers.

Focusing on the classroom as the sole nexus of change was inadequate because, although the reform had changed the core of classroom practice in many cases, it did not appear to have impacted beyond the classrooms into the central support systems of most of the schools. Nor had it impacted on the schools' leadership practices at all levels of the schools so they could support the changes being made in the classrooms in a more systematic and sustainable manner.

It came clear to us that it was necessary to develop a model for changing school leadership practices that was as transformative as that we had undertaken with classroom teachers. Therefore, just as the teaching model was developed to be responsive to and supportive of the learning needs of students, we needed to develop a model of leadership that was supportive of and responsive to the learning needs of teachers.

The GPILSEO model first appeared in a monograph in 2005 as a result of an investigation into what effective educational leadership of educational reform looked like. The study was funded by Ngā Pae o Te Māramatanga (Bishop & O'Sullivan, 2005). It was tested and revised with leaders in Te Kotahitanga project schools in the late 2000s, and in 2010 it was developed further in a book about how school and system leaders could scale up successful education reforms (Bishop et al., 2010). It was then used with school leaders in Phase 5, the last phase of the project in that year.

Phase 5 of the project ran from 2010 to 2013. The initial outcomes from this phase were very encouraging, showing the achievement of Māori students in the Phase 5 schools (as measured by NCEA levels 1–3) improved at around three times the rate of Māori in a comparison set of schools. This progress was higher than had been made at a similar time by the Phase 4 schools. In addition, by 2012, the number of Year 13 students achieving NCEA level 3 in Phase 5 schools was nearly three times what it had been 4 years earlier. Also, a very high proportion of Years 9 and 10 Māori students in Phase 5 schools (87%) reported that it felt good to be Māori in their school ("always" or "mostly"), and over 60% reported that their teachers "always" or "mostly" knew how to help them learn (Alton-Lee, 2015).

However, as I explained earlier, the funding approach used in Te Kotahitanga impacted upon the sustainability of the project. In the model schools were provided with external funding from the Ministry of Education to release staff to learn how to coach their peers in the ways of the new relational pedagogy. The funding provided would then be gradually reduced with the expectation that the schools would re-prioritise their own funding to sustain the project in their schools. However, now, some 10 years after funding ceased, in most cases this never happened, nor have the gains in achievement levels made in the Phase 5 schools or in most of the earlier phases of schools been maintained.

However, because most principals did not take ownership of the project in this way by re-prioritising funding and re-allocating staffing, they were not able to maintain the central institutions of the reform. What this meant is that they missed the opportunity to embed formative conversations within the institutional structure of schools, at a number of levels within the school, about the impact of teaching and leadership on student and teacher performance and progress. These formative conversations need to be undertaken within formal, structured opportunities created within the school in a regular, repetitive cycle for this specific purpose. And they are best led by competent North-East leaders who are able to direct the deliberations towards constructive and effective use of the preferred pedagogic intervention in ways intended. However, because of the reliance on external funding to fund the release of teachers to run these formative team meetings and coaching sessions, they were among the first things to be abandoned when the external funding was withdrawn. In other words, these infrastructural institutions never became embedded within the schools' support systems.

The use of external funding to release teachers from their usual teaching duties to coach others also limited the inclusion of a very experienced cohort of staff, the middle-level leaders within the school, and many times left them marginalised. This meant that the schools did not develop sufficient capacity among their leaders to undertake the necessary leadership roles. By releasing some "enthusiastic" staff for the coaching function, we limited the necessity to transform existing leadership roles. In effect, we developed a power structure separate from the existing lines of power and responsibility within the school. In this way, we created a separate cohort of "experts" whose function was reliant upon the external funding, and this function disappeared with the demise of that funding. What we should have been doing was to work within the existing authority and responsibility structures of the school. What was needed was middle-level leaders, who have responsibility for teams of teachers in parts of the school, to be supported to undertake a North-East leadership role.

As I identified earlier, all of these problems negated the development of what John Hattie (2012) has termed the collective efficacy of the school's staff, its parents, and the local community. It has been shown that, when this collectivity is engaged, the impact on student outcomes is huge, in the order of an effect size of 1.57. Ironically, the use of external funding meant that those project institutions and the specialist positions that were most likely to promote the collective efficacy of the staff, and which were designed to remain in the school, essentially disappeared once external funding was withdrawn from the schools.

At best, most of the project schools are now implementing some of the institutions of the project, with some teachers, for some of the time. Essentially it remains as an enclave in most schools. Only a very few schools have retained the project in all settings and, encouragingly, in these schools, evidence shows that Māori student achievement gains are outstanding, on par with those of their peers. In addition, because they have maintained the central relationship-based, culturally responsive pedagogy, they are also seeing their goals of promoting cultural sustainability being realised. In fact, a number of these schools have recently been included in the Prime Minister's Award for Excellence in Teaching and Learning in a proportion outweighing what we would expect to occur randomly or by chance.

This current iteration of the model in Figure 3.1 builds on and acknowledges earlier versions. However, since 2013, through a process of critical reflection on the details of the model and by working with educators from Cognition Education in their Relationships First programme,[15] a number of improvements have been developed. These include the further clarification over what constitutes the goal setting process, details of the pedagogy, the replacement of the broad term *institutions* with the more specific term *infrastructure*, clarification about actual leadership tasks, and functions and the inclusion of the concept of "learning partnerships" to include parents and families more effectively. However, perhaps the most crucial innovation has been addressing the issue of funding and the allocation of staffing. In this further iteration, it is made clear that the reallocation of funding and staffing is just as much a part of the process of transformation as the other dimensions of leadership. Hence, schools that are part of Cognition Education's Relationships First programme are expected, as they transform the roles and functions of their staff, to re-prioritise and re-allocate their schools' staffing and resources. The aim of this is to ensure that the existing resources of the school are used strategically in an ongoing manner so that their goals are realised.

The current iteration of the model is as follows.

---

15 https://www.cognitioneducation.co.nz/relationships-first/

Chapter 3 GPILSEO: A model for reform

Figure 3.1: The GPILSEO model—the institutional pattern for transforming a school into a North-East learning institution

North-East schools' leaders lead the development of the following dimensions of the model:
• **Goals:** SMART Goals[16] are collaboratively set at all levels of the school to focus on promoting learning excellence though an equity approach within a framework that ensures cultural sustainability by including Māori students' wellbeing, their cultural safety, identity, language, and culture as a base for learning. North-East schools' goals include those that focus on realising equity between Māori and non-Māori students within 2 years, Māori succeeding as Māori, and other marginalised students realising the benefits of the transformed school as well. School leaders realise these goals by strategically planning and de-cluttering the school.
• **Pedagogy:** A common code of practice is implemented. This is termed the North-East relationship-based pedagogy that includes culturally responsive and sustaining, dialogically interactive and formative-focused principles and practices. This pedagogy is instituted in all levels of the schools to ensure that all learners learn to become both successful task-orientated, self-regulating, and self-determining learners in ways that promote cultural sustainability. The common pedagogic code includes those acting as "teachers"; that is, as Leaders of Learning creating an extended family-like context for learning, interacting within this context in ways we know promote learning and monitoring the impact of teaching practices on student learning and modifying their practices accordingly.
• **Infrastructure.** Infrastructural institutions are developed within the school to support the effective implementation of the common code of pedagogic practice. Institutions that do not serve the purposes of the schools are discarded.
• **Leadership:** North-East leadership skills and knowledge of how to work within infrastructural support systems to ensure the effective implementation of pedagogic practices are distributed throughout the school.
• **Spread:** All teachers, leaders, parents, and community leaders are (or are becoming) involved in learning in ways that add value to students' learning.
• **Evidence:** Systems for evidence gathering and interrogation are developed so that decision making and problem solving at all levels of the schools are able to be evidence-based.
• **Ownership:** Collective ownership of the transformation, through strategic planning, resourcing and self-reviewing demonstrates the importance of the goals of the school.

When we consider the implementation of these dimensions in North-East schools, it appears that there is a sequence that most follow. The first step is to undertake an assessment of the current achievement and experiences of Māori students in the school. If this analysis shows disparities in outcomes and experiences, the principal commences the process of collaboratively setting goals for the school that address these disparities in outcomes and experiences. To ensure this occurs, the

---

16 These goals are Specific, Measurable, Attainable, Relevant, and Time-bound.

principal leads the development of a strategic plan that identifies how the goals will be realised, including those activities in the school that need to be discarded as not assisting in the realisation of their goals. The purpose of goal setting and strategic planning is to focus the whole school onto the urgent need to address problems of disparity in as short a time as possible.

The next important step is the implementation of the pedagogy as the central change agent, for, if this does not occur, structural transformations have little value. What we have found in North-East schools is that structural changes need to be implemented in response to and supportive of pedagogic innovations.

In the next phase of the sequence, following the goal setting and the implementation of the relationship-based pedagogy, schools move into transforming the support systems of the school. The purpose of this is to ensure the implementation fidelity of the pedagogy and specific teaching approaches over time, to add value to students' learning, and to ensure there is an evidence base for decision making and problem solving. These transformations include the development of a supportive infrastructure, the development of North-East leadership practices, the inclusion of all involved, and a means of gathering and using evidence for decision making and problem solving.

Ownership is central to each dimension of the model and is seen at each phase. Ownership means that principals take on the responsibility for:

- leading the collaborative development of goals
- the strategic planning necessary for the realisation of these goals
- focusing the school and removing "clutter"
- taking responsibility for providing their staff with effective professional learning opportunities so that they can become proficient in the long-term implementation of the relationship-based pedagogy including appropriate learning strategies and approaches
- providing a supportive infrastructure to ensure the implementation fidelity of the pedagogy

- ensuring leaders have the skills and knowledge to work within the infrastructure so as to provide instruction and monitoring of teachers' performance
- including parents and community leaders
- providing and using data-management systems
- taking ownership of the problems and solutions for realising the school's goals.

This sequence can be seen in Figure 3.2.

Figure 3.2: The Sequence of the implementation of the dimensions.

Phase 1. Goal setting and pedagogy
• **Goal setting.** Baseline data of Māori students' schooling experiences and achievements is gathered for future reference. Prospective North-East principals then lead the school's community to set SMART goals that are responsive to Māori parents' (as represented by government agencies) aspirations for Māori students to achieve on par with their non-Māori peers and to succeed "as Māori". School goals also include the objective that other marginalised students will also benefit from the transformation process. Prospective North-East leaders then develop and implement a strategic plan so as to transform the school into a North-East learning institution where these goals are realised. This includes removing those initiatives that don't assist the school to realise its goals.
Phase 2. The implementation of the North-East Leaders of Learning Profile
• This goal-setting process is followed by the implementation of an effective and proven Relationship-based, North-East **pedagogy** such as the *North-East Leaders of Learning Profile* across the school. It is this pedagogy that will realise the goals of improving Māori achievement *as Māori* and other marginalised students' achievement in multiple areas including academic, cultural, social, and leadership. It is within this pedagogic framework that specific literacy strategies can be implemented so as to ensure their ongoing implementation fidelity, sustainability, and efficacy.
Phase 3: The structural transformation of the school into a North-East learning institution
This phase consists of school principals leading the implementation of a number of support systems in the school to: • Institutionalise a supportive **infrastructure** that ensures teachers can learn and implement the principles and strategies of the *North-East Leaders of Learning Profile* with fidelity. This means that teachers are able to learn about and implement the dimensions of this pedagogy in their classrooms through their collective interrogation of the impact of their teaching practices on student learning performance and progress with learning. • Transforming the role and function of senior- and middle-level **leaders** so as to ensure that any initial coaching provided by outside experts is transferred to in-school North-East leaders. In-school North-East leaders can then coach teachers and other leaders to learn how to implement the *North-East Leaders of Learning Profile*, chair and guide North-East meetings at differing levels to interrogate evidence of student learning, and monitor the overall progress of all teachers, leaders, and the whole school towards its agreed-to goals.

- **Spreading** the reform to eventually include all teachers, leaders, and parents, families, and community leaders into Learning Partnerships in ways that add value to student learning.

- Ensuring that the school has a robust data management system to provide **evidence** of teaching practice and student performance. Principals then need to ensure that teachers and leaders are able to use this evidence of student performance in ways that support their teaching and leadership practices. Such use needs to ensure that whatever learning approach is chosen is done so with fidelity. Most interventions will come with a means of ensuring fidelity in its initial stages. Ensuring that this is maintained over time is a major leadership task.

Phase 4: Taking **ownership** *of the problems and solutions.*

This phase consists of the principal leading the collective ownership of the transformation process by:

- strategic planning to set the direction for the school's participants to realise their goals

- re-allocating the school's human and funding resources so as to ensure the school's support systems are implemented with fidelity

- engaging in a process of self-review to identify how well the school is progressing towards realising its goals.

Using GPILSEO for quality assurance purposes

In this way, principals are able to use the GPILSEO model to set their school up for the transformation into a North-East learning institution. Some will need outside assistance. Others will be able to address the means of implementing the changes themselves. Whatever the case, once the principal has led the identification of the changes that need to take place, and identified how they will go about implementing them, they and the other school leaders will then be able to use the GPILSEO model again for formative purposes to see how well the "learners" in their areas of responsibility are able to work within the various dimensions of the model.

The questions that principals need to ask of the team leaders, and team leaders need to ask of teachers in their area of responsibility include:

- How well are team leaders/teachers able to set goals for their own learning and for the learning for those whose learning they are responsible?

- How well do they understand the pedagogy to depth and make use of the pedagogy?

- How well are they able to work within the support systems designed to support the implementation of the pedagogy?

- How well are they able to undertake the North-East leadership roles necessary for the support systems to function effectively?
- How well are they able to work with others to ensure the collective efficacy of the staff is realised? How well are they able to include students' parents, families, and community leaders into the processes of learning?
- How well are they able to gather and make use of evidence of their own practice in relation to student performance and support others to do so?
- How well are they taking ownership of the processes of transformation in their area of responsibility by planning, resourcing, and reviewing their progress?

The model is also useful for use at the school level to see how well the school as an entity is undergoing its necessary transformation.

The questions that the North-East principal and senior leaders need to ask of their school include:

- How well are we going in realising the goals we have set in response to Māori parents' aspirations for their children to be successful learners? And for them to be successful learners as Māori?
- How well have we managed to implement the North-East relationship-based pedagogy (the *North-East Leaders of Learning Profile*)?
- How well have we managed to implement the support infrastructure necessary for the effective implementation of the preferred pedagogy in our school?
- How well have we managed to transform leaders' practice from primarily administrative to become North-East leaders who can work within the school's support infrastructure in ways that support teachers as learners?
- How well are our staff able to work with others to ensure the collective efficacy of the staff is realised?
- How well are we able to include students' parents, families, and community members into the processes of learning so as to add value to our students' learning?

- How well are our teachers, team leaders, and senior leaders able to gather and make use of evidence of their own practice in relation to student/learner performance and support others to do so?
- How well are we planning, resourcing, and reviewing our taking ownership of the processes of transformation?

In this way, school leaders can address John Hattie's three formative assessment questions: How they we going? Where to next? How are we going to get there? You will see that these are the same questions that teachers and students use in their classrooms so they too, can both become self-managing learners.

These questions can be presented in a rubric so that a quantitative measure is attached to each dimension at specified times of the year. In this way, the principal and senior leaders can monitor how well the school is moving towards the North-East.

In the next chapter, I will begin to detail the dimensions of the GPILSEO model as they are implemented in a North-East school. The first dimension is goal setting.

Chapter 4
Goal-setting and commencing the transformation into a North-East school

Introduction

This chapter commences the process of identifying how aspiring North-East leaders lead the transformation of their schools into North-East learning institutions. It deals with goal setting, that essential part of the transformation process that needs to be undertaken by teachers, team leaders, and principals in their respective areas of responsibility in order that all of their actions are orientated towards addressing those crises in education that have plagued our people and our society for far too long.

Goal setting is of fundamental importance to the creation of North-East schools because it signals the specific direction the school is intending to take in order to address the learning needs of, in this case, Māori students. Goal setting also identifies the school's prime objectives, includes the school's strategic means of realising these objectives, and identifies what would constitute appropriate milestones along the way.

Leading to the North-East: Ensuring the fidelity of relationship-based learning

Most goal-setting exercises for North-East schools are actually a statement of the leaders' dissatisfaction with the current situation in their schools. Generally, it is a realisation that the patterns of attendance, engagement, retention, and achievement (AERA)[17] measures for Māori students are not acceptable. Leaders are also expressing their dissatisfaction with how these AERA outcomes have been arrived at; that is, their dissatisfaction with the relationships and teaching and learning interactions that Māori students and their families have repeatedly told us negatively impact on their potential to be successful learners. This means that goal setting necessarily focuses on the interaction between the schooling experiences of Māori students and how these are reflected in the AERA measures.

As was detailed earlier, what we have found over the years about the pattern of relationships and interactions includes Māori students being the recipients of negative stereotyping because of their being Māori. It also includes their being treated negatively in classrooms because of deficit explanations for their performance by their teachers and other staff members and the lack of any visible caring if they are present, let alone being successful learners. Also included are Māori students' voiced concerns about the problems caused by their teachers having low expectations for their learning performance, providing limited curriculum content, repeating remedial strategies, continuing the use of ineffective boring "chalk and talk" teaching strategies, and using "behaviour modification" practices too often. All of the students we have spoken to over the years, both here and overseas, explained that these teaching approaches have made them into reluctant and unsuccessful participants in most educational settings.

In effect then, Māori students are only too aware that their ongoing academic achievement levels are more closely related to their being

---

17 While these measures are usually applied to student learning, they are just as useful as measures when the "learner" is a teacher or a more senior member of staff. For example, if a teacher or a team leader is absent, be it literally or figuratively, then this will signal to the Leader of Learning the need to follow up their absence, its reasons, and investigate possible means of addressing this situation. Similarly, if teachers or team leaders are not remaining on the kaupapa, and are reverting to a more traditional, non-productive pedagogy, or are not engaging in the work, and not making progress with their learning, then this will signal that the Leader of Learning has something that needs to be addressed.

Māori than are any attempts to realise their potential. In effect, negative stereotyping actually blames Māori students for their low performance. Further, Māori students and their families understand these toxic relationships to be a targeted attack on their identity as Māori. They report that mainstream classrooms are culturally unsafe places for them as Māori; they are not able to be themselves, to use their language and culturally based ways of making sense of the world to successfully participate in learning. Sadly, the effect of these negative experiences at school is not only to alienate Māori students from participation in the education system and in the wider New Zealand society, it also limits their abilities to participate in te ao Māori.

When we spoke to those parenting Māori students, they told us of their having had similar experiences when they were at school, and of their disappointment that these negative relationships and interactions were now intergenerational. They spoke of the need for schools to reach out to their children and establish caring and learning relationships along whānau lines. They were clear that this would see vast improvements being made in their children's learning outcomes. They were also convinced that schools establishing relationships with themselves in ways that were responsive to their aspirations for their children's learning would be an additional means of improving their children's learning outcomes. They were keen to participate in their children's learning journeys but could not see any ways that they could contribute because there did not seem to be any place for them in the school. These experiences create a cycle where their feelings of being rejected, coupled with school leaders' and teachers' feelings of bewilderment and frustration, make for a toxic recipe for non-communication.

1. The first part of a goal-setting exercise is to identify the current pattern of relationships and interactions in the school

A necessary step at the outset of the transformation of their school into a North-East learning institution is for an aspiring North-East principal to investigate whether this generalised pattern of relationships and teaching and learning interactions and their outcomes is replicated in their school. They can do so by two means. First is by an analysis of the current AERA patterns of Māori students in the school. This will help them to identify the need for achievement goals for Māori students. This analysis should also include all those other groups of students who are being marginalised in most schools in New Zealand by their supposed deficiencies. This analysis will enable them to set achievement goals for these other marginalised students as well. Of course, this analysis presupposes an efficient data management system is in place. If this is not the case, then this needs to be attended to with all due haste.

Secondly, this quantitative analysis of achievement needs to be accompanied by a qualitative analysis of Māori students' current schooling experiences in terms of the relationships and interactions that they are part of in class and also outside of classrooms. The outside dimension is also important because many Māori students have told us that, while they may get on well with their own classroom teachers, they are often subject to stereotyping behaviour from some other teachers in the playground.

As these measures of the relationships and interaction patterns will involve talking face-to-face with students, it will probably be preferable that someone from outside the school initially undertakes these conversations. This reduces the pressure of the power relationship that exists between teachers and students, allowing them to be more frank than perhaps they would be with their current teachers or school leaders. However, in time, school personnel should be able to take over these "students' voice" conversations once relational trust is built through the overall school's transformation process and the school has been developed into a North-East "whānau".

It is also important that a repeat conversation is conducted. I say this because, when we commenced the Te Kotahitanga project, we conducted these interviews with a number of groups of students in a range of schools. We found that, during the first interview, the students were generally quiet and rather subdued. However, on our return for a second follow-up interview, and importantly, as there had been no consequences from what they had said in the first interview, they were very open with their observations about what was happening in their school. These second and sometimes third interviews allowed us the opportunity to say to the students something like, "In the last interview, you said such-and-such. What did you mean by that?" This approach gave the students the opportunity to delve more deeply into their experiences and explain what they meant to them in more detail. It is important that young people are given this opportunity to reflect upon what they are saying rather than schools' leaders thinking that the first thing they say is what they really mean.

This qualitative approach is also far better than giving a survey to students where they only get a one-off opportunity to provide an answer. We found that, in some cases, by returning with the same questions, we were provided with extremely erudite and articulate descriptions of the problems these young people were facing at school, and the solutions offered were often profound and potentially very successful if they had been implemented. Having said that, a survey of Māori students' experiences can be useful as a touchstone of progress being made in the school towards the North-East. But a survey is actually a quantitative exercise, not to be confused with the depth and richness that is to be found in a qualitative activity.

In our conversations with Māori students, we used a simple set of questions asking them to tell us about their experiences of being Māori in this school. Opening activities asked students to tell us about themselves and how they were going at the school. We then moved onto asking them to expand upon some of the things they had raised earlier in the interview or had mentioned in the first round. This was usually all it took to get students talking about their experiences. It was enhanced of course by our talking with groups of students because it enabled them to bounce ideas off each other. At some appropriate time in the first interview, or more usually in a later session, we said to the group, "If we could tell your teachers how they could teach you so that you and your friends could be successful learners in their classrooms, what could you tell us to say to them?" This invitation often opened the flood gates, and, as I said earlier, many of the suggestions were very similar to those we had been reading in education textbooks. But their ideas were far more complex than those of many of their teachers whose solutions were severely curtailed by their drawing on deficit explanations that only provided limited, and negative, possibilities for Māori students' learning.

We also wanted them to tell us what it was like specifically to be Māori in this school. The students in many schools found this to be very hard to articulate clearly, to the extent that one day a group of students told one of our interviewers that it would be easier to show her than to tell her. So began the now-famous "smoking" story I recounted in *Teaching to the North-East*. To cut a long story short, it involved two random groups of duty teachers, zeroing in on a group of Māori students who were smoking cigarettes out on the rugby ground. This happened at two different times over the lunch break and resulted in their dishing out detentions for misbehaviour. What was significant, however, and this is what the students wanted our interviewer to see, was that there were two other groups of non-Māori students, similarly engaged in cigarette smoking out on the rugby grounds. To the amazement of our interviewer, they were left alone while the group of Māori students were disciplined, not once, but twice! The students then turned to her and said, "That is what it is like to be a Māori student in this school."

Collecting "student voice" in this way is not only useful for goal setting, but is also an extremely useful part of the ongoing quality assurance processes of the school to provide a base from which to measure how well the school is progressing with improving relationships and subsequent learning outcomes. North-East schools that are currently part of Cognition Education's Relationships First programme make use of this approach by following up the initial interviews by sampling student experiences on an annual basis. Their leaders find this information to be extremely valuable for monitoring the progress they are making towards the North-East. This information is also a major form of achievement assessment because the change in schooling experiences of Māori students is a powerful measure of the school's transformation.

It is also a very important check on the pedagogic direction that the school has taken to realise the goals they have set to improve Māori students' literacy and other learning. By this I mean, for example, many schools' leaders identify that the solution to Māori students' literacy learning difficulties is to implement a specific literacy learning approach in the school. However, unless this specific approach also addresses the wider relational and interaction concerns that Māori students have identified as limiting their opportunities to be successful learners, the initial gains made as a result of a new literacy approach may not be sustainable. In other words, goal setting should not just result in the introduction of a new approach to literacy learning, but rather it should also herald a wider pedagogic transformation.

Including teachers

It is also important to identify where most teachers in the school stand in relation to Māori student achievement. Again, outside experts are perhaps better able to conduct these interviews to reduce the potential that current power relationships may have to limit candid responses. The actual purpose of these initial interviews is to identify which discourses teachers are drawing from when explaining the patterns of Māori student achievement. This will identify for school leaders what sort of approach they need to take with their staff and how well their ideas of transforming the school are likely to be received.

Teachers need an opportunity to express how they feel when teaching Māori students. Principals need to know if they are angry and upset, feel that they are being blamed for the lack of progress of the Māori students in their class, frustrated by the students' attendance patterns and general demeanour, and are ready to leave the profession. It is the need to transform these types of experiences and understandings of both teachers and Māori students that is one of the main purposes of transforming the school into a North-East learning institution.

Goal setting is what guides the transformation. However, it is vital that prior to any attempts to engage in goal setting of the type suggested in this chapter, teachers' positioning regarding the discourses they are drawing from are identified, and their emotional responses are clearly understood. Apart from anything else, this evidence will supply leaders with a further baseline from which they can measure the progress their school is making towards the North-East. North-East teachers are not angry and frustrated, they are confident, competent professional educators. They are very secure in their abilities to relate and interact with Māori students in ways that ensure these students will achieve on par with their non-Māori peers, will be successful learners as Māori, and that the benefits of a North-East classroom will be shared with all its students. North-East teachers' ability to create caring learning relationships in their classroom enables them to do their job as teachers in ways that are satisfying to them as caring and competent professionals.

Including Māori parents, families, and communities

Developing relationships with Māori children's parents, families, and their communities so as to include them in their children's learning, including goal setting, needs to follow a similar pattern. Establishing relationships often means that aspiring North-East principals will go to community venues for meetings, understanding that expecting people who may have had a negative schooling experience themselves will be hesitant to come to the school itself. There are many ways that such meetings can be conducted and many possible locations. Whatever the case, the aim is to ascertain just what their aspirations are for the education of their children and how best schools might go about realising these aspirations. Again, this information is probably not going to be forthcoming at the first meeting, and follow-up meetings may be necessary.

The three case study school principals, whose experiences are detailed later in this book, are all experts at developing these parental and community relationships and they all have different stories to tell of how they go about this process. What they have in common, however, just as when relating and interacting with students and teachers, they understand that time is of the essence and an openness to "listen", and not "tell" is essential. The next important feature of these relationships is that community members need to see that they have been listened to, that they and their ideas are included in the ongoing developments of the school, and, overall, they have a place in the ongoing development of their children being successful learners.

Hence the need for inclusion of Māori students, their families, and communities into the process of goal setting. This means that principals who aspire to lead the transformation of their schools into North-East learning institutions will then be supported by community members to lead the collaborative development of a number of goals, specific objectives, and expected outcomes for the school in ways that are responsive to Māori peoples' aspirations for the education of their children. It is vital that parents, families, and the local community are involved in this process from the outset because the closer their aspirations are to those of the school, the better will be the achievement of their children.

One further implication of including parents, families, and community members into the process of goal setting is that it develops an accountability mechanism that assures community members that the school will be answerable to them for the ongoing and sustainable improvement in their children's educational outcomes in culturally sustainable ways. Schools that are actually at odds with the aspirations of their community need to create responsive relationships with their local community and, when their leaders do, they will receive support and assistance.

As a result, North-East leaders talk about their schools being a *whānau* where they have deliberately developed a pattern of inclusivity that involves a spiral of regular input, feedback, and participation from students, teachers, parents, families, and community members in ways that direct their school's activities and add value to students' learning.

Through this process of collaborative goal setting, these school-wide goals are then able to be replicated in team settings and classrooms across the school so as to ensure coherence of the whole-school approach.

So, in many ways, school principals commencing the process of North-East goal setting is, as Helen Timperley et al. identified in 2007, actually a positive response by school leaders to the totally unacceptable circumstances that are affecting Māori students currently and an expression of dissatisfaction with their schools' current performance in addressing them. It is their refusal to accept differences in outcomes being based on ethnic or other group membership. Therefore, goal setting is not just a desirable activity that affirms the current direction of the school. It actually sets out to disrupt the current patterns of relationships and interactions by being primarily outcomes and performance focused. In doing so, leaders are seeking to reorientate the school towards providing an education that is responsive to Māori peoples' aspirations for improving achievement in ways that ensure cultural sustainability.

2. What do North-East goals look like? A SMART analysis

I will now turn to a consideration of the three goals that feature in this book in terms of how they address the concerns Māori students and their families voice about the current pattern of relationships, interactions, and outcomes. The three goals are:

- Māori students will be achieving on par with their non-Māori peers in our school within 2 years.
- Māori students will succeed "as Māori".
- Other students, currently marginalised from being successful learners, will also benefit from the changes made in the school to benefit Māori students.

To analyse the potential effectiveness of these goals, I will use the SMART acronym that identifies the characteristics of effective goals. There are many such methods for goal setting, but I have found this one to be useful because of its clear focus and time frame. This theory states that goals need to be Specific, Measurable, Achievable, Relevant, and Time-bound.

These three North-East goals are **specific.** There is no mistaking the focus of these goals. They focus on what is often a hidden issue in many schools. That is, that Māori students' achievement is more to do with their being Māori rather than anything to do with schools addressing their potential. The first goal, for example, is a clear statement that the school intends eliminating the current gaps between Māori and non-Māori achievement. And in short order.

The second goal of Māori succeeding "as Māori" is responsive to the current schooling experiences of most Māori students in mainstream, English-medium schools. It is essential that this focus is part of goal setting because, as identified earlier in this chapter, many Māori students understand the current pattern of relationships and teaching and learning interactions to be an attack on their identity as Māori. It is that serious. They feel that they are not valued and wanted by their teachers and by the school as a whole. Hence a goal that states that Māori will succeed as Māori turns the whole situation on its head by saying that it is not just enough that Māori students achieve on par with their non-Māori peers, they must do so in ways that affirm them as Māori—which, after all, is what most mainstream schools do for their more successful clients.

What this means is that any pedagogy chosen to realise the first goal of improving Māori students' achievement to be on par with their non-Māori peers will also need to be culturally responsive to the aspirations of Māori people that their identify is affirmed by such a pedagogy. In effect, this means that any teaching approach needs to have a focus that is broad and culturally sustaining; not just on improving literacy learning.

The third goal is also specifically aimed at improving the academic and "cultural" experiences of other marginalised students by using the same methods as those being used to address Māori students' learning needs. Again, the implications are that it is not just a matter of improving literacy learning by introducing an approach; the context within which it is introduced is equally as important.

These three goals are also **measurable** because the school can use the same data gathering system for both Māori and non-Māori students. However, here is another issue we found at the outset of the Te Kotahitanga project. Many of the schools that had entered the project did not differentiate student achievement data along ethnic lines at that time. They had a student data management system that allowed them to do so; it was just that they did not see the need for this finer-grained differentiation. Since then, of course, a greater awareness of the need to differentiate data has spread throughout the sector so it would be very difficult to find a school now that did not have evidence in this form. Nevertheless, setting goals about reducing achievement differentials will alert the school's leaders to the need to examine their student data management system to ensure it can differentiate data in this way.

Of equal concern, we also found that once AERA measures were differentiated along ethnic lines we often found that leaders used deficit explanations to explain any differences in outcomes. I recall this happening on a number of occasions. For example, one response I recall vividly was leaders blaming parents for attendance differences once the pattern was revealed, rather than looking at what was happening to Māori students in their school's classrooms. Hence it is vital that any intervention includes a means of leaders challenging their own deficit explanations for differences in outcomes and a means of interrogating the impact of teaching practices on students' performance. Otherwise, all the differentiated data in the world won't of any use to realise the schools' goals.

These three goals are also **achievable** given the changes identified as part of the GPILSEO transformation process. Perhaps some school leaders might be sceptical, but the three case studies in this book will confirm this assertion. It is entirely possible to realise these goals in this time frame identified. In fact, as for the first goal, recent reports from the BSLA approach show that it is entirely possible to see that "achievement gaps evident at school entry level between Māori and non-Māori have significantly closed after just 10 weeks of BSLA teaching" (A. Macfarlane, 2022, personal communication). Also, earlier reports from this project showed that little if any difference remained between Māori and non-Māori students following earlier implementations of this approach (Gillon et al., 2019). Hence, that which has been accepted for decades—that differences in literacy skills and knowledge on school entry will remain, often for the rest of the students' time at school—is in fact readily challengeable and changeable.

However, nothing will change if the gaps are accepted as inevitable and nothing is done to address them. Once school leaders interrogate their own assumptions about Māori students and question if in fact they are accepting something that should not be accepted, perhaps addressing their own explanations for differentiated outcomes in their school being along ethnic lines, it is entirely possible to change matters. From this agentic positioning, leaders can set SMART goals with confidence that they will be realised given an effective model of change such as GPILSEO.

Goals being achievable is a major function of goal setting because it ensures that school leaders orientate all of the actions, roles, and tasks of the school community towards realising these goals. It is important that leaders acknowledge that maintaining the status quo will simply realise the same outcomes as always. School leaders need to acknowledge the need for them to lead the transformation of the central pedagogic and structural systems of the school so that all actions undertaken in the school will lead to realising these goals.

It is vital to reiterate that it is not just a matter of changing an approach to teaching but rather it is also important that leaders change the pedagogy and the support systems within the school to ensure that the teaching approach is implemented with the fidelity necessary for its successful long-term implementation. These pedagogic transformations need to be built on the creation of a culturally responsive context for learning. The structural transformations need to include those systemic supports teachers need to ensure they are able to implement the pedagogic transformation on an ongoing basis. The structural transformations that are the subject of later chapters in this book include the function of the meetings teachers attend, the role of leaders in supporting teachers' learning and sustaining effective pedagogic practices, who is included, and how data are gathered, displayed, and used. As we have seen, unless this latter transformation takes place, a new approach to teaching literacy learning might well see immediate and rewarding gains but, given the tendency for teachers to modify teaching approaches if they are not supported to maintain implementation fidelity, long-term sustainability of these gains is unlikely.

As I identified earlier, our schools are constantly being reminded by the Ministry of Education—as the prime agency of the government, acting on behalf of the people of New Zealand—of the need for schools to produce equitable outcomes through the implementation of an excellent education. Indeed, there is an air of urgency from all system-level leaders and politicians that this current pattern of inequality must be addressed forthwith. Similarly, the messages about the need for Māori students to achieve as Māori in ways that are responsive to Māori peoples' aspirations for the education of their children are unequivocal. Schools' goal setting needs to be responsive to these imperatives in ways that are entirely achievable, understandable by all involved in the schools' whānau, and within a realistic time frame.

Setting these goals is a matter of ensuring that the pedagogy and the support systems within the school are **relevant** to their potential for the goals being realised. If the current achievement patterns in your school are similar to most other schools in New Zealand (that is, inequitable), it will be necessary to question if the current pedagogic and support systems are fit for the purpose of realising the school's goals. However, if the answer is that they are not sufficiently supportive, the question becomes one of "What do we need to do to make sure they are?" This subject is detailed further in Chapter 8 in the section on self-review as evidence of ownership.

The **time frame** is a further important consideration. As I identified above, it is quite possible to see achievement gains in very short periods of time when new approaches to literacy or even other curriculum areas are introduced. In fact, short time frames for goals are essential to ensure staff motivation and focus are maintained. There is no need to drag it out. "Get it sorted and get on with other things" would be my approach. Goals that have very long time scales are more likely to be unsuccessful because of the difficulty of maintaining focus as other demands on time and resources come along. The other outcome of short-term-focused goals that are tightly focused on student achievement is that they also address any desired long-term cultural changes that are needed. In other words, often what are long-term "culture-of-the-school"-type goals will actually be able to be addressed by leaders focusing on short-term, achievement-orientated goals.

It is very important that time frames are responsive to parental and community aspirations. This means that they must not be captured by the school's time frame. What may be seen as parents being unrealistic by the school's leaders may in fact be seen as "provider capture" by the parents. As a result, school leaders will need to be purposely consultative with their staff, especially those who may still be drawing upon deficit explanations about Māori student potential. There again, just as the need to investigate if the school's data management systems are fit for purpose, there is a signal here that perhaps some teachers' mind-frames might not be conducive to the school realising its goals. In this way, this will be signalling to school leaders the need for them to engage in this issue with their staff in ways that all participants can retain their dignity and their jobs of course, but the goals of the school will be realised.

The third goal in this set is that transforming the school to better support Māori students will also benefit others who are currently being marginalised from being successful learners by what they bring to school being seen as deficiencies rather than potentialities.

Two examples of how to generate acceptance of the need for a new approach

When inducting new school leaders, facilitators/coaches, and teachers into the Te Kotahitanga programme, we used a large teaching space at one of our local Māori-medium wharekura, Ngā Taiatea. We did this for a number of reasons. Among these was that they had a space that was not used by the school every day, so we could use it as a fundraising activity for the school. It also gave the students an opportunity to practise manaakitanga ki ngā manuhiri. When we brought the new inductees to the training sessions, we were all welcomed by pōwhiri. Added to this experience, some of the students also helped their parents cater for us during induction sessions; again, as a part of this fundraising activity based on manaakitanga.

However, we also had an ulterior motive which was that we wanted to show our inductees, who were all from mainstream schools, just what a large group of successful Māori students actually looked like en masse. I remember arriving at the kura and being welcomed at the pōwhiri by the whole school, not just the kapa haka group. All of the students were present. They all knew the waiata and the haka pōwhiri and the appropriate kawa and tikanga. However, what was wonderful to see was the demeanour of all the students. They were all happy to be there. They looked us in the eyes and smiled. They were really pleased to see us and to show us how competent they were in this setting. They had pride in their participation and achievement that showed clearly in their faces and their ahua; their whole beings reflected their pride and wellbeing.

When I asked the principal, "How are the Māori students' other achievements at this school?", he replied that they were doing extremely well in NCEA, for example. With great pride he showed me their NCEA achievements, which were excellent. The students at this medium-sized, decile 1 school were outperforming their Māori and non-Māori peers in adjacent higher decile schools. However, their achievements were not limited to Māori or English medium. A major focus of the school was students learning Spanish and Japanese with all the cultural ways of understanding that these languages entailed. Indeed, part of the fundraising was to provide opportunities for students to travel to these countries to immerse themselves in other language groups' ways of making sense of the world. In this way, Māori-medium schools are not limiting their students' curriculum, but are building on their competence as learners so they can not only participate in te ao Māori and the wider New Zealand society, but they can also become "citizens of the world", building on their confidence as Māori.

Over the years, a number of hui participants expressed their admiration for what this host school was accomplishing. They also spoke of their own schools—the downcast eyes, hunched shoulders, and a general air of despondency among the Māori students. They also lamented the poor attendance patterns, limited engagement with learning, and the low achievement levels of the Māori students at their and similar schools. Most importantly, they determined that it would change. Their Māori students would look like those at Ngā Taiatea Wharekura. Job done!

A second example of how it is possible to address teachers' drawing on deficit discourses to explain Māori students' educational performance in a non-confrontational manner is by using narratives of students' and teachers' experiences such as those in Bishop and Berryman (2006). We found that providing teachers and school leaders with an opportunity to read and consider the impact of these mostly negative experiences to be a very effective way of their considering where they stood in relation to these stories. In this way, teachers reading about Māori students' schooling experiences provided them with a vicarious experience of what it was like to be a Māori student in classrooms and schools similar to theirs. These were often salutary experiences because, most often, they were unaware of what it was like to be a Māori student in their school or classroom. Many teachers were very quiet when they read these stories and determined to do something about the negative, toxic relationships they were reading about. This obviated the need for arguments about whether we should be focusing on the learning needs of Māori students. It negated any arguments about why we should be focusing on supporting Māori students and simply resulted in teachers asking how they might go about changing these horrible experiences for Māori students in their class and school. Again, job done.

Any approach to transforming a school into a North-East learning institution will be met with some resistance. It is vital that this initiative does not descend into arguments about "Why does the school need to focus of Māori students?", or "Why do we need to change what we have been doing successfully for years?" The problem with this happening at the outset of the reform process is that all that happens is we get better at the argument. Both sides put their point of view and both leave with their views unchanged. There will not be any ready changes in Māori students' schooling experiences and achievement, which, after all, is the main goal. So, it is important that we engage teachers and leaders in a process that skips over the need for an argument. This process needs to engage all staff in what, after all, is only a short-term activity; in improving Māori students' achievement outcomes to be on par with non-Māori students, in ways that they are able to be successful as Māori. And above all, no one will be harmed in the process.

3. The need for objectives and a strategic plan

The need for these analyses of current positionings and practices is further reinforced when we consider the need for a strategic plan with specific, measurable objectives to be developed. Following the defeat of the All Blacks by the Irish in July 2022, there was an outpouring of anguish. Among them was Zac de Silva, a business coach, who wrote in the *New Zealand Herald*[18] that the current leadership needed to develop a strategic plan to change how they were going to realise their goal of winning the Rugby World Cup the following year. He also identified that the first step in this process was to engage in some soul-searching to identify the root cause of the problem. He warned that this might be an uncomfortable experience, but it was necessary in order to enable them to move on to strategically planning how they could achieve their goals. He suggested that finding someone to blame is probably not the most productive thing you could do, remembering that when you point the finger at someone, there are three fingers pointing backwards at yourself. He then recounted the now-legendary story of how the All Blacks' coaches, led by Sir Graham Henry with Wayne Smith and Sir Steve Hansen, after some dire performances by the team, "came up with a brilliant strategy at the end of 2007, to give us a close-to-guaranteed

---

18 https://www.nzherald.co.nz/business/zac-de-silva-what-a-business-coach-would-do-with-the-all-blacks/IKOPKPUENWWJE2NHYVON64SJ2Y/

chance of the glory four years later, which came to fruition" by their winning the Rugby World Cup.

To Zac de Silva, a strategic plan is an overview that sets out how you will achieve your goals. It requires big-picture thinking. If you have a poor strategy, no matter how necessary or important your goals, or how good your culture or staff are, you will not succeed in realising your goals. It is when leaders take ownership—that is, responsibility for developing a strategy, and for the performance of their staff—that the potential for change is realised.

4. Goal setting also requires of school principals that they lead the de-cluttering of their school

By de-cluttering I mean that, when I talk to groups of principals, one of their biggest gripes is the huge number of initiatives they are offered, often with supporting funding, that they are expected to incorporate into their schools. A recent, yet to be published at the time of my writing this book, is a book by Arran Hamilton, John Hattie, and Dylan Wiliam (in press). The focus of the book is "de-cluttering". They term it "de-implementation" and they provide their readers with a systematic means of identifying and removing those initiatives in schools that don't add any value to the school realising its goals. This concept is revolutionary and is absolutely vital if schools are going to be able to realise their goals in a timely fashion. If school leaders are not ruthless in pursuing their goals, they will never be realised. A major part of making it happen it clearing the way ahead by de-cluttering.

As mentioned earlier, Elizabeth Forgie emphasised that keeping the focus of her school on the main goals of raising Māori student achievement in a culturally sustainable way meant they needed to "stick to their knitting". This meant that she had to be ruthless sometimes in turning away new offerings, many of which came from the Ministry of Education, especially given that many initiatives come with funding that could prove very useful in straitened times. She was absolutely convinced of the need to de-clutter and stay that way in order to realise the goals of the school. She also realised that, while some of the school's goals were realised within 2 years, there was potential for the means of sustaining these outcomes to improve. For example, while they achieved parity between Māori and non-Māori students in level 2 NCEA baseline statistics within 2 years, they still had work to do to get both groups up to the now-current level where nearly all students at Kerikeri High School achieve this qualification. The fact that these approaches took some time to mature was no impediment. If they needed time to be fully matured, then so be it. It was time they got.

A problem is created for school leaders when a further innovation is introduced to the school before the previous one has had time to become embedded. Then to the consternation of leaders, teachers, and students, a further innovation is introduced on top of the first two. The result is that none of them are implemented in the way they were designed to be; that is, with the fidelity needed to ensure the expected outcomes. And when they do not produce the outcomes that were intended, blame for the failure of the innovation to realise its goals is sheeted home to the leaders, the students or the teachers. The problem is actually with the layering of innovations and the lack of time for any one innovation to be implemented with the fidelity necessary to realise its expected outcomes.

When we introduced the Te Kotahitanga project at one very large high school, they had 80 different innovations running in the school! Each one had its own agenda, funding, and staffing allocations. Each had been added onto the existing core curriculum of the school over time in a cumulative manner that had more to do with the purposes of the innovation than with the goals of the school. Five years after the implementation of Te Kotahitanga, the school had five initiatives, all of which were focused on realising the school's goals. During these years, the school saw a huge gain in Māori student achievement taking place. Along with the implementation of the Te Kotahitanga pedagogy and support systems, the de-cluttering of the school's initiatives had played a very significant part in realising their goals.

Summary: The main purposes of goal setting

The main function of goals and objectives is to set the necessary directions for change. Goals orientate all actions, at all levels within the school including classrooms, team levels, the whole school, and the wider community towards their realisation and exclude those actions that do not contribute to the achievement of the goal.

This power of orientation cannot be over-emphasised because there are many calls on Leaders of Learnings' attention—both at the school and classroom level—so much so that the less-disciplined will be side-tracked from what is important for improving Māori and other marginalised students' learning. Goal setting is a powerful means of maintaining focus and orientation for sustainable learning to occur. As Robinson et al. (2009) suggest from an in-depth study of leadership, "Goals focus attention and lead to more persistent effort than would otherwise be the case" (p. 96). Also, persistent, sustained effort is what is necessary to improve educational outcomes for those students currently denied success. In other words, goal setting at its simplest channels leaders' energies and actions into finding ways in which the goals will be achieved and prioritises their actions in the face of multiple demands on their time and resourcing. This narrowing of focus and enhancing a sense of purpose increases the likelihood of goals being realised.

Along with these innovations, principals need to lead the development of a strategic plan and (re)allocation of staffing and funding to realise these goals and objectives. These goals are then able to be used as part of the school's quality assurance process where they can measure how well they are progressing towards the realisation of these aspirations. SMART goals enable formative quality assurance activities to be used to evaluate progress being made toward reaching the objectives of the school, how well the steps along the way that will achieve the agreed-to outcomes of their collective efforts are being implemented, and whether the time frame within which the goals can be realised is being kept to. These objectives are encapsulated in the strategic plan the leaders have developed. The strategic plan is a means that North-East leaders have for realising their goals.

And perhaps above all, the value of goal setting is in being able to identify arrival points, for if you do not have a plan, how do you know where you are going, and also how do you know if you have arrived in the North-East?

Overall, collaboratively developed goals that are responsive to Māori peoples' aspirations for their children to be highly successful learners who are confident and competent in te ao Māori, the wider New Zealand society, and the wider world set the scene for all the activities in North-East schools. Now the task before the schools' leaders is to set the process of transformation in motion by implementing a relationship-based pedagogy that includes culturally responsive and sustaining, dialogically interactive and formative-focused principles and practices. The next chapter details what this entails.

Chapter 5
Pedagogy: The North-East Leaders of Learning Profile

Introduction

The main agent aspiring North-East principals' use for realising their schools' goals is pedagogy. In North-East schools, the pedagogy used is the *North-East Leaders of Learning Profile*. This pedagogy is relationship-based; it includes culturally responsive and sustaining, dialogically interactive and formative-focused principles and practices. It is this pedagogy that ensures the transformation of their schools into North-East learning institutions.

Because of its centrality, it is important to know what I mean when I use this term. *Pedagogy is a theory of practice that consists of a set of principles that guide and direct teaching practices.* This means that, while it may appear that the major gains in student achievement are made through the implementation of specific literacy approaches for example, it is important to note that these approaches need to be implemented within a set of pedagogic principles that we know are those that ensure Māori students make gains in learning and cultural sustainability. This is especially so if the school's leaders want to sustain these gains in student achievement. These broad principles include *creating* a whānau context for learning, *interacting* dialogically within this context in ways we know promote learning, and *monitoring* the impact of these learning processes on student performance and progress. It is these principles and what they entail that create the context within which specific literacy strategies, for example, are able to be implemented. What these principles consist of is detailed in this chapter and how they are developed in practice is explained in the three case studies later in this book.

The North-East Leaders of Learning Profile

The pedagogy used in North-East schools is relationship-based because, when teachers, team leaders, and principals are able to create caring and learning relationships in their respective areas of responsibility, they are able to do their respective jobs most effectively. Simply put, effective North-East leaders care for and support their staff. Subsumed within this relational context for learning are culturally responsive and sustaining pedagogies so that learning builds on learners' cultural ways of making sense of the world. It also includes dialogic interactive pedagogies that ensure that learners are able to participate in learning in ways we know are most productive. These include drawing on learners' prior knowledge, the use of formative assessment processes, and co-constructing learning through the use of power-sharing strategies. The relational pedagogic framework also includes a formative focus that enables Leaders of Learning to monitor how well those learners whose learning they are responsible for to successfully engage in task and process learning.

This is the pedagogy that is used by North-East teachers in their classrooms when relating to and interacting with Māori students. What is of importance to this book is that the same pedagogy is used by the principal and middle-levels leaders in their respective areas of responsibility. They do so in the whole school and North-East team meetings respectively to support the ongoing learning and development of those team leaders and teachers for whom they are responsible. In other words, principals and team leaders, acting as Leaders of Learning, support the learning, performance, and progress of learners in their area of responsibility. For example, just as teachers are Leaders of Learning for the students in their classes, principals and senior leaders are Leaders of Learning for the whole school and team leaders. Middle-level (team) leaders are Leaders of Learning for those in the part of the school for which they have responsibility. How the pedagogy is used by North-East teachers was detailed in my earlier book on this topic, *Teaching to the North-East* (Bishop, 2019). How it is used by team and senior leaders, including principals, is the subject of this chapter.

North-East schools using the same pedagogy at each level of the school means that their students are guaranteed a common learning experience, teachers can learn about the pedagogy and reinforce their learning, and leaders are able to model the preferred pedagogy for teachers and students.

It is when there are different means of establishing relationships and interactions in schools that problems with implementation fidelity occur. Probably the most problematic for our purposes in this book is that, if different pedagogies are used at different levels of the school, staff at one level do not know what is happening at other levels, which is one of the main causes of variability of practice. It also means that goals are not reflected from one level to another, thereby limiting the potential for all involved to contribute to the realisation of the school's goals.

Whereas when the whole school is transformed into a North-East learning institution, the same pedagogy guides practice at each level of the school. What is important in a North-East school, however, is that all involved are supported by others in various roles and levels of responsibility in the school to be successful learners. This is what is meant by a "whole-of-school" or a "whānau" approach to pedagogy. "Whole-of-school" does not simply mean that all involved in the school have the same goals or even that they do the same things. It means that they have a common means of realising these goals and the school's support systems support them to do so in a coherent and commonly understood manner.

Implementing the profile

Once the decision has been made to begin the transformation of the school into a North-East learning institution, it is probably important that assistance is sought from outside experts to support the teachers, team leaders, and the principal with the myriad tasks and under-standings that are involved in transforming their respective areas of responsibility, be they a classroom, a team area, or the whole school.

Essentially what will change are the goals, the pedagogy, the infrastructure, the roles and responsibilities of leaders, who is included in the transformation and how they are included, the use made of evidence, and the strategic planning, resourcing, and reviewing of the transformation. A tall, but necessary, order.

What does the North-East Leaders of Learning Profile look like at the school-wide level?

There are three parts to the profile of what makes an effective North-East Leader of Learning. These include *creating* a whānau context for learning, *interacting* within this context in ways we know are most effective in supporting learning, and *monitoring* the impact of their teaching practices on learners' performance.

Part 1: Creating a whānau context

The first part of the profile that needs to be implemented is the extended family-like, whānau context for learning. This relational, culturally responsive context for learning needs to be implemented at all levels of the school including the whole school, teams, and classrooms.

North-East Leaders of Learning reject deficit explanations for all learners' learning

The first dimension of this part of the profile includes the understanding that relationships and interactions between the leaders and staff, between staff, parents, and families, and between teachers and students, are based on their rejecting negative stereotyping about others. This is important because negative stereotyping results in deficit explanations about other peoples' performance with consequent negative responses and interaction practices. John Hattie's meta-analyses identifies that negative stereotyping has an effect size of -0.33; a profoundly negative influence on learning and achievement. He explains that it is outranked only by illness, anxiety, and boredom in terms of its debilitating impact (Hattie, 2012). In our many interviews with Māori and other Indigenous students, both in New Zealand and in other countries, it is clear that they know only too well the impact of these toxic experiences on their potential to be successful learners.

In contrast, schools that exhibit effective relational contexts and interactions are based on respectful, agentic positioning by principals, other leaders, and teachers. I realise that I have been going on about the impact of this form of theorising or explaining performance a lot in this book, but if implementing a means of rejecting this form of explanation for Māori students' or teachers' performance is not "front and centre", as a central part of the reform process, then it will be very difficult to realise the goal of establishing a North-East school. The major impact of ongoing negative stereotyping by staff members about the performance of others is that any attempts to realise the goals of the school will be undermined and rendered impotent.

Māori-medium schools like Ngā Taiatea Wharekura, where we used to take our Te Kotahitanga inductees, provide a useful model because, in my experience, they do not have the issue of deficit explanations for staff or Māori student performance to deal with. This is because these are their family and as one of my own family's kaumātua told me once, "Be careful what labels to ascribe to your ancestors or family members, because if you use negative terms about them, you are in fact using negative terms about yourself." In other words, when a school is a whānau, all the children and staff are members of the whānau, the extended family, and must be treated as such.

This means that, in North-East schools, I hear school leaders and teachers talking about the students in the same ways that the school leaders and teachers in Māori-medium schools do. They talk about the children as if they were members of their own whānau, including their accepting all the responsibilities that this entails. These school leaders and teachers do not talk about their children in deficit terms. They do not explain why some of their children do not or cannot make the same progress as do other groups of children in their care. They take their being responsible for the learning of all their children very seriously. And, if some children are having difficulties, they do not categorise them negatively because of their ethnic or other group origins, but identify their individual learning needs and attend to these.

North-East principals and team leaders relate to and interact with other staff members in the same manner. They talk about their team leaders or teachers as if they were part of their family with needs and aspirations that they need to respond to. North-East leaders accept their responsibility to ensure that their staff members become successful professionals. They do not explain that some of them are "not up to it". Instead, they make it possible for all members of staff to be included in the school's success criteria by becoming North-East teachers or leaders.

North-East school leaders care for and have high expectations for their teachers' learning

There is clear evidence of this relational context for learning having been created in North-East schools because the leaders demonstrate that they care for and have high expectations for the learning of their teachers or team leaders. This means that team leaders will have been supported to learn how they can support the teachers in their teams to create relational contexts in their classrooms. Initially, this task will probably need to be undertaken by an outside expert, but gradually, team leaders need to learn how to take over this task themselves, thus ensuring the longevity and embedding of these practices into the daily life of the school. Similarly, principals will probably need outside support for their team leaders' learning their new roles and responsibilities, but they will gradually need to learn how to take over the task themselves; this being a major milestone on the road to becoming a North-East school.

At the school-wide level, evidence of the principal and senior leaders caring for, and demonstrating high expectations for teachers' learning, and indirectly for their students' learning, is seen by their provision of effective in-school PLD opportunities and processes for team leaders, and in turn, teachers. These PLD provisions will be characterised by collaborative, evidence-based, decision making and problem solving that focuses on improving practice, not changing the teachers. These in-school PLD processes will be aligned with the school's vision, values, goals, and targets and will support teachers to effectively implement their school's common code of pedagogic practice. And what is of prime importance is that these learning opportunities are ongoing, built into the day-to-day activities of the school.

In this way, leaders reinforce the impact successful teachers have on student learning and provide them with the means of being successful. The purpose of supporting team leaders and teachers in this way is to ensure that they are able to support the learning of their teachers and students in the best way possible. They will not be left on their own to determine how best to teach their students because we know that collaborative decision making and problem solving are among the best ways of reducing variability in teaching practice and ensuring implementation fidelity.

In addition, it is important to emphasise that caring for someone else's learning is not just providing support for their wellbeing, health, and cultural knowledges, but also, in an educational context, it means taking *responsibility* for their task and process learning and not dismissing learning difficulties with deficit explanations.

It also means that, just as teachers are expected to provide a culturally responsive context and interactions with students in their classrooms, principals and team leaders are expected to build upon their teachers' cultural understandings and ways of making sense of the world. In this way, modelling what it means to implement a culturally responsive pedagogy. This approach will also become increasingly important as the teaching force diversifies over the coming years.

North-East Leaders of Learning know what their learners need to learn and how to ensure this occurs: Including specific literacy learning approaches is part of this dimension

Specific literacy learning approaches such as those associated with "balanced" or "structured" literacy learning approaches fit into this part of the profile by teachers knowing specifically what learning needs to take place and how it might best be accomplished. In other words, implementation fidelity of literacy learning approaches is actually part of their overall caring about their students' being successful learners. It is not just something desired by the principal. Similarly, this pattern of using specific, tested, teaching approaches is replicated by principals, for example when determining the best literacy learning approach for their school.

By this I mean that it will only be through detailed analyses and assessments of students' learning needs compared to current teaching practices that principals will be able to identify the need for either a revamped "balanced" literacy or the newer "structured" literacy approach. Similarly, it will only be through similar detailed analyses and assessments of teachers' learning needs in relation to their current teaching practices and their students' outcomes that team leaders will be able to identify their teachers' learning needs. The same pattern is repeated for principals and team leaders.

If, on the other hand, principals take on a new approach to literacy learning in their school because a new approach is offered by the Ministry of Education, and it has external funding attached to it, then the new approach is not likely to a have long-term positive impact on the school. One of the major impediments to successful education reform is the "magpie effect"—something that looks new and shiny will be the solution to a school's literacy learning problems, especially if it has funding attached to it; that is, thinking that simply shifting approaches to literacy learning will solve all problems. As I have said previously, there may well be a period of initial success with this transference to a new approach, but the causes of the problem of teaching variability and sustainability will still remain in the school. The long-term prognosis will not be encouraging.

However, if the decision to change literacy learning approaches, or indeed to remediate the current one, is made in response to a detailed analysis, including assessments of students' learning needs in relation to current teaching practices, then it is far more likely that whatever is decided will be effective in the long term. This will be because it will be clear what changes need to be made to the school's support systems in order to ensure what the new, or existing, approaches need to ensure their long-term implementation with fidelity.

Outside assistance will probably be needed initially to ensure that the specificity of the approaches is implemented in ways that initially ensure their expected outcomes, then teachers' learning needs to be supported by North-East leaders working within the support systems introduced into the school for this purpose. This includes the use of formative assessment to ensure that their teaching was effective and the monitoring of their practices to ensure the students' progress with learning using the strategy was being sustained. Strategies on their own do not make a sustainable difference, albeit they are essential; pedagogy and supportive structural innovations do.

Māori succeeding as Māori

North-East schools are responsive to the increasing call by Māori people for mainstream schools to support their children to be successful learners *as Māori*. It is what every member of migrant groups who come to New Zealand also wants. They want their children to be successful at the academic pursuits of schooling, but not at the expense of their language and culture. The opposite has been the pattern in New Zealand. Māori children commonly come from English-speaking homes due to the education policies of the past that promoted the learning of English at the expense of their home language. This remains the case for most Māori students today, even when they attend Māori-medium schools and, traditionally, mainstream schools have done little to support their learning of te reo Māori.

Migrant families also wish their children to maintain their language, but the traditional pattern has been that the home language of migrant families is gone by the third generation. This means that their children cannot converse with their grandparents in the family's home language. North-East schools value the languages and cultures the children bring to school. They introduce means of supporting home language learning and extension that includes explicit teaching of languages. This approach is supported by their using culturally responsive pedagogies that enable the ways that diverse students make sense of the world to be the basis for further learning. They not only teach the academic skills but also pride themselves on nurturing and bringing out the authenticity of the students' languages and identities. Māori (and other previously marginalised) students at these schools achieve highly in their work, showing little if any difference between them and their non-Māori peers—a far different picture than has been the case in the past. Māori children graduate from these schools with their mana intact.

The meaning of cultural competency

In this way, schools and teachers are implementing what is being called "cultural competency". Many people misunderstand this call for cultural competency by suggesting that teachers need to learn and teach a number of Māori concepts, including whānaungatanga, manaakitanga, and tiakitanga, which is a legacy of the dominance of transmission pedagogies. On the contrary, cultural competency means teachers need to exhibit these competencies so they can better support Māori students' learning, focus being on the students' learning, not the teachers.

The use of the term "extended family or whānau" metaphorically means that people can expect values of caring, support, and learning (manaakitanga, tautoko, akoako) to come to the fore, that they will be supported, their ideas nurtured, their identities fostered, and they and the group will prosper. Hence it is important that teachers and leaders learn what it means to create and interact within such a context; they do not need to learn how to teach about these contexts to Māori people. Māori people know what they mean already.

Hence to see a school and its classrooms that have been developed as a whānau, an extended family,[19] is to see a totally different learning environment with different roles and responsibilities that effectively support all learners' learning compared to those traditionally developed for the transmission of knowledge. This collaborative context is an excellent place for communication, for shared decision making and problem solving, for constructing shared understandings and meanings; all ideal conditions for the promotion of learning.

In summary, North-East leaders *create* an extended family-like, whānau context for learning in their school or their area of responsibility by:

1. *rejecting* deficit explanations for learners' learning
2. *caring* for and *nurturing* the learner, including their language and culture
3. *voicing and demonstrating* high expectations for their learning
4. *ensuring* that all learners can learn in a well-managed environment so as to promote learning
5. *knowing* what learners need to learn.

Part 2: Interacting dialogically within this context

In North-East schools' classrooms, the creation of a caring and learning relational context for learning is fundamental to teachers being

---

19 In Māori, this is described as being the process of *whakawhanaungatanga*. The prefix "whaka" means "to make". The word "whanaunga" means extended family relations or relatives. The suffix "tanga" means it is a noun form. Thus, whanaungatanga means relationships. Put whaka in front of it all and you have a word, whakawhanaungatanga, that means "establishing extended family-like relationships".

able to use those dialogic teaching and learning *interactions* we know make the most difference for learning. In fact, we have shown that those teachers who have not been supported sufficiently to learn how to create whānau contexts for learning in their classrooms are not likely to be able to use those learning interactions we know most effectively support learning.

Similarly, in North-East schools, the creation of a caring and learning relational context for learning is fundamental to team leaders being able to use and model the use of those teaching and learning *interactions* we know make the most difference for teachers' learning. The same can be said for the relationships and interactions created between team leaders and the principal. If the skills and knowledge necessary for creating these learning contexts have not been learnt by the respective leaders, their potential to support the learning of those for whom they are responsible is severely hampered.

This means that learning how to create a whānau context for learning is fundamental to teachers and leaders being able to use those learning interactions we know have the greatest impact upon learners' learning. Therefore, it is just as important that principals and team leaders learn how to create these learning contexts so that they can then use those learning interactions that are most effective in supporting learners in their areas of responsibility, be they team leaders or teachers. These interactions include using learners' prior knowledge, using formative assessment practices, co-constructing learning, and using power-sharing strategies.

Building upon and including learners' prior knowledge

Building upon teachers' and team leaders' prior knowledge is fundamental to motivating these staff members to participate fully in reforming their and the school's teaching practices. We found in the Te Kotahitanga project that bypassing the prior knowledge and understandings of (especially senior) staff members is a major cause of resistance to the change process. Hence, opportunities for teachers, team leaders, and principals to provide evidence of their prior knowledge about the preferred pedagogy, support systems, and what is involved in taking ownership of the problems being faced by the school is an essential part of the proposed transformation of the school.

Many teachers will have had experiences and detailed knowledge of what is being proposed. Just as with students, it is important to build on these prior skills, knowledge, and understandings so that staff members feel included and not excluded. This process is fundamental to a culturally responsive pedagogy because it enables people to bring how they make sense of the world to the deliberations and problem-solving conversations that support learning. However, it is also important that conversations about "prior knowledge" do not derail the pursuit of learning conversations about what the evidence of student performance and teaching practice is showing. Keeping to the evidence is what keeps the process on track.

Using formative assessment practices: Feedback and feed-forward

The second task to learn is how to receive and provide feedback. John Hattie found from his analysis of the power of feedback, that the most effective form of feedback was that from the learner to the teacher. In this case, this is from teachers to the team leaders or from the team leaders to the principal.

Many people struggle with receiving feedback on their teaching efforts and their initial response is often different from what is expected. It is a very difficult skill to learn, especially for someone who has essentially been working on their own for years, and successfully so, at least in their own eyes and in the eyes of many of their students, just not all. Teachers find their first interaction with "student voice", for example, to be sometimes confronting, especially if they have no real notion of what is happening for Māori students in their school. However, once the initial experience is over, teachers are very keen to hear from students about the impact of their teaching on students' learning. This is often encouraged informally and proves to be very useful as a base for co-constructing learning activities. As well, student voice, collected formally—for example, on an annual basis—is now being used in many schools currently on the North-East trajectory in the Relationships First programme. This summative picture is very useful to plot how well the school is progressing; its formative use is also used to provide steps that can be taken to improve these experiences.

It is important to prepare team leaders and principals for feedback of this sort. The reason being that receiving feedback without being prepared psychologically and emotionally can be confusing and challenging. When provided in a suitable relationship, feedback from teachers to team leaders and team leaders to principals about what they already know and understand about the common pedagogy, what errors or misunderstandings they are making when working with their team of teachers or students as the case may be, and how best they may support staff members to improve their practice, is all very useful information to build upon.

In addition to this "teacher to leader" feedback, there is a need for leaders, acting as North-East leaders (to be detailed in Chapter 6), to provide feedback to teachers on their practice. For this to occur effectively, an observation schedule, related to the preferred code of pedagogic practice, needs to be used.

This feedback includes a range of feedback functions. These include task feedback which are precise responses to the teachers' observed practices and include comments on learning progression and processes so far. A second form is process feedback. This involves the provision of precise responses about the observable and verbal understandings the teacher exhibits about the functions of learning processes when providing learning opportunities for their students. A third is feedback for self-regulation, probably the most important for teachers. This form of feedback aims to support teachers to make their new learning part of their internal monologue about where they go to next—that is, developing their learning "toolkit" so that they can draw from it in response to the learning needs of their students. This form of feedback also enables the teacher to develop the skills necessary to request feedback and further dialogue as they learn. They can then articulate where they need support and, in turn, respond to the feedback they are receiving from their students.

Formative assessment practices also involve the provision of feedforward which are precise responses from their team leader that guide the teacher to their next steps in the *task*, to make learning progression and *processes* clear and indicate what might help them to check, *self-regulate*, that they have been successful. Such learning can further improve upon the formal sessions by teachers engaging informally with one another. It is important that they can articulate where they need support, and, like most learning situations, being able to articulate an appropriate question rapidly improves the chances of arriving at a useful answer.

Engaging in co-construction activities

A further powerful means of supporting teachers' learning is the provision, within the professional learning opportunities being provided to teachers, of opportunities for teachers to collaboratively deconstruct tasks and to co-construct next teaching steps and success criteria. Here, learning scenarios are provided by leaders to enable teachers to bring their own understandings and perspectives to the learning, in dialogue with others, in order for them to make their own sense and thereby include these approaches in their own repertoire. In this way, teachers are enabled to be co-enquirers; that is, to be raisers of questions and evaluators of questions and answers. In this manner, learning is reciprocal, and understandings are co-created.

Using power-sharing strategies

At all levels in the school, these dialogic interactions are facilitated through the use of power-sharing strategies. These include dialogue, co-operative learning, narrative approaches, and learner-generated questions to facilitate learning interactions such as using learner's prior knowledge, feedback, feed-forward, and co-construction. These strategies are used to enable teachers to work co-operatively and to learn how they may themselves promote the creation of non-dominating learning relationships within their classrooms and/or learning spaces.

A summary note about the use of dialogic interactions

The learning interactions described in this section between team leaders and the teachers in their teams are the same as those occurring between the team leaders when they meet with the principal (or in large schools, with a senior staff member). The principal interacts with the school's team leaders by drawing upon their prior learning, listens to their feedback on their actions, provides their team leaders with feedback and feed-forward on their practice, and co-constructs understandings with them. Apart from the benefits of the principal supporting the team leaders' learning about how best to support their teachers' learning, principals are also appraised about what is happening in the school in terms of how well staff members at all levels are moving towards realising the school's goals and where additional assistance might be needed.

Of course, what makes this approach even more powerful, self-generating, and self-perpetuating is that these principles are exactly the same as those that teachers are expected to implement in their classrooms/learning spaces. So by all teachers' being immersed in practices that operationalise these principles that they need to be using with their "learners", they are then able to more effectively implement these practices themselves.

In summary, Leaders of Learning *interact* within the whānau/family-like context they have created in ways we know promote learning by:

1. *drawing* on learners' prior learning
2. *using* formative assessment: feedback
3. *using* formative assessment: feed-forward
4. *using* co-construction processes
5. *using* power-sharing strategies.

Part 3: Monitoring for sustainability

The third main part of the pedagogic framework of North-East schools is a means of seeing how well the learning is being embedded and therefore sustained. This is accomplished by Leaders of Learning, be they team leaders or teachers, monitoring how well their "learners" are not only able to use the preferred pedagogy but how well they able to implement and use those support systems that sustain the pedagogy as the key means of supporting students' learning.

Monitoring in this way is formative in function because it informs the leader about the impact of their teaching practices on the performance of their learners. It also identifies ways they may need to modify their practices so as to enhance learners' performance. As described above, the monitoring that occurs between teachers and students in classrooms is replicated by the monitoring that takes place between team leaders and the teachers in their teams. The same pattern is replicated between team leaders and the principal (or an appropriate senior-level leader).

Team leaders and principals firstly need to learn how to become North-East leaders (how this occurs is covered in the next chapter). When this is underway, part of their activities as Leaders of Learning will be to engage in supporting "their" learners, in their respective areas of responsibility, to learn how to implement the preferred pedagogy in their classrooms or team meetings as the case may be. They will then need to monitor the performance of those learners for whose learning they are responsible. They will learn how to do so by assessing how well their learners are able to:

- set goals for their own learning, for the learning of others, and to teach others how to set and use learning goals as a focus for their learning

- create whānau relational contexts for learning, interact dialogically within these contexts, and monitor how well their learners are progressing with task and process learning

- participate in North-East meetings. These are meetings established in the school for teachers, and team leaders in turn, to collaboratively interrogate evidence of learners' performance in relation to evidence about the efficacy of teaching practices. How these meetings are established and work in practice is detailed in Chapter 6, but suffice it to say at this point that the reason for these meetings is firstly to make use of the effectiveness of collaborative decision making and, secondly, to reinforce the importance of focusing on modifying teaching practices in relation to student performance rather than modifying students' behaviour while leaving teaching practices untouched

- take leadership roles so as to be leaders of the learning of others

- work with others including parents and family members to collaboratively interrogate evidence of learners' performance

- use evidence of student and their own performance to determine their next teaching steps and how to improve their understanding of what taking responsibility for their own learning entails

- take ownership of their own learning and apply lessons to new situations as they arise.

This pattern is repeated by the principal or principal-level leaders in the school. They will need to identify how well their team leaders are able to use the preferred pedagogy themselves in their team's meetings and associated follow-up sessions. They will also want to know how well their team leaders are able to set goals for their own learning, work within the infrastructure, take North-East leadership roles, include others, use evidence, and take responsibility for their own learning.

Principals will also want to know if their team leaders are effectively supporting the teachers in their teams to set goals and so on—and if their teachers are able to do so as well with their students. Where the evidence suggests something different is happening, then supportive feedback and feed-forward, provided within a respectful, relational context, can be used to assist the team leader back onto the North-East pathway. This may appear to be a movement towards compliance to some recipe for change. While I am aware of this concern, this is not a recipe. It is a formalised supportive context that ensures that teaching variability is addressed and removed.

This detailed description is summarised in Figure 4.1 below. When reading the details of the diagram, just replace the word "learner" with who you are responsible for. For example, if you are a teacher you will see "learner" as "student". If a team leader, you will see "learner" as "teacher". Principals see "learner" as "team leader". In fact, it might be easier to reproduce this profile with the appropriate people identified in the place of "learner".

The whole profile

Having detailed each part of the *North-East Leaders of Learning Profile* above in this chapter, it is now equally important to show the whole profile and to detail what each of the 17 dimensions of the profile mean in action. This reproduction is necessary to illustrate that the profile is not three separate parts but is really made up of three interacting parts that influence and impact upon each other as shown in Figure 5.1.

Figure 5.1: The *North-East Leaders of Learning Profile*[20]

North-East Leaders of Learning create, interact, and monitor

Part One: North-East *Leaders of Learning create* a family-like context for learning by:
1. *Rejecting* deficit explanations for learners' learning, which means that: • deficit explanations are not used to explain learners' performance • agentic talk is clearly articulated, and learners are encouraged as they succeed • errors and mistakes are seen as opportunities to learn, not insurmountable problems • learners' language, culture, and heritage are seen as assets and not as hindrances to learning.
2. *Caring* for and *nurturing* the learner, including their language and culture, which means that: • learners can bring their own cultural experiences to the learning interaction/ conversation • culturally appropriate and responsive learning contexts are provided for and created • learners' prior learning is utilised and built on.
3. *Voicing and demonstrating* high expectations, which means that: • activities are cognitively challenging • there are high expectations of learners' learning and behaviour • interactions include talk about learner capability to set and reach short- and long-term goals • what is expected of learners is clearly identified as is what learning involves.
4. *Ensuring* that all learners can learn in a well-managed environment so as to promote learning, which means that: • the lessons/interaction are well organised with clear routines for learners to interact and learn individually and as a pair or group • teachers/leaders use non-confrontational interaction and management strategies • teachers/leaders know how to promote learning through the use of effective dialogic interactions.
5. *Knowing* what learners need to learn, which means that: • Leaders of Learning know their subject knowledge • there are models and exemplars to support learners to know what success looks like • Leaders of Learning incorporate routine subject knowledge with pedagogical imagination.

---

20 This version of the profile first appeared in Bishop (2017) and was expanded in Bishop (2019). It was also expanded for use by Cognition Education in their Relationship-First Programme. No doubt it will continue to evolve in an iterative manner as we engage with more learners.

Leading to the North-East: Ensuring the fidelity of relationship-based learning

Part Two: North-East Leaders of Learning *interact* within this whānau/family-like context in ways we know promote learning by:

1. *Drawing* on learners' prior learning, which means:

- using activities that enable learners to activate what they know already, see that their cultural (sense-making) knowledge is acceptable and legitimate, know what they may need help with, and know what they need to learn
- using this information and other assessment/observation data with learners explicitly to inform the learning intentions and the pace of the learning.

2. *Using* formative assessment: Feedback, which means that:

- a range of feedback is sought from learners to provide evidence of the impact of teaching practices on learners' performance
- a range of feedback (including task, process and "self-regulation" feedback) is provided on learning efforts by the learner
- learners are able to practise their learning and request feedback as they learn. They can articulate where they need support.

3. *Using* formative assessment: Feed-forward, which means that:

- a range of feed-forward is provided. These are precise responses that guide the learner to their next steps in the task, to make learning progression and processes clear and indicate what might help them to check that they have been successful
- learners are able to practise their learning and request feed-forward as they learn. They can articulate where they need support.

4. *Using* co-construction processes, which means that:

- models and exemplars of successful learning are provided to support learners to deconstruct tasks and to co-construct success criteria
- learning tasks enable the learner to bring their understandings and perspectives to the learning in order to make their own sense
- learners are able to be co-enquirers, raisers of questions, and evaluators of questions and answers
- learning is reciprocal; knowledge is co-created.

5. *Using* power-sharing strategies

- A range of power-sharing strategies (including collaborative interrogation of evidence from in-class observations, collaborative interrogation of evidence of student performance, learners' questions) are provided to facilitate learning interactions (like using prior knowledge, feedback, feed-forward, and co-construction).
- A range of power-sharing strategies are provided to deliberately promote learning by allowing learners to work co-operatively.
- Opportunities are provided for learners to learn with and from each other in order to reinforce non-dominating relationships.

Part Three: North-East Leaders of Learning *monitor* learners' progress (using the GPILSEO model) by collecting qualitative (e.g., voices) and quantitative (e.g., objective/ standardised data) evidence of learners' progress and performance in a variety of ways to demonstrate that they and other learners are able to:
GOALS: Set goals for their learning, which means that: • learners set specific, measurable goals for improving AERA[21] measures • learners clearly demonstrate that they understand what they are learning and know when they are successful.
PEDAGOGY: Articulate how they learn best, which means that: • learners demonstrate their understanding of the appropriateness of practices that they are able to use to promote their learning • learners acquire an in-depth understanding of the underlying theoretical principles of how and why they are learning so that they can use their learning flexibly when new situations and challenges arise.
INSTITUTIONS: Explain how they can best organise learning relationships and interactions, which means that: • learners demonstrate how they organise ways of relating and interacting in learning settings • learners demonstrate understanding of the role and function of institutional/ classroom structures and modes of organisation that support learning • learners demonstrate their ability to be engaged in individual and collaborative evidence-based, problem-solving activities.
LEADERSHIP: Participate in leadership roles and functions that are responsive, proactive, and distributed, which means that: • learners explain how they are able to work with others and how they can take on leadership roles and functions • learners are able to initiate, and take responsibility for, their own learning and the learning and development of others.
SPREAD: Include others in the learning context and interactions, which means that: • learners are able to include others in individual and collaborative evidence-based, problem-solving activities • learners are able to describe who they learn with best and explain why • learners are able to describe who else needs to be involved in their learning.
EVIDENCE: Provide evidence of how well they are going and what progress they are making, which means that: • learners' AERA data are used in a "formative to summative sequence" of purposes • AERA data are used to inform students/teachers/coaches about where to take their learning (evidence informing their practice) and the learning of others for whom they are responsible • AERA data are used in a cumulative manner to indicate progress over time.
OWNERSHIP: Take ownership of their own learning, which means that: • learners are able to explain what they need to learn next in order to reach their goals • learners are seen to be responsible for their own learning and for the learning of others • learning needs are based on analysis of patterns of learning of one's self and of others.

21 Attendance, engagement, retention, and achievement. See footnote 17.

Leading to the North-East: Ensuring the fidelity of relationship-based learning

Verification of the dimensions of the North-East Leaders of Learning Profile

It is important that our work is able to be verified by other sources of evidence. That the various dimensions of the profile are effective is attested to by John Hattie's synthesis of meta-analyses of possible influences on students. This analysis was initially developed in 2009. Since then, he has revised and added to the list of effects so that now there are over 265. While he cautions against using them too specifically, the positioning on the range of effects is very useful to see the potential impact of a variety of influences on student achievement. Therefore, something that has an effect size of -0.33 like stereotyping, is egregious and has to stop. However, "those effects with positive effect sizes also range from those effect sizes of 0.00 to +0.15 which are designated 'developmental effects,' +0.15 to +0.40, 'teacher effects' (i.e., what teachers can do without any special practices or programs), and +0.40 to +1.20 the 'zone of desired effects'".[22]

Clearly, the latter range is itself progressive—the higher the effect, the more useful it will be to implement this practice. Collective teacher efficacy, for example, has a huge effect of 1.57, one of the highest John Hattie has ever seen—hence my insistence that school leaders need to operationalise this strategy instead of leaving teachers to work on their own, an activity that has a very low effect size. My including effect sizes from time to time in the text is simply to reassure readers that what I am talking about is not only from my own research but is also reinforced by a huge amount of evidence collated over a number of years. Among Hattie's reasons for developing this range of effect sizes is to get leaders and teachers to reflect on their practices using evidence and move forward by looking at those practices that we use every day and collect evidence to give us a better understanding of how they work.

In Table 5.1, I have used John Hattie's effect sizes to verify the impact of the various dimensions of the *North-East Leaders of Learning Profile*, that picture of what an effective teacher of Māori students does in their classroom and also that which effective North-East leaders do in their schools. What is really important for the purposes of this book,

---

22 https://visible-learning.org/
    hattie-ranking-influences-effect-sizes-learning-achievement/

is that most if not all of the activities in this profile have a medium to high effect upon students'/learners' achievement. This means that their use is to be encouraged.

Table 5.1: Mapping John Hattie's effect sizes onto the *North-East Leaders of Learning Profile*

North-East Leaders of Learning Profile	John Hattie's meta-analyses of effect sizes of teaching practices for improving student achievement: –0.4 is maturation. Above 0.4 is the zone of desired effects. The higher the number, the better the effect.
Part One: They *create* a family-like context for learning by:	
1. *Rejecting* deficit explanations for learners' learning	Teacher–student relationships 0.52 Teacher not labelling students 0.61 Conceptual change programmes 0.94
2. *Caring* for and *nurturing* the learner, including their language and culture	Māori students' qualitative reporting
3. *Voicing and demonstrating* high expectations	Self-reporting grades 1.33 Teacher's estimate of achievement 1.62
4. *Ensuring* that all learners can learn in a well-managed environment so as to promote learning	Elaboration and organisation 0.75 Evaluation and reflection 0.75 Deliberate practice 0.82 Learning intentions (planning and predicting) 0.76 Using deductive approaches to problem-solving 0. 61
5. *Knowing* what learners need to learn	Teacher credibility 0.90 Interventions for students with learning needs 0.75 Reciprocal teaching 0.75 Phonics instruction 0.70 Direct instruction 0.60 Explicit teaching strategies 0.57

Leading to the North-East: Ensuring the fidelity of relationship-based learning

Part Two : Leaders of Learning *interact* within this whānau/family-like context in ways we know promotes learning by:	
1. *Drawing* on learners' prior learning	Prior knowledge 0.93 Prior abilities 0.94 Strategy to integrate with prior knowledge 0.93
2. *Using* formative assessment: Feedback	Feedback 0.75 Providing formative evaluation 0.90
3. *Using* formative assessment: Feed-forward	Scaffolding 0.92 Planning and predicting 0.76
4. *Using* co-construction processes	Cognitive task analysis 1.29 Problem solving 0.68 Setting standards for self-analysis 0.74
5. *Using* power-sharing strategies	Classroom discussion (as an opportunity to provide feedback) 0.86 Reciprocal teaching 0.62 Self-efficacy/regulation 0.92 Conceptual change programmes 0.99 Jigsaw method 1.20 Meta-cognitive strategies 0.60 Co-operative learning. 0.55
Part Three: Leaders of Learning *monitor* learners' progress (using the GPILSEO model) byL	Response to intervention 1.29 Strategy monitoring 0.58
GOALS: Set goals for their learning	Appropriately challenging goals 0.59
PEDAGOGY: Articulate how they learn best	Cognitive task analysis. Strategies emphasising learning intentions 1.29 Help seeking 0.72
INSTITUTIONS: Explain how they can best organise learning relationships and interactions	Collective teacher efficacy 1.57
LEADERSHIP: Participate in leadership roles and functions that are responsive, proactive, and distributed	Leading teacher learning and development 0.84 (Robinson, 2011) Comprehensive instructional programmes for teachers 0.75

SPREAD: Include others in the learning context and interactions	Collective teacher efficacy 1.57
	Family engagement 0.49
	Parental involvement 0.50
EVIDENCE: Provide evidence of how well they are going and what progress they are making	Provision of formative assessment 0.90
OWNERSHIP: Take ownership of their own learning	Assessment capable learners (self-regulated learners) 1.44
	Self-efficacy 0.92
	Transfer skills 0.86
	Setting standards for self-judgement 0.62
	Self-verbalisation and self-questioning 0.55

Summary

What is obvious when visiting a North-East school is that a common code of pedagogic practice is seen in all classrooms and learning spaces, and this code also guides the relationships and interactions between school leaders and teachers and parents, families, and community leaders as well. In North-East schools, this common code of practice was described in *Teaching to the North-East* as the *Relationship-based, Leaders of Learning Profile*. However, I have decided to change the name to the *North-East Leaders of Learning Profile* to emphasise the importance of the North-East being the position where effective relationship-based pedagogy, led by North-East Leaders of Learning, takes place.

However, instead of worrying about the name too much, it is how this pedagogy of relations is implemented in North-East schools that is so important. It is by implementing this profile in their school that principals and all of the staff can arrest the tendency for variability in teaching practice that perpetuates poor student learning outcomes. This pattern consists of teachers, team leaders, and principals, acting as Leaders of Learning *creating* an extended family-like context for learning in their learning spaces, *interacting* dialogically within this context in ways that we know effectively support learners' learning, and *monitoring* learners' progress and the impact of the processes of learning by assessing how well learners are able to complete learning tasks and learn how to become self-managing learners.

What this is signalling is a radical change in principals' and team leaders' roles, especially in secondary schools where the focus for team leaders is more often on the content of the curriculum to be delivered rather than on their supporting teachers to be effective developers of relationships and interactions. Principals in secondary schools are certainly not commonly seen in classrooms but have developed systems where this role is devolved to leaders at other levels in the school. Whatever the case, as Viviane Robinson identifies, the closer the leader gets to the "action", the more effective they are. It is the implementation of the common code of pedagogic practice described in this chapter throughout the school in ways to be detailed in the coming chapters that enables them to do so.

The book now turns to the support systems that are necessary to ensure the effective implementation and sustainability of this pedagogic pattern.

Chapter 6
The need for support systems

Introduction

Once the goals have been developed, the pedagogy has been introduced, and the specific teaching practices determined, it is important that leaders develop and implement in-school support systems. These support systems are needed to ensure the new pedagogic practices continue to be implemented with fidelity after the initial period of enthusiasm is over and before any support provided at the outset finishes. In this way, the leaders ensure the gains made in student achievement are sustained. Included in this development is the means of transferring the skills and knowledge necessary for these systems to function from outside experts to the school's leaders.

These support systems include:

- building a responsive infrastructure to ensure the pedagogy is implemented with fidelity in the long term
- transforming leadership practices to support teachers' learning and development by working within this infrastructure
- including all teachers, leaders, parents, and community leaders into learning partnerships so as to add value to students' learning

- developing systems and practices for gathering and using evidence of performance for formative purposes.

This chapter deals with the first two of these dimensions—infrastructure and leadership—because of their interconnectedness.

Infrastructure and leadership—the keys to ensuring North-East pedagogy is implemented with fidelity

North-East schools provide infrastructural support systems that are specifically developed to support the implementation fidelity of the *North-East Leaders of Learning Profile*. But before I deal with what the infrastructure looks like in practice, it is important to know what infrastructure means.

In everyday use, infrastructure most often means things like the roads and railway lines that enable a society or economy to function. Bolman and Deal (2006) identify that:

> infrastructure ranges from and includes school management
> structures, organisation, and reporting systems, such as staffing
> role allocations and capability-building procedures, decision-
> making processes, through to the symbolic representation of what is
> important to the school. (p. 33)

What is important about schools' infrastructure is that, while we understand that it is teachers in classrooms who are the engine room of educational reform, as was identified previously, Richard Elmore (2004, p. 4) reminds us that "the key to change is teacher action supported by responsive structural reform". Responsive means the way it supports the implementation of the *North-East Leaders of Learning Profile* with fidelity.

The importance of North-East leaders engaging with teachers within the infrastructure

We know from Viviane Robinson (2011, p. 11) that principals and other school leaders have a "large positive impact on student learning by leading teacher learning and development". Among the many activities leaders undertake, this action is the most effective that school leaders can engage in to further enhance student learning in their schools. It has an effect size of 0.84, almost twice the effect size of any other action that leaders undertake. This means that the closer leaders get to the "action" (that is, the interface between teachers and students), the greater their impact upon improving student outcomes.

In North-East schools, they do so by creating, implementing, and working alongside teachers within responsive (infra)structural institutions in their schools that are focused on improving teachers' professional learning and development. This important leadership function is not left up to chance. It is built into the institutional structure of the school so as to promote and sustain gains made in student learning outcomes.

Of course, there are many other actions leaders must undertake to support the improvements in student learning. These include goal setting, strategic planning, de-cluttering initiatives, establishing support systems, including all teachers, parents, families and community leaders in formative deliberations, developing the use of evidence-based decision making, strategically allocating funding and resources, and promoting means of reviewing progress towards the North-East. It is important to emphasise that these actions are not standalone. They are interconnected activities that are actually a means to an end which is to enable leaders to effectively focus their support on teachers' learning and development. Key among which is leaders supporting teachers within the schools' supportive infrastructure.

I have termed this complex set of actions North-East leadership because it is these leadership actions that supports the implementation of the *North-East Leaders of Learning Profile* at all levels of the school with fidelity. And we know that it is the implementation of this profile with fidelity that ensures that Māori and other marginalised students are able to become and remain successful learners on their own terms.

In effect, this approach takes the focus off leadership practices as such and focuses leadership practices across the whole school on student learning. It is this spread and focus that creates the school as a North-East learning institution.

This focus is also different from generic forms of instructional leadership, for example, because of North-East leaders' attention to using those pedagogic principles and practices we know makes a difference for Māori students.

Unless school leaders have this focus, they could direct teachers, team leaders, or principals towards actions that don't necessarily lead to the realisation of the school's goals. For example, if a leader was to focus teachers on using what we know are effective interactive teaching strategies without ensuring they knew how to create a whānau context in their learning settings, they would be promoting Teaching to the North-West. Similarly, if the leader were to promote relationships as being sufficient for improving outcomes—the key means of changing student learning outcomes—transforming teaching interactions would be ignored. They would be promoting Teaching to the South-East. I doubt if anyone would promote Teaching to the South-West (low relationships and low teaching skills), but we do know that Māori students do not learn in any of these three locations. Hence the need for Leaders of Learning to focus on supporting their "learners" towards the North-East because this is where Māori students know they will be able to become successful learners.

Therefore, by using the term "North-East leadership" I am emphasising that the main task of all leaders is to ensure that all teachers and leaders are supported to implement the *North-East Leaders of Learning Profile* with fidelity. In this way, North-East leadership ensures gains will be seen in Māori and other marginalised students' learning outcomes and sustained. This will be due to programmatic coherence, and we know, again from Viviane Robinson (2011, p. 13), that "when programme coherence is higher, then teacher professional learning opportunities are likely to be more productive". Further, the focus of North-East leadership is crucial for promoting the collective efficacy and responsibility of teachers and leaders in interrogating the impact of teaching practices upon learners' learning (what has been taught, how it was taught, and what was learnt). It does so by building upon students' prior learning, interacting in ways we know promote learning and monitoring the progress learners have made. It is this process that makes the difference to learning at all levels because North-East leadership has a specific focus—that is, Leading to the North-East.

The role of infrastructure and leadership in North-East schools

While it is necessary for principals to initiate the transformation of the school into a North-East learning institution, it is vital that all leaders are involved in the process of transformation. Leadership actions are central to this happening. However, they need a structure to act within, otherwise, as previously explained, just as teachers' actions are prone to variability of implementation, so too are leadership practices. It is the infrastructure that North-East leaders work within that is of major importance for teachers' learning because it ensures schools implement and maintain effective North-East teaching practices with fidelity by making it part of the "business as usual". Usually, as I said earlier, infrastructure means the physical structures of an institution. It may include this if it has an impact on pedagogy, for example, but—more importantly—it is the systems that support the humans in the buildings to relate and interact with each other in ways that promote learning that makes up the infrastructure. It is this meaning of the term that is used in this book.

Infrastructure has a number of functions in North-East schools. *The first function of the school's infrastructure* is to address the tendency for variability in teaching or leadership practices. We know that literacy interventions, for example, need to be implemented with fidelity in the long term to ensure that their impact upon student learning is as it was intended and is not diluted. Most interventions come with a means of ensuring fidelity during its initial implementation. However, it is once the initial implementation period is over that the problems arise. This tendency for fidelity to be compromised once the initial implementation is over is why schools need an infrastructure that focuses on making sure this does not happen.

We also know that the most effective way that teachers can improve student learning is through collaborative problem solving and decision making. It could be left to happenstance, where often teachers will talk with another on a casual basis about specific learning issues some of their students are facing. However, it is far more effective when these conversations are institutionalised and timetabled within formal meetings and teachers learn how to use these meetings to improve their teaching practice. These meetings are designed for the specific purpose of teachers collaboratively interrogating evidence of student performance in relation to their teaching practices so as to collectively determine the future direction of their teaching. This is especially important so as to ensure the effective implementation of a previously agreed to and understood teaching strategy or a wider common code of effective pedagogic practice. Led by a knowledgeable North-East leader, infrastructure in the form of these meetings provides the means of ensuring the tikanga of the teaching processes and pedagogy are maintained.

However, it needs to be emphasised that just the physical act of getting a group of teachers together is in itself not going to activate the collective efficacy of the group. It must be more than just a collection of teachers hoping for or talking about good outcomes. What is needed is leadership that ensures that each person involved is able to make a contribution, that they are listened to, and that others can benefit from their input. And above all, there needs to be a means whereby evidence of the impact of teaching practice on student performance is able to be collaboratively interrogated.

A guide to the best way to chair such a meeting is the leader themselves being able to implement the *North-East Leaders of Learning Profile* in the process. When the chair of the group ensures that the deliberations are run within a context that is whānau-like, the group will be able to use those learning interactions we know foster learning. For example, a context where there are no deficit explanations for performance, and listeners care for what is being said and who is saying it, will mean that others will listen carefully with empathy to what is being considered. Where there are high expectations for the outcomes of the group's deliberations and it is based on an understanding that they will know what it do and what needs to be learnt, will be a productive setting for learning where to take your teaching to next.

John Hattie—who has recently identified the power of collective efficacy through his most recent meta-analysis as being the most effective action that teachers can engage in in terms of its impact on student learning—emphasises the importance of the social context that is created by the group's leaders, and also of course its members. It is the group members' willingness to listen to others, to empathise, to tolerate, to contribute, to receive feedback, and to provide feedback to others in ways that are respectful and determined to be productive. It is these skills and dispositions that enable the deliberations to realise the wisdom of the collectivity. Also necessary are North-East leaders' skills to channel the deliberations away from "war stories" and accounts of frustrations and anger to be solution-focused. This latter skill is essential in these trying times for teachers who often do not see any solutions to problems that seem insurmountable. Skillful leaders move teachers from feelings of frustration and anger to being solution-focused by deliberate actions.

In such a context for learning, North-East leaders can then engage teachers in those teaching and learning interactions we know promote learning most effectively. These include leaders drawing on teachers' prior knowledge so that it can be built further. I recall hearing teachers' voicing their frustration at Te Kotahitanga facilitators who did not recognise the expertise and prior experience of group members, especially among older, more experienced staff members who felt they were being patronised. Group deliberations run as a whānau will also enable teachers to receive feedback on their proposals, to provide feedback and feed-forward to others on their proposed actions in relation to evidence of student performance. Remember that receiving feedback is one of the most challenging actions that teachers need to learn to do and time and tolerance will be well rewarded.

And above all, when the participants are enabled to co-construct solutions in ways that acknowledge their individual efficacy, then the collective efficacy of the group will be realised. It is these "impact" focused deliberations about the evidence of student performance that are what realises the collective efficacy of the group. Above all, in this way, the leaders channel the deliberations of the group's members towards assessing the impact of current practices on student learning and how to improve this impact. Improving student learning is the focus, and realising the collective efficacy of the group's members is the task of the leaders. Again, it is not something that can be learnt overnight, but, with guidance from an outside expert—because it has been determined that this will be a long-term process within the school—efforts to run effective meetings will be rewarded with clear evidence of improvements in student learning outcomes.

In addition, the deliberations are not just about resources, planning, or assessment practices. It is vital that the conversation focuses on the impact that teaching and learning practices are having or will have on the outcomes of the collective decision making. In turn, this provides the group with the agenda for the next meeting where the first item is to consider the impact of what teaching practices were decided upon at the previous meeting.

A second reason for the introduction of a North-East infrastructure in schools is to ensure the sustainability of teaching practices and pedagogy that we know make a difference for Māori and other marginalised students' learning. The tendency to revert to traditional practices or modify new approaches is very strong once the initial support has finished. Unless the reform processes are embedded as part of the school's core business as usual, the reform will suffer from competing priorities, changing demands, and will be especially vulnerable when the principal or other strong advocates of the reform leave. An effective infrastructure will ensure that teachers gain an in-depth understanding of the principles underlying the *North-East Leaders of Learning Profile* and gain proficiency in implementing effective teaching practices over time. This support also means that they do not have to struggle with the effective use of approaches in their classroom on their own. In this way, placing the new pedagogies at the centre of school routines ensures ongoing sustainability with fidelity.

A third reason is that responsive infrastructural reform is a form of structural transformation that has been proven to support teaching and learning. Most other forms of structural reforms—reviewing governance systems, changing class sizes, and removing streaming, for example—in themselves rarely bring about changes in student learning outcomes. Advocates of these single-factor solutions would do well to refer to John Hattie's meta-analyses of effect sizes. Non-streaming, for example, has an effect size of 0.09. Many single-factor solutions have similar low (effect size) impact on student learning outcomes.

However, having said that, a number of these actions are very useful for improving the relational context for learning by improving students' feeling of wellbeing. It is just important to clearly identify the purpose of the intervention and not confuse wellbeing outcomes with achievement gains.

Chapter 6 The need for support systems

It is clear that North-East schools succeed in changing and improving teaching practice and subsequent student outcomes by starting with changing teaching practices. They then implement supportive structures so as to ensure these effective teaching practices are sustained with fidelity. This then further supports teacher learning and collaborative decision making and problem solving.

Overall, the role of infrastructure is to support teachers and leaders to gain a sound and deep theoretical understanding of the *North-East Leaders of Learning Profile* while they learn how to use and implement it in their classrooms and schools. This acquisition is necessary because we know that this form of pedagogy is what makes the difference for Māori students' learning outcomes. Understanding it deeply also means that teachers are able to respond effectively when they encounter different circumstances rather than their resorting to a recipe or assumptions about the learners. It also provides a means of them developing a commitment to implementing this code of practice in their classrooms or teams because of its effectiveness.

The teaching process used in North-East schools

Teachers, team leaders, and principals learning about the *North-East Leaders of Learning Profile* and how it works in action involves a teaching process. The teaching process that is used in North-East schools is used at a variety of levels by whomever is responsible for the people in their area of responsibility. That is, it will be used in classrooms by teachers with their students. It will be used in team meetings by team leaders with the teachers in their team. It will also be used in the whole school setting by the principal (or their deputy) and their team leaders. It is the teaching practice that we used in Te Kotahitanga schools and that which is used in Relationship First schools.

It is similar to that described in a recent paper by Shaun Killian.[23] In this paper, he reviews what John Hattie and Robert Marzano, two well-known meta-analysts of effective teaching strategies, agree upon as being the most effective teaching approach to ensure learners learn

---

23 https://vtss-ric.vcu.edu/media/vtss-ric/documents/s2s-strand-2/2021-2022-session-a-non-accessible/session-b-accessible/quality-core-instructions/VCU-3396_02aag_8 StrategiesRobertMarzanoandJohnHattieAgreeOnR1V2.pdf

most efficiently. It is a deductive approach, where learners are taught how to apply general principles to evidence of specific problems, preferably initially in association with other learners or more-knowledgeable others. This process of problem solving enables learners to apply previously learnt skills and knowledge to new situations in relation to a preferred set of understandings. This process of interpersonal learning is then used by individuals to later engage in intrapersonal reflection on a daily basis on problems by reference to an already learnt sets of skills and knowledge. This process enables teachers, for example, to move from their previous practices of using assessments for summative and categorising purposes to more formative purposes where they use assessment and other evidence of their students' performance to guide and direct learning.

This approach has proven to be more effective than inductive approaches where learners seek general principles from specific situations. Hattie's effect size for this deductive approach to problem solving is 0.61, whereas he found that, when a problem is addressed through what is known as "discovery learning", the effect size is 0.15. What this means is that learning is more effectively promoted when learners are able to refer to their prior understanding of a set of principles and practices, such as those in the *North-East Leaders of Learning Profile*, to address new problems, rather than their having to come up with answers themselves. A further benefit of this approach is that, when this deductive approach is used across the school, it serves to maintain the fidelity of the preferred common code of effective teaching practices.

The teaching process is detailed below. In detailing the parts of the process, I have used the term "teacher" to include actual teachers, team leaders, or the principal in their roles as Leaders of Learning. I have used the term "learner" to include teachers as learners, team leaders as learners, and principals as learners.

The Hattie/Marzano model identifies that an effective teaching practice should include the following.

1. The "teacher" identifies *a clear focus* for the lesson in terms of learning intentions.

2. This needs to be followed by some form of *overt instruction* of what needs to be learnt. Direct instruction at this time is very

effective and essential to identify to the learner what needs to be learnt. It is important to emphasise that direct instruction does not equate with transmission approaches—the traditional "stand and deliver" approach. Rather, it is important that the "teacher", acting as a Leader of Learning, needs to provide "learners" with the content details in ways that demonstrate "pedagogic imagination" so as to engage them in learning the new principles and practices with cumulative opportunities for practice.

3. The next step is the provision of *multiple opportunities* for "learners" to *familiarise* themselves with the content by their actively building on their prior cultural and topic knowledge. This is a vital step in the process of implementing a relationship-based pedagogy that includes a culturally responsive and sustaining focus because it enables the "learner" to bring how they understand and make sense of the world to the dialogue that ensures learning can take place on their own terms.

4. The next part is where "learners" are provided with *multiple exposures* to the content and its implementation, with appropriate feedback to ensure implementation fidelity as intended. Multiple opportunities to engage with the new content is essential to enable learners to internalise new information.

5. In association with the multiple exposures is the provision of opportunities to engage in *reciprocal feedback and feed-forward*. This has multiple functions including "learner" to "teacher" feedback; that is, "learner" providing "teachers" with information about their performance in relation to their "teachers'" teaching actions. It also provides "teacher" to "learner" feedback; that is, where "learners" are provided with responses as to how the "teacher" sees their performance with both task and process learning. It is also useful for identifying directions "learners" could take their learning to enhance both task and learning how to learn.

6. The provision of multiple opportunities to *apply* their new knowledge is the next step in the learning process. This is an effective deductive process of applying new knowledge to problem solving. It has a far greater impact than "learners" trying to

solve problems without a prior set of knowledge to work from. It is also more likely to result in "learners" being able to extrapolate their understandings to situations beyond the present, hence building flexibility into learning. In this way, being able to apply new knowledge to problems provides opportunities for "learners" with diverse backgrounds to make sense of the new content by reference to their own prior knowledge.

7. Working together to *collaboratively address* problems is next because it is far more effective than individual efforts and results in better outcomes for all. Such approaches allow "learners" to support the learning of others in how best to apply their previous learning of the topic at hand. Power-sharing strategies such as co-operative learning, "learners'" questions and collaborative deliberations about evidence of progress with learning are particularly effective for this purpose because they allow "learners" to make purposeful contributions to the learning of themselves and others so that all can gain mastery of the topic. Co-operative learning in this way is also very useful for supporting follow-up intrapersonal learning and application.

8. Building *self-efficacy*; that is, the individual's belief in their capacity to act in the ways necessary to reach specific goals is the final step. This means developing self-managing and self-regulating skills and knowledge that will allow the individual to realise the goals. This is the key outcome of the teaching approach outlined above. Self-efficacy is a key determinant for "learners" being able to continue to learn because it provides them with confidence that what they are learning is useful and how they are learning is effective. It also enables them to identify what they need to do and what support and "help" they should seek. Further, it assures them that they have a means of sustaining their abilities to learn when the "teachers" are no longer there.

In effect, there are four parts to this teaching process:

- INDUCTION. This includes actions 1 to 3 which consists of the "teacher" providing the "learner" with a clear focus on learning intentions, an explicit exposition of the content, and an opportunity for the learners to engage with the content to become familiar with it.
- TRIALLING. This includes actions 4 and 5 where "learners" are provided with multiple opportunities to implement the new learning and be provided with feedback on their emerging understandings of the content.
- APPLICATION. This includes actions 6 and 7 where "learners" apply their knowledge to a new or their own situation and work together to collaboratively address evidence of learning problems and identify solutions.
- REFLECTION. This consists of action 8 which provides "learners'" with an opportunity to build their self-efficacy to realise and consolidate their and others' learning goals.

These parts of the Hattie/Marzano teaching process can be understood in terms of the *North-East Leaders of Learning Profile*. Figure 6.1 identifies how these four parts can be positioned alongside the profile to identify how they map onto each other.

Figure 6.1: How the *North-East Leaders of Learning Profile* is implemented using the Hattie/Marzano Teaching Practices model

North-East Leaders of Learning Profile	Hattie/Marzano Teaching Practices
Part 1: Teaching practices need to be conducted within an extended family-like context for learning which is characterised by: • rejecting deficit explanations • caring for learners • demonstrating high expectations • knowing what needs to be learnt (e.g., literacy and numeracy content) • knowing how to promote learning (e.g., overt instruction followed by "assessment for learning").	INDUCTION. Team leaders need to: 1. provide a clear focus for the lesson 2. offer overt instruction 3. engage learners with content
Part 2a: Interacting in ways that promote learning through the provision of feedback on teaching and learning.	TRIALLING 4. provide multiple exposures 5. engage in reciprocal feedback
Part 2b: Interacting in ways we know promote learning through drawing on prior knowledge and the provision of opportunities to co-construct learning.	APPLICATION 6. learners apply knowledge 7. learners work together
Part 3: Monitoring of teachers', team leaders', and principals' abilities to be self-managing learners by using the GPILSEO model.	REFLECTION 8. building learners' self-efficacy

The Hattie/Marzano teaching process can be used for inducting team leaders and principals into being North-East Leaders of Learning

In this section, I am going to focus on how team leaders induct and support teachers in their area of responsibility to become and remain North-East teachers. They do so by themselves learning how to work within the changing roles and responsibilities of being North-East Leaders of Learning. Following this consideration of what team leaders do to support the learning of the teachers in their team, I will detail how principals or principal-level leaders support the learning of the team leaders in the school.

The reason I am focusing on the roles and responsibilities of team leaders is their central importance to the school for the ongoing implementation with fidelity of the North-East pedagogy—and, as we know, North-East teachers implementing the *North-East Leaders of Learning Profile* with fidelity is the key to the successful improvement of Māori students' learning. However, probably just as important is the support they receive on an ongoing basis from North-East leaders. North-East teachers are not left to their own devices. They are supported by North-East leaders. This support ensures that they do so as to sustain the gains made by Māori students.

In order for team leaders to support their teachers to implement and use the *North-East Leaders of Learning Profile*, they need to learn how to work within the infrastructure that the principals have established for this purpose.

This infrastructure consists of four interacting dimensions.

INDUCTION. Firstly, an *induction process* provides "learners" with a clear focus of the *North-East Leaders of Learning Profile*, offers overt instruction about what needs to be learnt, and supports "learners" to engage with the principles and practices of the profile *(Hattie/Marzano steps 1 to 3)*.

TRIALLING. Secondly, opportunities for teachers to trial the new pedagogy in their learning spaces is provided. This trialling is supported by leaders providing a series of observations and feedback sessions to assist teachers to embed these practices.[24] *(Hattie/Marzano steps 4 and 5)*.

APPLICATION. Thirdly, North-East meetings offer "learners" multiple opportunities to apply their new knowledge of the *North-East Leaders of Learning Profile (Hattie/Marzano steps 6 and 7)*.

REFLECTION. Fourthly, opportunities are provided to identify if "learners", be they teachers, team leaders, or principals, are able to take ownership of their own learning *(Hattie/Marzano step 8)*.

Each dimension includes parts of the eight steps of the Hattie/Marzano teaching process. In Figure 6.2, I have identified how the Hattie/Marzano teaching process is used in North-East schools to induct and support team leaders (and principals) into how to support the teachers in their team to implement and use the *North-East Leaders of Learning Profile* with fidelity.

---

24 These sessions have been identified as among the most effective forms of professional learning that can be provided for teachers. However, it must be emphasised that these are not an end in themselves, but part of a more comprehensive process. The Education Hub has a number of videos on this topic that are well worth viewing. See https://theeducationhub.org.nz/introducing-instructional-coaching-in-schools/

Figure 6.2: The relationship between the *North-East Leaders of Learning Profile*, North-East schools' infrastructural support system, and the Hattie/Marzano teaching process

North-East Leaders of Learning Profile	North-East schools' four-part infrastructural support system	Hattie/Marzano eight-step teaching process
Part 1: Induction process needs to be conducted within an extended family-like context for learning which is characterised by: • rejecting deficit explanations • caring for learners • demonstrating high expectations • knowing what needs to be learnt • knowing how to promote learning.	Support system 1: INDUCTION A clear focus, direct instruction, and familiarisation opportunities are provided.	1. A clear focus for the lesson 2. Offer overt instruction 3. Learners engage with content
Part 2a: Interacting in ways we know promote learning through the provision of feedback and feed-forward on implementing the principles of the profile.	Support system 2: TRIALLING. Multiple observations and feedback opportunities are provided.	4. Give feedback 5. Provide multiple exposures
Part 2b: Interacting in ways we know promote learning through the provision of opportunities to co-construct learning.	Support system 3: APPLICATION. North-East meetings provide multiple opportunities to collaboratively apply skills and knowledge so as to build self-efficacy and self-management skills and knowledge.	6. Learners apply knowledge 7. Learners work together
Part 3: Monitoring of teachers', team leaders', and principals' abilities to be self-managing learners by using the GPILSEO model.	Support system 4: REFLECTION. Follow-up monitoring and coaching ensures that teachers, team leaders, and principals are building self-efficacy .	8. Building learners' self-efficacy

Details of the infrastructural support systems that team leaders use to support teachers' learning and development

Infrastructural Support Number One: Induction

The first infrastructural support system consists of an *induction process* that integrates the first three parts of the Hattie/Marzano Teaching Practices model—that is, the focus for the learning, the actual content, and an opportunity for learners to engage with the content; in this case, the *North-East Leaders of Learning Profile*.

The initial focus for the learning needs to include statistical evidence of educational disparities, preferably from within the school, and the consequences of this situation over time. It should also include narratives of Māori students' schooling experiences. This approach, albeit inductive, has proven to be a very powerful way to introduce the need for new teaching relationships and interactions. The narratives in the book, *Culture Speaks* (Bishop & Berryman, 2006), or narratives of Māori students' experience from their own school specifically gathered for this purpose, are essential to provide teachers, team leaders, and principals with a vicarious experience of what it is like to experience racism and prejudice on a daily basis and how this impacts upon students' learning and identity. This often provides teachers with a sobering experience, and most participants determine to address these often negative experiences following this exposure. As mentioned before, gathering these voices annually also provides schools with an excellent measure of how well they are progressing towards the North-East.

Creating this context for learning makes it possible for the leader to explicitly present the details of the *North-East Leaders of Learning Profile* as a research-based set of pedagogic principles, with appropriate specific examples of teaching practice that, when implemented with fidelity, results in improved achievement and wellbeing of Māori students. This teaching can consist of practical workshops, online lessons, or information sharing mini-lectures about the specific approach. However this is achieved, explicit details of the principles and practices of the *North-East Leaders of Learning Profile,* including any specific literacy or teaching strategy, need to be provided at this time. Then learners need to be provided with opportunities to engage within the content so as to learn how these literacy strategies—and the wider common code of pedagogic practice including the dialogic interactions we know improve learning—can be applied in their own classrooms, teams, or school settings. Teachers are thus supported in a variety of ways to engage with the content, actively drawing on their prior learning in ways that ensure both surface and deep learning of the principles and practices detailed in the profile. At the same time, team leaders are able to be inducted into their new roles and responsibilities in order to take over from the outside experts in due course.

In Te Kotahitanga we used a marae for this induction process because here we could begin to induct teachers and school leaders into what it means to be culturally competent as well as the content of the profile. It provided them with a culturally safe context for learning, which in turn allowed us to an opportunity to engage them dialogically with learning the content. Providing learners with hospitality, food, and comfort goes a long way towards assuring them that you are on their side and are going to support them.

So, in this way, the metaphor of whānau is expanded to include manaakitanga (hospitality and caring) in action. We don't talk about it. We do it. And it also models how teachers can create similar contexts in their classrooms. However, it is not all comfort and singing Kumbaya because some of the induction process is very confronting, especially when student voice is used to provide teachers with an experience of what it is like to be a Māori student in their school. On many occasions when we provided these stories, teachers could not believe that this sort of thing would be happening at their school. It is confronting and upsetting when you realise that the school you think is going well is actually causing grief for many of its students, and these are an ethnically identifiable group. For example, it is possible that many teachers will be unaware of why the Māori students are not attending or, when they do come, they are "absent", mentally. On the other hand, the use of student voice on an annual basis is proving to be a very effective means of keeping schools on the path to the North-East and is a strategy to be encouraged.[25] Similarly, classroom interactions are not all warm and fuzzy. But we do know that improving Māori students' experiences of

---

25 One such example is seen in the Motueka Kāhui Ako. https://gazette.education.govt.nz/articles/authentic-voice-collection-empowers-motueka-kahui-ako/

being successful learners is the key to improving behaviour. The other way round is the common approach in our schools and it is not working. I have seen classroom behaviour patterns, albeit over time, change from challenging to exciting because of *Teaching to the North-East.*

Infrastructural Support System Number Two: Trialling

In North-East schools, the induction process is followed by targeted, in-class observations with follow-up coaching sessions undertaken by a knowledgeable other.[26] Teachers are observed, initially by outside experts shadowed by team leaders, as they implement the various dimensions of the profile in their classrooms. In this way, team leaders gradually learn how to provide teachers with responses as to how they see teachers' performance with both task and process learning and directions they could take to enhance both. At the same time, there is also an opportunity for the teachers' results to inform the team leader about how effective their teaching actions have been. A third process that occurs in these meetings is that the teacher is encouraged to develop an understanding of what the evidence from the observations is showing. In this way, the team leader's and teacher's interactions provide opportunities for co-constructing understandings of what is happening and to develop joint determinations about where to next. This latter part of the process is important for moving teachers towards being responsible for their own learning.

Infrastructural Support System Number Three: Application

The third main support system is structured and timetabled *"North-East meetings"*. Within these meetings, teachers are supported by their team leaders to collaboratively interrogate evidence of students' performance in order to evaluate the impact of their teaching practices on students' learning. They are then able to modify their teaching practices in ways that ensure ongoing learning of both task and process learning. In these formally structured meetings, led by team leaders, "learners"—be they teachers, team leaders, or the principal—are provided with multiple opportunities to apply their knowledge, work together

---

26 An excellent resource for leaders is provided by the Education Hub. It covers a range of issues that principals and other leaders should consider when implementing a coaching and feedback cycle in their schools. https://theeducationhub.org.nz/an-introduction-to-instructional-coaching

to achieve better outcomes, and build self-efficacy and self-managing skills and knowledge.

These formal meetings provide opportunities for conversations to focus on learning as opposed to behaviour. It is these timetabled, formal meetings that provide teachers and team leaders the opportunity to meet to use formative assessment processes to improve students' or teachers' learning that are at the centre of sustaining the gains that are made in North-East schools. These types of meetings are common in the literature and have many names, but they are called North-East meetings here because the focus is on supporting Leaders of Learning at all levels in the school to use the North-East Leaders of Learning Profile to improve learners' learning. It is vital that these meetings become a regular part of the school's infrastructure and are not allowed to be modified, diluted or even abandoned. Fidelity of the process of collaboratively interrogating evidence of student performance in relation to teaching practices is vital to sustain the school as a North-East learning institution.

These meetings ensure that teachers are not isolated, but work together, supporting each other's progress and performance. Teachers have always done so informally, but in North-East meetings, these deliberations are formally part of the daily work routine and are understood to be an essential and ongoing part of the infrastructure of the school.

It is also important to acknowledge that Infrastructural Support Systems Numbers Two and Three are actually two sides of the same coin. The first side enables the learners, the teachers, team leaders, and principals to begin to develop an in-depth understanding of the *North-East Leaders of Learning Profile*. The second side enables them to engage in multiple opportunities to collaboratively improve their understanding of the content of the *North-East Leaders of Learning Profile* and the processes of learning associated with its implementation. This means they can then build a means of sustaining these practices in their classroom when they are on their own.

Infrastructural Support System Number Four: Reflection
Team leaders are also supported to learn how to use the GPILSEO model to see where and how they need to modify the caring and

learning whānau relationships they are developing and the interactions they are using with their teachers in their team. As was detailed earlier, they do so by asking:

"*Are the individual teachers in my team, whose learning I am responsible for, able to:*

- *set* goals for their own learning and use their performance to guide their learning towards these goals
- *achieve* at task performance, and understand what and how they are learning
- *participate* effectively in the learning infrastructure
- *participate* in leadership roles and functions
- *include* others in their learning
- *use* evidence of their current performance to identify their next learning steps
- *take* ownership of their own learning; be self-regulating and self-determining learners?"

North-East team leaders use a mixture of expository and responsive coaching teaching

As the North-East Team Leader moves through the four steps of the North-East infrastructure with the teachers in their team, it is important that they use different teaching approaches for each of the steps. In practice, the "teaching" approaches used initially by the outside expert, which are then transferred to the team leaders, are a mixture of expository teaching and responsive coaching. At the outset, it is necessary for the North-East leader to provide details of the *North-East Leaders of Learning Profile* and how it can be implemented in classrooms. It is also at this stage that details of a proven "structured" or "balanced" literacy approach can be introduced. The overriding principles and practices of the induction process guide the leading of learning.

In the next step of the teaching process, the observations and feedback, it is important that the North-East Leader of Learning uses coaching practices. In this way, they will both listen to feedback from teachers as to how well they are supporting their learning of the new approaches, and they will need to be able to provide feedback and feed-forward to teachers on their progress and performance. This coaching approach is very focused on supporting the learner to understand how to implement the profile and its associated practices in their respective classrooms or team meetings.

When conducting North-East meetings, the role becomes more of a facilitator of the deliberations about what the evidence before the group means. The task is to facilitate discussions and guide them towards resolution based on reference to the *North-East Leaders of Learning Profile*.

Monitoring how well teachers or team leaders are becoming task-proficient and self-managing learners themselves and are being supportive of the learning of these skills in others again requires the North-East team leader to be a coach. Learning conversations based on the evidence of practice derived from the application of the GPILSEO model to their practice will support learners to become leaders of their own learning.

The overall approach used by North-East Leaders of Learning is to support the people whose learning they are responsible for, to learn about and how to implement the *North-East Leaders of Learning Profile* in their respective areas of responsibility. It is important that all involved in the school are engaged in this activity. As will be detailed below, we learnt the hard way in the Te Kotahitanga project the dangers of creating a small cohort of "experts" in the school. It is far more effective in terms of sustaining the gains being made in student learning that the primary role of leaders changes from "administrative" to being "North-East leaders".

The role of outside experts

It is perhaps useful that this infrastructural pattern is introduced into North-East schools by outside experts at the instigation of the principal. It is vital that the principal understands what is involved in transforming the school to become a North-East Learning Institution. It is also important that the whole process of the transformation is clearly understood by the whole staff and community leaders from the outset so they can see where the school is heading—that is, to the North-East.

The outside experts will then need to commence the process of inducting the teachers (including team leaders in their role as teachers and principals if they are teaching students) into the new approaches and pedagogy to ensure early gains in achievement. These early gains are vital to demonstrate to teachers and team leaders that the effort involved is worthwhile. Nothing succeeds like success. As the three case study schools detailed later in this book demonstrate, early success in realising the schools' previously unattainable goals within 2 years had a very strong motivational effect on ongoing effort, implementation fidelity, and sustainability of the new practices.

During the induction process for teachers and team leaders, the outside experts will need to demonstrate how to create a whānau context for learning, and interact dialogically within this context. This is important for modelling this principle in practice and it also provides team leaders and teachers with an experience of just what it means to participate in a learning setting in the full knowledge that they will not be subject to deficit explanations about their performance with the subsequent tasks. They will also experience what it means to be cared for as learners and to interact in a "high expectations" context. In this way, they will begin to experience what it means to be a learner in a culturally safe and responsive context. Being able to bring who you are and how you understand the world to the conversation of learning has been shown to be a very powerful motivator.

The outside experts will also support team leaders to learn how to induct teachers into the process of transforming their pedagogy by initially providing explicit details about the Profile, how to implement observations and feedback sessions, how to lead North-East meetings of their teams of teachers and how to monitor the impact of their teaching practices on teachers' learning. They will also need to include considerations of how these all fit together into an iterative process of ongoing learning and improved practice. Team leaders will be able to learn these skills and knowledge by shadowing the outside expert as they work with the teachers.

How outside experts can assist principals

The third action of the outside experts is to induct principals and principal-level leaders into how they can best support their schools' team leaders by learning how to induct new team leaders[27] into their roles and responsibilities, observing and providing feedback on how well their team leaders are undertaking observations of their teachers, and conducting North-East meetings populated by team leaders. In the meetings of team leaders run by the principal or their nominee, team leaders collaboratively interrogate evidence of how well students are performing in their teachers' classrooms, and how well their teachers are implementing the *North-East Leaders of Learning Profile* and, where necessary, how they might improve their practice so as to improve their teachers' practice and, indirectly, student outcomes.

In smaller schools, North-East meetings for team leaders can be run by the principal. However, in larger schools, this is probably unrealistic so it may be necessary to delegate this responsibility to other designated members of the Senior Leadership Team (SLT) who then work with a group of team leaders. In which case, the SLT members would be delegated to undertake observations and provide feedback to individual team leaders and to lead team leaders' meetings. In smaller schools then, there will only be two layers of North-East meetings; those populated by teachers led by a team leader, and those populated by team leaders and led by the principal. However, in larger schools, a third layer of meetings will be necessary where SLT members engage with the principal to interrogate evidence gathered from the performance of the schools' team leaders' observations and North-East meetings, as well as evidence gathered from meetings led by team leaders. As in the other meetings, these data will be used for both summative and formative purposes. In this case, the North-East meetings led by the principal are where the senior leaders engage with evidence of student and teaching performance at the school level to identify both a summative picture of how well the school is progressing towards its objectives, and a formative investigation of "where to next" and how we might proceed in that direction.

The benefit to the principal of this arrangement in a large school is that, although the principal may not be able to take part in the actual

---

27 An excellent paper on this topic of how leaders can use formative assessment approaches for teacher learning is by Helen Timperley. https://www.educationalleaders.govt.nz/Leading-learning/Professional-learning/Using-evidence-in-the-classroom-for-professional-learning

Chapter 6 The need for support systems

coaching and formative deliberations with teachers, they will be able to collate the evidence from a range of meetings being conducted for this purpose and, in this way, be able to maintain their overview of what is happening in the school and monitor how well they are progressing towards realisation of their goals. Figure 6.3 illustrates how this overlapping infrastructure could be arranged in a large school. Note that parents, families and community members are represented alongside these activities so that they can be included in formative deliberations at any level.

Figure 6.3: The distribution of North-East meetings in large schools

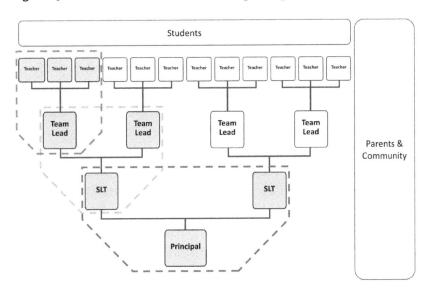

The need to build North-East skills and knowledge within the school

What the outside experts are doing is supporting principals and team leaders to add a further set of skills and knowledge to their roles and responsibilities, or, better still, to delegate the administrative responsibilities such as finance and human resources and prioritise the instructional. When this happens, they are able to learn how to become North-East leaders. North-East leaders are those who have the responsibility, including the skills and knowledge, to teach teachers and team leaders both inside and outside of the classrooms of the school. As I explained above, part of the transformation of the school is to gradually move away from the instruction and support provided by the outside experts so as to transform leadership roles and responsibilities to a situation where staff members of the whole organisation are engaged in teaching others at one level or another. In this way, they become learners themselves by their participation in the collaborative deliberations of their colleagues about the evidence of students' or teachers' or team leaders' performance and the impact of their collective practices on learners' progress. Just as teachers' roles are transformed to their becoming leaders or learning in a North-East school, so too are the roles of other members of staff transformed to them also becoming Leaders of Learning of teachers, for example, or the learning of team leaders. The whole aim is for no one to be left on their own but to operationalise the benefits of collective efficacy across and within the school.

We found out the hard way in the Te Kotahitanga project how important it is that school leaders take on the responsibility of institutionalising infrastructural support systems and North-East leadership practices in their schools. This necessarily includes strategically resourcing the practices. The Te Kotahitanga project used external funding to provide schools with a separate group of specialists, many released from their duties within the school and also many from other agencies from outside of the school such as Resource Teachers: Learning and Behaviour (RTLBs) and School Advisory Services. This group was trained by our PLD team to run the induction process, to implement the observations, and run what we then called "co-construction" meetings. It was our need to maintain fidelity of the PLD process for research purposes that meant that this relatively small group of highly trained people were assigned these tasks within the schools.

However, this arrangement created a number of problems that limited the potential for sustaining the project. The first was that involving "external" specialists in transforming the school bypassed existing positions of authority and pools of expertise within the schools. Secondly, this approach did not allow for the development of coaching capability to spread widely among the staff. This was unfortunate because one of the main purposes of the project was to support teachers and other staff to become Leaders of Learning using coaching and formative assessment approaches, rather than transmitters of knowledge. Both of these actions left key, experienced people out of the process of education reform and meant that they were not part of the transformation. Apart from their possibly feeling ignored and resentful, they didn't have "skin in the game", and, as a result, they were not as committed to the transformation as were the principals, for example, and this often caused unnecessary tension and misunderstandings. In effect, we missed the opportunity to mobilise the collaborative strength of the whole staff, that includes the collaborative conversations based on evidence that occur among all of the staff of North-East schools. Hattie identifies this collaborative decision making as being probably the most effective thing that school personnel can engage in to improve student achievement. But if only part of the staff understand or are engaged in this activity, and if they are not the ones who hold positions of responsibility, then the possibility of sustaining the infrastructure is severely limited, which in turn limits the potential for sustaining the gains made in student outcomes. In short, the model of externally funded expert facilitators precluded the development of collective capacity within the schools that would have contributed to sustaining the project. Hence the school leaders need to plan for the transition from outside experts to in-school leaders. This will necessarily be something undertaken differently by individual schools according to their differing circumstances. However, whatever the case, it needs to be done, and the sooner the better.

Conclusion

There will be few school leaders who do not realise the implications of this North-East mode of leadership and infrastructure. These changes will not only impact teaching practices, but also will impact human resources, funding, power relationships, networks, lines of authority, and how the school represents itself to and includes its community. In short, a culture change is proposed. What the model suggests is a change in the central organising policies and practices of these schools. I make no apologies for this as it is clear that our current practices are maintaining the status quo of disparities being determined by ethnicity, not the realisation of individuals' potential. Clearly, there is something profoundly wrong within our schools that this situation has been allowed to continue for decades with all the negative consequences for the individuals involved and for the whole society.

Of course, there will be resistance to change, just as there will be some who are over-zealous in their support of change. Nevertheless, it has to happen, and this chapter sets out the key institutional and leadership changes needed and how they can be undertaken.

It is vital that principals do not get distracted by the latest "single factor" solutions that are constantly promoted. Education reform is a complex process. There are many models for change in numerous publications but probably one of the best currently exists in New Zealand. It is the Kāhui Ako model where school leaders can work together to collaboratively interrogate evidence of their school's performance in ways that identify pathways they can take so as to transform their schools into North-East learning institutions. Again, some Kāhui Ako are not working optimally, but those that are provide an effective model for others to emulate in the future. Outside help will probably be necessary to keep Kāhui Ako achieving optimum outcomes, just as outside help is needed to implement the *North-East Leaders of Learning Profile* within a school. Whatever the case, it is the collaborative effort of implementing the *North-East Leaders of Learning Profile* across schools that is proving to be an effective model of responding to the changes in teaching practice, roles, and responsibilities among the various staff that are fundamental to institutional change in our schools. In other words, the extension of the *North-East Leaders of Learning Profile*'s practices across a set of interrelated schools provides leaders with collaborative support for addressing implementation issues as they arise in a far more effective and sustainable manner than principals working on their own.

In the next chapters, I will address how the remaining parts of the GPILSEO model—spread, evidence, and ownership—contribute to the enhancement of Māori and other marginalised students' learning in ways that sustain the gains being made by the transformations made so far in pedagogy, infrastructural support systems, and leadership.

Chapter 7
Spread and evidence

Introduction

In this chapter, I address how two further support systems of the GPILSEO model contribute to sustaining the gains being made by the transformations made so far in pedagogy, infrastructural support systems, and leadership. The first is a consideration of how well principals and other leaders are able to involve others, including students, all teachers, other leaders, and parents, families, and community leaders in ways that add value to students' learning. The second is how well principals and leaders are able to create means whereby evidence of student performance can be used to support and improve their teaching and leadership practices.

Spread: Enhancing the transformation of the school into a North-East learning institution by including teachers, parents, and community leaders

Spreading the reform to include all concerned is extremely important for sustaining the gains being made in Māori and other marginalised students' performance. Probably the first necessity is to include all of the school's staff in the reform as soon as possible. This is not only important for their own professional learning, but it also provides all students with a common learning experience between classes and between levels of the school—rather than the lottery effect that is so common in our schools today. These common learning experiences also minimise the disruptions caused at major transition points in primary schooling and the daily subject-based movements common to secondary schooling. Overall, it makes it possible for the other parts of the support systems to eradicate variability of teaching practice; as we know, this is one of the most limiting factors for Māori and other marginalised students' learning.

North-East schools have different means of including all staff into the transformation process, the means being specific to the particular school's circumstances and communities. However, probably the most common approach is to commence with a small cohort of either enthusiasts or key personnel, then expanding to rapidly include all others. Whatever the case, the leaders need to ensure that they are making it possible for all staff to be successful participants because it is important that they model the idea of whānau which means that you work with who you have—you don't eradicate some because they may not agree with you.

However, there are implications of this level of support for teachers as well. Once the school's principal has led the process that has determined the pathway they are going to take, taking the pass option is not acceptable professional practice. Indeed, in some North-East schools, it becomes a condition of employment that new teachers will teach in ways specified by the school—that is, by implementing the *North-East Leaders of Learning Profile.*

In this way, the North-East pedagogy of caring and learning relationships, dialogic interactions, and monitoring for formative purposes becomes a whole-of-school pedagogy because it is used by all leaders and teachers to support the learning of those whose learning they are responsible for. In practice, teachers use this pedagogy to support the learning of students in their learning spaces. Team leaders use the common pedagogy to support those teachers in their team for whose learning they are responsible. The principal uses the pedagogy to support the learning of those team leaders for whose learning they are responsible.

In this way, all leaders of the school are able to experience what it is to be a Leader of Learning, just as they are expecting teachers to learn how to teach in this manner in their classrooms. They do not tell them what to do, but rather model the principles-in-action at their level of the school for those for whose learning they are responsible. The principles and practices of learning are the same—these principles guiding practices at all levels of the school. This means that team leaders are able to support teachers more effectively because they are knowledgeable supporters, rather than being an outside observer or an administrator. They know what the common code of pedagogic practice consists of and are able to offer assistance and direction to teachers' learning and implementation in what is truly a whole-school approach.

Parents, families, and community leaders are also included and are sometimes taking the lead in the learning process

Similarly, North-East leaders are supportive and inclusive of parents, families, and community leaders by including them in GPILSEO deliberations.

The Education Review Office (ERO) undertook a study of school–family relationships in a 2018 research study. This study involved 40 medium-sized primary schools, many of them in low socio-economic status communities across New Zealand. The sample of schools was made of those "with increased numbers of students achieving at or above the expected standards as they moved through the upper primary years (Years 5 to 8)" (Education Review Office, 2018). In the best examples, ERO found that "teachers involved most parents in goals and next learning steps with their child" (Education Review Office, 2018, p. 1); that is, in formative learning approaches. These schools were particular to involve the parents of students who were at risk of underachieving, responding quickly to evidence of students' progress so as to address learning issues before they affected other parts of the child's education.

The most effective schools also involved parents in genuine learning relationships and interactions which resulted in even greater gains in student achievement, and these developed *alongside* gains in students' feelings of self-worth and ability to be a learner. In this way, these results challenge the theory common among educators that improving self-esteem and wellbeing *leads to* improvements in learning. It is not an either/or debate. It does not work that way. Improving learning outcomes is *associated with* improvements in self-esteem and wellbeing. Both are built on teachers creating a whānau context for learning in their classrooms which enables pedagogic change to occur and also improves students' feelings of self-worth and identity. An approach that seeks to promote wellbeing on its own, trusting that this will somehow ensure academic gains, is promoting a necessary but not a sufficient condition.

The simple reason is that the "self-esteem first" approach does not require teachers to change their practice. It requires them to support children's feelings of wellbeing through activities that are seen to be culturally appropriate, which means that they can carry on teaching as before, problematically not teaching in ways that we have shown lead to changes in achievement in the long term. Again, it is the student who has to change.

There is reported evidence that Māori students engaging in kapa haka at high school do better academically.[28] There is no debate about the benefits of kapa haka to re-indigenise lives and be a major way to reconnect Māori students with Māori values and improving wellbeing. However, the danger of this finding is that teachers might think this is sufficient to ensure Māori students will become successful learners at what the school is offering and that they will not have to change their pedagogy. Changing pedagogy is necessary, especially at senior primary and secondary school where literacy learning, for example, is fundamental to subject learning. No manner of improving self-esteem is going to help Māori students become competent with senior maths, for example, in the long term without commensurate changes in maths teaching! My understanding is that, unless pedagogic change accompanies any gains in Māori student achievement associated with their engagement in kapa haka for example, it will not be sustained because the means of sustaining the gains are not present.

---

28 https://www.nzherald.co.nz/kahu/m9-clinical-psychologist-dr-kiri-tamihere-waititi-moves-between-both-worlds/3KFX6SFHF5A2XAIBGCJPEJZQXM/

In fact, there is some evidence that improving academic achievement may well lead to improvements in wellbeing and self-esteem. In some schools in the Te Kotahitanga project, we noticed that, as Māori students gained self-respect due to their becoming successful at classroom activities, they began to seek further means of affirming their identities as Māori. An Education Review Evaluator we spoke to noticed the increase in the number of Māori students taking te reo Māori at Okaihau College during their visit to this medium-sized Northland college. They asked the students the reason for this increase. The students explained that, before, the whānau unit and Māori language classes were seen as a "dumping ground" for naughty kids, and they didn't want to be part of that. They explained that it was now cool to be Māori at this school because they were achieving well in all their subjects. They felt that to be Māori was now OK, and so they were comfortable to engage with identifiably Māori learning. Being Māori at Okaihau College had a high status now, not low.

Aggregated data from Te Kotahitanga also showed this pattern. The teachers who primarily focused on promoting wellbeing moved their practice to the South-East, not the North-East, and Māori students explained to us that they did not learn in these South-East classrooms. In fact they explained that, in terms of improving their learning, the South-East classrooms were no better than the South-West classrooms that had been the most common type prior to Te Kotahitanga. The South-East classrooms were more pleasant to be in, but that was all. However, for many teachers in the project, the self-esteem and wellbeing of students became an end it itself, mainly because it improved behaviour. Whereas, for the students it was a means to an end. Improving learning is a complex process including improving learning relationships and interactions.

The importance of learning interactions

Besides creating a context within the school that supported parents' involvement in the development of children's feelings of self-worth, confidence, and resilience, the ERO study emphasised the importance of including parents in formative approaches to learning. This means that they identified that one of the key components of genuine learning partnerships is the regular and honest sharing of all achievement and progress information that teachers collect. Teachers and parents look at the actual assessments together, by using a wide range of communication methods (including three-way conversations) and they discuss "the strengths and possible reasons for any visible progress or confusions for the child, ... [especially in, but not limited to] the first two years the child was at school" (Education Review Office, 201, p. 2). The focus of the successful partnerships is to work especially closely with parents of children who needed to accelerate their progress. There is also a great deal of sharing of information about the actual teaching approaches being used, including the learning intentions and likely benefits and next learning steps.

What is also significant is that these relationships are not just one-way. Teachers working in schools that exemplified the best examples of this approach in the ERO study also listened to what the parents might suggest and acted on the suggestions. Parents know their child best, their interests and concerns, and can identify anything getting in the way of children's learning. All the parents spoken to as part of the study valued the opportunity to be fully engaged with their children's learning, especially if their child had specific learning needs or needed to accelerate their progress. "In the most successful schools, every parent was involved and contributing to their child's learning. Parents expressed their gratitude for the genuine support that teachers and leaders provided to their families" (Education Review Office, 2018, p. 3). The report's authors summarise their findings:

> Leaders and teachers in these schools avoided making negative assumptions about parents' willingness to contribute to their child's progress. Instead, they:

- built strong and ongoing learning relationships with parents and whānau,
- fully and honestly shared assessment information about the child,
- listened to parents' ideas about how they could help and what support they needed,
- provided details about the language, strategies and approaches the child used at school,

- provided materials and internet links for parents that needed them,
- regularly communicated with parents to share and hear what was working and what they all (the child, parent and teacher) should do next.

The way leaders and teachers valued and worked with parents was key. Teachers did not just talk at parents; they worked with parents who could then fully contribute to their child's learning. Every school had such productive and genuine learning partnerships, "especially for children who need additional support to achieve success with some aspect of their learning. Partnerships established in Years 1 and 2 were built on further as the child moved through the school" (Education Review Office, 2018, p. 6).

In this way, the inclusion of parents into learning partnerships also contributes to the ongoing implementation of North-East pedagogy because it is by using a Relationship-based, culturally responsive pedagogy that promotes the use of formative assessment approaches that parents can be included in this manner. Further, the need for ongoing fidelity of the implementation of the pedagogy is also ensured because parents and community leaders are not going to accept any reversion to the previous achievement patterns once they have seen what is possible.

There is a further trend occurring in North-East schools. From the initial positionings of learning partnerships, many parents, families, and community leaders are turning from being learners in this responsive system to becoming Leaders of Learning themselves. Often this is initially through the transmission of skills and knowledge, but increasingly it is involving them monitoring how well their learners are making progress with new skills and understandings so as to modify learning processes. This is proving to be of immense value for improving Māori student achievement and wellbeing. An example of this taking place over time is detailed later in the case study of Kerikeri High School in Chapter 11.

Evidence

As I identified earlier, a recent survey by Nina Hood of the Education Hub asked teachers what they considered to be the most difficult teaching practice they had to undertake. The overwhelming response was using evidence of student performance to determine their next teaching actions—in other words, to use formative teaching practices. What is extraordinary is that this approach has been promoted in schools for decades because it is a very effective means of improving students' outcomes. Yet it remains the most difficult action that teachers are expected to use.

We know that the key to learning new skills and knowledge is being provided with multiple opportunities to gain familiarity with the new content and also to practise implementation. This process also requires that learners are provided with corrective and forward-focused feedback, opportunities to apply the new skills and knowledge alongside others in ways that build self-efficacy. However, if teachers are not provided with these opportunities to learn in the way we know works most effectively (as was identified in the Hattie/Marzano teaching process in Chapter 6), they will find it difficult to use formative approaches. Also, if the dominant pedagogy in the school remains transmission, then teachers won't use formative assessment approaches, but rather will stay with summative.

However, what if schools do promote the use of dialogic, interactive pedagogies based on formative analysis of learners' performance as do many primary schools today? Why then are teachers still finding formative assessment practices difficult to implement? It is the same answer: the lack of formal, institutionalised opportunities to practise formative assessment practices on a daily basis. North-East schools demonstrate the need for schools to provide teachers with clear understandings of what constitutes evidence, clear means of collecting evidence, and structured means of collaboratively interrogating evidence so as to determine next teaching steps and to understand the processes of learning. In other words, the answer lies in the infrastructure developed in North-East schools because it is one thing to gather evidence of student progress and performance, but it is entirely another to be supported to make sense of this information in ways that will inform future practice. This is a skill that needs to be learned, and it is best learned with others.

In North-East schools, decision making and problem solving are based on evidence gathered from a range of sources. These include student performance in formal assessments and day-to-day learning activities. Evidence of teacher performance about how well they are implementing the profile is gathered by classroom observations conducted by their team leaders. Evidence of team leaders' performance is gathered by the principal from observations of how well they are implementing the profile with their teachers. This layering of evidence reinforces the implementation of the common code of pedagogic practice throughout the school, supporting the use of common approaches to learning by all members of the school staff. Parents are also included in this pattern of using evidence of student performance to add value to their children's learning. None of these people are recipients of transmission pedagogies that privilege one part of the learning partnership. Rather, the power over learning is in the relationship; evidence being used to improve the learning of all involved.

The need for effective data management systems

Of course, this all presupposes that schools will have or will develop effective student data management systems that will provide individuals and teams with timely and precise collations of evidence of student performance and teachers' practice. Gaining expertise in interpreting these data is a further skill that will need to be developed among the students, staff, and parents of the school. These formative skills grow with time as participants become more familiar with the patterns shown and are able to understand the relationships between various sets of data. One example from the ERO report of Te Kura Tuatahi o Papaioea – Central Normal School (one of the case study schools in this book) is where

> [the] deliberate selection and use of the schoolwide student tracking and management system enables analysis of relevant student data and information about teaching practices and is used effectively to evaluate and inform goal setting. (Education Review Office, 2019a)

The process of data collection and developing skills and knowledge of how to use this evidence is clearly something missing in many of our schools today but is a major focus of North-East schools' leaders.

I now turn to the last piece of the GPILSEO model. This final dimension is what makes it possible for school principals to successfully lead the transformation of their schools to become North-East learning institutions. It is done by their taking ownership of the problems their school faces, reflected in their goals and strategic plans, so that they are able to realise these goals. Taking ownership of these problems means they take responsibility for implementing the means identified in the rest of the GPILSEO model as ways that will ensure their goals are realised.

Ownership features in each of the other dimensions. North-East school leaders take ownership—that is, responsibility for the goals, the means of implementing the North-East pedagogy, and the support systems needed to ensure the gains made are sustained.

How they do this is the subject of the next chapter.

Chapter 8
Ownership

The final piece of the puzzle as to what makes it possible for school principals to successfully lead the transformation of their schools to become North-East learning institutions is their taking ownership of the problems they identify in the analysis they undertake as part of their goal setting. Taking ownership of these problems also means they need to take responsibility for the solutions selected in ways that will ensure their goals are realised.

Taking ownership of the problems means that principals must lead their schools' addressing inequitable student achievement patterns, including the "literacy crisis", Māori succeeding as Māori within mainstream, English-medium schools, and other marginalised students realising similar gains.

Taking ownership of the solutions means that principals must lead their school to take ownership of the means of addressing these problems. These include:

- setting goals for equity, excellence, and cultural sustainability for all students, not just for some
- implementing a pedagogic approach that ensures that these goals are realised

- implementing in-school support systems that ensure the pedagogy is implemented with fidelity over time, value is added to learning, and decision making and problem solving are evidence-based. These systems include infrastructure, leadership, means of including parents and community leaders, and evidence

- taking ownership of the approach by planning, resourcing, and self-reviewing so that the support systems work as designed over time.

Evidence that the school is taking ownership

There are three pieces of evidence that will show how well the school is heading to the North-East. These three actions—planning, resourcing, and self-reviewing—strategically focus all of the school's actions so as to realise their goals.

The first piece of evidence that a school is taking ownership of these problems and solutions is seen in their strategic planning documents where who has been involved in the production of the plan and how the school's leaders are going to realise their goals are identified. The strategic plan will include details of what pedagogy will be used, the support systems that will be implemented to ensure the pedagogy will be implemented with the designed fidelity, and the resourcing and self-review process that will be used to identify how well the school is progressing towards realising its goals.

The strategic plan will also include details of the ways in which the goals are to be realised in terms of their being specific, measurable, achievable, realistic, and within a specified time frame.

The second main piece of evidence that the school is taking ownership of the problems identified and the solutions chosen is the way the school is undertaking the allocation of human and funding resources. The strategic reallocation and realignment of staffing resources will determine, for example, how the changes in leadership tasks and responsibilities will be implemented so as to ensure the support systems necessary for the transformation of the school are able to function as intended. Details will be found in the documents about the specific nature of the role and responsibilities of the principal, senior leaders, and team leaders in terms of their tasks within North-East meetings for team leaders and teachers.

It is important to emphasise here that most of the staffing funding required for the transformation of the school into a North-East learning institution is already in the school, but it is being spent on activities that do not realise North-East goals. For example, middle-level leaders are crucial to supporting teacher learning and development. However, in modern schools they are often over-burdened with administrative tasks. They need to be freed up to reorientate their focus to leading teacher learning and development.

I realise that this is easy to say, but hard to achieve. However, this reorientation of leadership tasks and responsibilities is crucial for supporting teachers so that they can ensure that Māori and other marginalised students are successful learners on their own terms in the long term. If it is not done, then the support systems for teachers will not work, and if they do not work, then implementation fidelity of teaching approaches will not be assured. And if they are not assured, then teachers will modify and dilute the effectiveness of teaching approaches. As a result, the school's goals of equity and cultural sustainability will not be realised. This reorientation of team leaders' task and responsibilities may take some time and careful deliberations, but looking elsewhere for funding, while it is in your school, will not be very productive, certainly not in the long term.

The strategic realignment of community–school relationships will determine how the school will build learning partnerships with their local Māori community and those of other diverse groups so as to add value to their students' learning. How parents, families, and community leaders will participate in planning, problem solving, and decision making will also be made obvious.

The strategic reallocation and realignment of funding resources is necessary so that the focus of the school remains on successfully addressing the North-East goals in the long term.

The third piece of evidence that a school has taken on the responsibility of owning the problems they face and the solutions to these problems is their planning for self-review. Self-review is a means of identifying how well the school is progressing towards its goals of equity, cultural sustainability, and spreading the benefits to others. Self-review is a means whereby professionals address problems presented to them in ways that involve them taking responsibility for their actions. Of course, most schools engage in self-review processes. Indeed, they are now required to report this to ERO as part of their ongoing review process.[29] What emphasises that a school is a North-East learning institution is that their self-reviewing process is focused on how well the school is implementing those dimensions of the GPILSEO model that ensure schools address the learning needs of Māori and other marginalised students. These include goal setting, culturally responsive pedagogies, support systems, and ownership strategies.

In detail, the self-review process will include a means whereby the principal and senior leaders will assess how well the leaders and teachers in the school are implementing the preferred common code of pedagogic practice in their classrooms and across the school. Also assessed will be how well they have restructured the school to provide teachers with supported learning opportunities and institutionalised collective ways of interrogating evidence of student performance and teacher practice. They will also need a means of identifying how well they have institutionalised North-East leadership practices, spread assessment practices and dialogic interactions to include parents and families, prioritised evidence-based decision making and problem solving, and taken overall ownership of the means of realising their goals.

An example of the sorts of questions school leaders will need to ask of their actions in their self-review process include:

- How well are we implementing the preferred pedagogy within classrooms and across the school? How well is the pedagogy realising our goals? How will we know?
- How well does the provision and direction of the professional learning opportunities offered to staff members and community leaders support the preferred pedagogy?
- How well do the policies and infrastructural systems of the school, including the meetings teachers are expected to attend, provide them with the necessary capacity to support them to use the preferred pedagogy with fidelity over the long term?

---

29 https://ero.govt.nz/how-ero-reviews/schoolskura-english-medium

- How well are the different roles, tasks, and responsibilities of senior and middle-level leaders enabling them to support teachers to implement the preferred pedagogy?
- How well are our means of including parents, families, and community members adding value to our students' learning? How do we know?
- How well do we use evidence of teaching practice in relation to student performance? How do we know?
- What is the degree to which our school's ownership of the problems facing its Māori students reflected in our commitment to planning for and funding the solutions?
- How well is our self-review process providing us with evidence of our progress to realising our goals?

These questions will give school leaders baseline information about the directions their school needs to take for realising their goals.

What does it mean to take ownership of a reform process?

As I have mentioned before, it is probably realistic to say that most principals are going to need assistance from outside experts for the initial stages of the process of transformation. For example, they will probably need help with gathering the qualitative evidence of Māori students' and their teachers' experiences of their relationships and interactions. They will certainly need assistance with the implementation of any new literacy learning approach and its wider pedagogic frame so as to ensure that it its initial implementation is done with fidelity. They will then need help with learning about the coaching interactions that will need to take place in the infrastructure once it has been implemented. In all, there is a lot to be done and outside knowledge will be extremely useful, if not vital.

However, it is also vital that principals and school leaders take ownership of the means of transforming their school into a North-East learning institution by ensuring they maintain the fidelity of the implementation of all of the GPILSEO dimensions. This is absolutely necessary in the face of competing and changing priorities that will impact on the ongoing fidelity of the reform over time. This means that the term "fidelity" or "tikanga" does not just relate to the pedagogy. It relates to teachers' actions and how they are supported by responsive structural reforms, over time. In other words, fidelity relates to all the dimensions of the transformation; the goal setting process, the pedagogy, the support systems, the leadership, who is included, and how evidence is used.

This means that, unless ownership includes all the GPILSEO dimensions, as soon as the outside experts leave, the dilution of the process and the diminution of outcomes for Māori and other marginalised students will commence. In other words, if the means of realising the school's goals are not firmly in the hands of the school's leaders, the dissolution will start.

I suggested in an earlier book that the koha is a suitable metaphor for such a process of schools' leaders taking ownership of the reform. A koha is a gift to assist with the cost of running a hui. Depending on the actual tikanga of the marae, at some time towards the end of the pōwhiri, someone will pass over a koha (nowadays it is usually money) to the hosts to assist with funding the coming event. On many marae, it is placed out in the middle of the marae ātea by the final speaker of the manuhiri. Sometimes it is handed over to a member of the mana whenua in person, but it is a part of the proceedings that usually goes without a hitch.

However, it must not be forgotten that receiving the koha is up to the hosts. It is up to them if they will "pick it up" as it were. The fact that the koha is "laid down" in some way or other, means that the manuhiri are acknowledging the mana, the power of self-determination of the hosts to receive the koha. The hosts can reject the koha, which means that the proposed hui is over before it starts in fact. On the other hand, by picking up the koha, the hosts are signalling that they will accept that which the manuhiri are bringing with them and they will take care and ownership of it with all the responsibility this entails.

This means that when schools' leaders "pick up" the koha, the process of reform in this case, that is offered by the outside experts, they are signalling that they will take care of this means of reform. In doing so, they are assuring the original "owners" of the reform process that they will implement it in the way it was meant to be implemented; that is, with fidelity. They are also assuring the original "owners" that they will ensure that their school is transformed in ways necessary for the kaupapa and the outcomes to be sustained, so that the goals of equity, cultural sustainability, and spreading the benefits to others are realised over time. And above all, they are saying to Māori and other marginalised students, their parents, families, and community leaders that they have the means to realise their collaboratively set goals and they are taking on the responsibility for the future of all of our children, not just some.

The next three chapters are case studies of North-East schools that have realised the North-East goals of equity, cultural sustainability, and spreading the benefits to others, within 2 years. These are inspirational stories and will illustrate what taking ownership of the means of realising these goals means in practice.

Chapter 9
Introduction to the case studies and Case Study 1: Sylvia Park School

In the next three chapters, I am going to provide details of three schools that fit my idea of what makes a North-East school. The principals of these schools do not use this term, but I am sure you will see what I mean about North-East schooling in practice after you read about these three remarkable leaders and their schools.

The three schools are quite different, in different parts of the country. There are two primary schools: Sylvia Park School in East Auckland, led until recently by Barbara Ala'alatoa; the other is Te Kura Tuatahi o Papaioea – Central Normal School in Palmerston North, led by Regan Orr. There is one secondary school, in Kerikeri, Northland, led by Elizabeth Forgie until her recent retirement in 2022.

The three principals are all experienced leaders of learning institutions. Barbara Ala'alatoa had extensive leadership roles at Auckland University and the Ministry of Education prior to her 18-year tenure at Sylvia Park. Regan Orr had previously been principal of two primary schools until his relatively recent arrival at his current school. Elizabeth Forgie had led Kerikeri High School for 28 years prior to her retirement. For the last 18 of these years, she has led the inclusion of the Te Kotahitanga programme in her school. Both Barbara and Elizabeth have been, and continue to be, active in national-level educational leadership roles. Regan is prominent and well-known nationally for his advocacy and leadership in the promotion of "structured" literacy approaches.

All three schools have realised the three goals that run through this book; that is, they all managed to use literacy learning approaches that raised Māori to reach parity with their non-Māori peers. They did so by providing a pedagogy and whole-school support systems that saw Māori students being able to succeed as Māori. And they were also able to include other previously marginalised students in the benefits of this schooling approach.

What is interesting for the purposes of the thesis of this book is that they all used different approaches to raising literacy learning outcomes. At Sylvia Park, Barbara Ala'alatoa led the revitalisation of the "balanced" literacy approach over 18 years ago. At Te Kura Tuatahi o Papaioea – Central Normal School, Regan Orr has led the implementation of a "structured" literacy approach quite recently. At Kerikeri High School, Elizabeth Forgie led the implementation of a "literacy across the curriculum" approach within a wider pedagogic and structural reform programme introduced as part of the Te Kotahitanga project which commenced in her school in the early 2000s.

The leaders' achievements can be seen in terms of the GPILSEO model

The first thing I look for when I visit any school is how well their Māori and other potentially marginalised students are faring in literacy, numeracy, and other achievement outcomes. Whatever the schools' leaders say about what they are doing is irrelevant if the achievement results do not match their practices. Hence, the first evidence I will provide in these three case studies will be the achievement gains made by the school in terms of the three North-East goals detailed in this book. Then, I will follow the sequence of the GPILSEO model to provide details of how each school realised the three North-East goals. These details include:

- **goal** setting
- implementation of a **pedagogy** as the key agent for realising the goals

- the support systems designed to ensure the pedagogy is implemented with fidelity, learning is enhanced, and an evidence base for decision making and problem solving is provided. These systems include an **infrastructure, leadership, spread, and evidence**
- how the schools took **ownership** of the planning, resourcing, and self-reviewing needed for the support systems to work effectively.

I have used current or recent ERO reports to provide evidence of the achievement outcomes of these schools and also of the various dimensions of the GPILSEO model of change. My reason for using these reports is because they are easily accessible to the New Zealand public on the ERO website or on the respective schools' websites. These reports are produced by reviewers who undertake visits to different schools on a weekly basis. They are very experienced observers. They see many schools and they know a great school when they see it. Their reports are produced in language that is readily accessible to most adults, or is able to be interpreted or translated readily. Most of all these reports are very useful to schools' leaders, as they guide schools' learning directions in terms of how well the schools are realising their goals and objectives.

The details from the relevant ERO reports of the three schools illustrate what effective North-East schools' achievement patterns and teaching and learning practices look like. In terms of the GPILSEO model, the first thing they did was to collaboratively lead the setting of goals that orientated the actions of all of the schools' activities and personnel towards the realisation of these goals.

They introduced their specific literacy learning approaches within a pedagogic framework that was, in my terms, relationship-based and also used what John Hattie and Robert Marzano have identified as being among the best approaches to teaching in the world. Because they did this, not only did they manage to improve Māori students' academic outcomes rapidly, they did so in ways that acknowledged their mana as Māori. The approaches they introduced also saw improved learning for other students who would usually be marginalised from the benefits of learning by their supposed "deficiencies".

They then implemented structural improvements in their schools that were aimed at supporting the pedagogic approaches they had instituted. These included the development of infrastructural support systems so that teachers were supported to implement the pedagogic framework, including any specific literacy learning approaches, in ways that will ensure they are implemented with fidelity in an ongoing manner.

They all led the transformation of leadership roles to become supportive of teachers' learning. Initially, they all called upon outside expertise to lead the introduction of the specifics of the new literacy and other pedagogic approaches, but soon they began the process of transferring these skills and knowledge to leaders in their own schools so as to ensure sustainability of these practices.

They all ensured that all of the staff in their schools were able to participate in the reform by providing them with the best professional learning opportunities they could find. They then developed the best infrastructural support systems and leadership practices they could to ensure their teachers were able to implement the new approaches with ongoing fidelity.

They all included parents, families, and community members and leaders in formative deliberations in ways that added value to their students' learning. They all did so in ways that included students' families not just as participants, but increasingly as initiators of learning.

Their collective approaches to decision making and problem solving were based on the effective and efficient provision of evidence of student performance in relation to what their teachers and team leaders were providing for "their" learners.

Above all, the all took ownership of the means of transforming their schools into North-East learning institutions. They did so by planning the best ways to achieve their goals, strategically resourcing and allocating staffing and engaging in processes of self-review so as to identify how well they were progressing towards realising their goals and where they had to go next to further the process of transformation.

An advance organiser to guide your reading

I am providing this detailed introduction to these three remarkable schools as an advance organiser to guide your reading so that you can identify and highlight the various parts of the GPILSEO model they have implemented while you read through these stories.

Of course, there are other North-East schools out there. There are many, but I might suggest there are not enough to make a dent in the ongoing pattern of educational disparities being along ethnic lines. We clearly need more North-East schools.

Remember that the first step to realising the goals in this book about Māori students achieving on par with non-Māori, and as Māori, and of other marginalised students also benefiting, is leaders' refusal to accept differences in outcomes based on ethnicity, group membership or beliefs. This means that because they are prepared to be primarily outcomes and performance focused, this pattern of disparities can be changed. And it can be changed very rapidly. All it needs is belief and conviction that it can be done, followed by the actions shown by these courageous and exemplary school leaders.

Case Study 1 Sylvia Park School

Introduction

Sylvia Park School is a decile 2, full primary school in East Auckland. The school serves a diverse student population of 560 students, 30% of whom are of Tongan descent, 28% NZ Māori, 23% Asian, and 7% Pākehā, with smaller groups of other students, mostly of Pacific Island descent, making up the student body. There is a "mainstream" section of the school where teaching is via the medium of English, and there is a Māori bilingual unit of three classes. There are approximately 32 teaching staff with a smaller team of support staff.

I am very grateful to Laurayne Tafa of TafaEd, also an ex-principal, for introducing me to her colleague, Barbara Ala'alatoa, who has recently retired after being the principal of this school for 18 years. Barbara has had a wide and varied career in education including teaching and leadership roles in other primary schools in South Auckland, lecturing at Auckland College of Education, co-ordinating school improvement at the Ministry of Education, and taking the inaugural chair for the Education Council of New Zealand. She is currently the chair of Te Aho o Te Kura Pounamu (formerly The Correspondence School). She is an Officer of the New Zealand Order of Merit for her services to education.

The achievement patterns of this school

As I said in the introduction to this section, my primary interest in any school I visit is the achievement levels of the Māori and other marginalised students in the school. Nothing else matters to me if the Indigenous students are not achieving on par with their non-Māori peers, and if the school is not able to ensure that this achievement is not at the expense of their identity as Māori.

Goal 1. Māori achieving on par with non-Māori students within 2 years

At Sylvia Park School, the principal was able to assure me that the achievement outcomes of their Māori and other often marginalised students, such as those of Pacific Island descent, were on par with their non-Māori peers. In fact, as you will see from their ERO reports cited below, their Māori and Pacific students are achieving at rates above those of the national levels. The principal explained to me that, following the introduction of a revitalised "balanced" literacy approach over 18 years ago, Māori and Pacific students' achievement rates accelerated to reach parity with their non-Māori peers "in a very short time". That this pattern of accelerated achievement for these students was sustained is verified in an ERO report that followed some time after the introduction of the revitalised approach had seen the earlier gains.

> Raising student achievement is the absolute purpose of trustees, senior managers and staff. Students make accelerated rates of progress in reading and writing. Analysed achievement information for the end of 2009 indicates that the majority of students achieve well in reading, with over 80% achieving at or above expected national levels for Years 7 and 8. Achievement information in writing for students in Years 4 to 8[30] suggests that students' rate of progress is significantly higher than the national rate at all these year levels.
>
> Separate achievement information for Māori and Pacific students is collated and analysed. This indicates that Māori and Pacific students make double the rate of progress in comparison to national average mean scores in reading, and more than triple this rate for writing.

---

30 These figures for mainly Māori and Pacific students compare very well to the figure of 56% of all students nationally.

Achievement information also suggests that Māori students who receive bilingual education achieve better than those in mainstream. (Education Review Office, 2010, n.p.)

Four years later, the reviewers were clearly satisfied with that the patterns of achievement identified earlier were being maintained and emphasised the reasons for these accomplishments.

[t]he school enacts its vision to empower students to stand tall and be proud. Students are clearly at the centre of adults' decision making … Students and teachers have also collaborated to create their own identities within their whānau. At the same time they have retained a strong sense of loyalty to the school as a whole. …

Students' enjoyment and understanding about their learning is also highly evident. They thrive on the school's culture of high expectations and inquiry. Students' aspirations and ambitions are valued and they are empowered to achieve them. As a result, students show a strong sense of belonging and pride in their school. … Māori students achieve well and school leaders place a high priority on ensuring positive outcomes for Māori students. …

Other significant strengths of this school include a school culture which affirms whakawhanaungatanga, manaakitanga and kōtahitanga. (Education Review Office, 2014, n.p.)

Goal 2. Māori succeeding as Māori

The second goal of North-East schools is to ensure that Māori students do not have to leave who they are, their identity, at the school gate when they come to a mainstream, public school. North-East schools build on, rather than reject, what young people bring to school with them in ways that reinforce their cultural identity, thus ensuring cultural sustainability. Again, the ERO reviewers saw this happening at Sylvia Park School.

Educational success as Māori is very well supported and promoted. The kaupapa of the school is strongly bicultural and Māori students benefit from this approach. The school has a well-developed kawa and deep understanding of tikanga Māori that is a part of regular school practice.

A range of opportunities are available for Māori students to explore their language, culture and identity. Bilingual learning opportunities gained through Te Puna Waiora result in Māori students who are confident and demonstrate high aspirations for their success ... Māori students in the mainstream benefit from a curriculum and a school culture that affirms their identity. (Sylvia Park School ERO report, 2014, n.p.)

Goal 3. Other marginalised students also benefit from the transformation of the school to be a North-East learning institution

The third goal of North-East schools is to support the learning of those groups of students who are currently most likely to be marginalised from the benefits that schooling has to offer them by what they bring to school being seen as deficiencies rather than potentialities. We saw above that Pacific children are achieving equitably alongside their Māori peers at Sylvia Park. The ERO reviewers were also able to identify evidence that this benefit was spread to other children as well.

Trustees, senior managers and staff know about the progress of groups of students, including students for whom English is an additional language. (Education Review Office, 2010, n.p.)

Equitable outcomes are evident for diverse groups of learners. The school finds ways to embrace the language, culture and identity of students to enhance their learning outcomes. Students with additional learning requirements receive very good support from caring and well trained staff. (Education Review Office, 2014, n.p.).

The question now is how did this school achieve these North-East outcomes? When telling the story of Sylvia Park, I will follow the GPILSEO sequence of goals, pedagogy, infrastructure, leadership, spread, evidence, and ownership to identify the process the principal led the school through. I will use relevant ERO evidence of the changes that the principal led so that they could realise the school's equity and cultural sustainability goals.

The need for goal setting, which commences with an analysis of the current situation

On her arrival at the school, the new principal undertook an analysis of the then current situation. This analysis was followed by a goal-setting exercise.

Reflecting recently on her arrival at Sylvia Park, Barbara Ala'alatoa described the place as being in disarray. They had had five ERO reports in 6 years.[31] Teachers were working in isolation from each other. They talked to each other of course, but rarely about learning and students' progress. What was also clear was that there was huge variability in teaching practice because there were no collective activities. Nobody knew what was happening in each other's classrooms. No one was supporting anyone to improve their practice and there was no means of doing so even if they had wanted to engage in such practices. Each teacher was on their own. Nor was there any inquiry or means of inquiry into students' achievement data and very little data on teachers' practice apart from that primarily of a summative nature from compulsory appraisal visits by senior staff members.

This situation needed a radical response. What happened is described later, but firstly, the school's leaders needed to identify what they and their parents and local community expected of the school. Barbara Ala'alatoa explained that it became very clear that their main goal had to be to raise achievement. "We were very clear about our mission which is to get great outcomes for our children." This vision remains the guiding principle for Sylvia Park School today. On their current website, their first statement is about "setting children on a pathway to life-long learning". They also identify that the three North-East goals

---

31 ERO reports are produced following school evaluation visits by reviewers from the Education Review Office. The aim of these visits is to investigate how well a school is meeting its goals and objectives. Repeat visits are a means of monitoring the improvements that were recommended in the previous year's report. A high frequency of repeat visits means that the school is not doing well in terms of implementing the means of realising its goals and objectives. Five visits in 6 years is a serious matter. High frequency of returns like this signals a low functioning school. In contrast, high performing schools tend only to be reviewed every 5 years. Indeed, Sylvia Park had not been reviewed since 2014; a measure of the confidence that the ERO reviewers have in the transformed school.

that run through this book are central to this overview. In their own words, they identify that:

> Literacy (reading and writing) and Numeracy (mathematics) have always been a priority at Sylvia Park School within a balanced, broad and place based curriculum. We want our learners to find their passion, experience success and know who they are and where they belong.[32]

Pedagogy

From her analysis of the school on her arrival 18 years ago, the new principal identified the primary need was for a strategic plan to address reading because of its foundational importance. She understood that, if left alone, the students' literacy learning skills would not improve, and, consequently, their self-perception as learners and their motivation to learn would continue to suffer as well. In short, because achievement results were appalling and as reading was the basis for most other forms of learning, here is where they began. She explained that "[w]e can't talk about agency and efficacy for our kids if they are unable to access news and information that they then do meaningful things with; not just at school, but in their lives" (personal communication, 10 June 2022).

However, she also knew that, when introducing a new way of teaching reading into the school, it was important that she as the "new broom" did not sweep all previous practice or indeed, people, before her. She understood this to be a dangerous principle if the new leader is trying to encourage teachers to engage with new approaches. In this case, the principal began with the teachers who were already there and with what they were already familiar. This was the old Schooling Strategy that consisted of "quality teaching at all times in all classrooms, being evidence-based in your practice and a learning focus on relationships with whānau".

She explained that this approach helped them build upon the teachers' aspirations and desires to improve the students' literacy results. This approach enabled them to use their prior knowledge and skills, engage their willingness to interrogate data when supported to do so,

---

32 https://www.sylviapark.school.nz/

and to lift their focus beyond the school gates; to see the importance of including families in the children's learning. "We have a really strong belief about what will create that, great teaching, every day in every classroom. The second part of that is being evidence-based, so you know we use data, kids' data ...".

It was also very important to call the teachers to action. By this she meant that they needed to realise how powerful they were as teachers. They could have a major impact upon their children's lives, and it could be negative or positive. Barbara Ala'alatoa continues, "The other part of sharing the national strategy was to let them know that we were all part of a greater plan—a plan that would see us play our part in creating a nation where *all* people could thrive. This could only be achieved as a collective." Before this, teachers working on their own did not have a belief in themselves as being agents of change. They tended to believe that the status quo of low achievement was inevitable and normal. This had to be disrupted and replaced with a feeling of all teachers and families working towards a greater purpose.

They also drew on the Ministry of Education's Best Evidence Syntheses for evidence-based information about the best ways to approach literacy learning. They did not go looking for different approaches. Rather, they delved into the practices they already knew about. However, this time, they wanted them to be implemented with fidelity right across the school. These included ELP (Effective Literacy Practice); deliberate acts of teaching, guided reading, shared reading, shared language with instructional writing, conferencing interactions, and guided home reading and writing activities—what is now called a "balanced" literacy approach. The result was that over 2 years "we saw incredible changes in student achievement". The school's leaders were able to go back to teachers and say "Look what you have done. That's what powerful teaching does. You have made a material difference in kids' lives."

A common code of effective practice was instituted within the school in order to provide children with a common, positive experience of being successful learners. The importance of all teachers taking part in the process of reform was emphasised so that children had common experiences within year levels and as they progressed through the school.

Along with other North-East schools, the common code of practice has the following characteristics. It consists of a means of creating an extended family-like context for learning, and interacting within this context in ways we know support learning. And equally as important is their monitoring of students' progress on identified tasks, and the impact of the processes of learning on students' performance and understanding of those dimensions of being self-regulating learners. The ERO reviewers noted that, at Sylvia Park School:

> High quality teaching practices are evident throughout the school. Leaders and teachers have a shared understanding of effective teaching practices. ... Leaders prioritise the urgency for teachers to support students not achieving sufficiently to make accelerated progress. Teachers use achievement information well to evaluate student progress ...

> The curriculum continues to be broad, holistic and affirming of students' cultural identities and heritages. Pacific and Māori contexts are very evident. The curriculum emphasises inclusive practices, affirming students' wellbeing and promoting students' empathy for others.

> Students are challenged and inspired by meaningful, open-ended inquiries that provide a clear purpose to their learning. They have opportunities to contribute to the design of learning experiences. Students demonstrate a strong sense of social justice and respect for environmental sustainability.

> The school's learning environments are adapted to suit student learning preferences, interests and needs. Thoughtful use of technologies enhances learning opportunities and supports students to be self-managing learners. Classrooms are well resourced, vibrant places for student learning. (Education Review Office, 2014, n.p.)

Infrastructure: How they achieved the transformation in teaching practices

The first thing to happen was the development of collective practice. "We had to pry open our classroom doors so we could engage in a practice analysis that would help us to challenge each other and support each other. We also had to establish a base line of practice that enabled us to see if what we were doing was actually working." In order to do so, they developed their own matrix of what an expert teacher of reading looked like and also what constituted each step towards this ideal type.

They developed a specific observation schedule used to provide feedback to all teachers in the school on the commonly developed and understood expectations about how to teach literacy. Classroom observations and support sessions were developed to enable the teachers and support people to point to where they were positioned along the continuum of expertise and what was needed to move them from one position to the next. The teachers found this approach to be very useful because it set out just where they needed to go in terms of acquiring the skills and knowledge they needed to become a really effective teacher of reading. Teachers were able to place themselves on the continuum. But it was not left up to them to work it all out for themselves without their having any idea on how they were going or how they could modify and improve their practice—they were constantly supported to implement the improvement strategies.

The school's leaders also developed a school-wide dataset of student achievement criteria in relation to teacher practice so all teachers and leaders could see the improvements in student learning as teachers' practice changed and improved. It gave them a situational analysis that further drove improvement.

They sought outside support from experts in literacy and, more importantly, in coaching.[33] This support enabled team leaders to learn how to undertake classroom observations and provide supportive feedback and feed-forward about how teachers could improve their literacy teaching practices and make progress along the continua towards being an effective teacher of literacy.

Sylvia Park School began by institutionalising (that is, making an action an ongoing part of the day-to-day business of the school) a means of de-privatising the classrooms so that the teachers could collectively interrogate evidence of student progress in relation to teachers' practice. This is done in ways that identify the next learning steps and

---

33 This help came from The Literacy Professional Development Project (LPDP) and Cognition Education.

the teaching practices that will support these steps and directions. Such new institutions replace existing practices with meetings that use evidence for formative purposes so that teachers practice using formative assessment processes in ways that promote student learning. They also learn how to teach students to make use of evidence of their own performance in formative ways.

These meetings were institutionalised in at least two levels in the school. The first was for classroom teachers in their year-level teams, led by their year-level team leader. Their team leaders led the development of teaching and learning in ways that supported the improvement of student learning and outcomes. The second level of these meetings was at the whole-school level, a meeting run by the principal, where deputy principals and senior team leaders collectively interrogated school-wide data on student achievement and teaching practices to identify the next learning steps and teaching practices that will be needed at a school level to support these learning steps and practices.

> An integral part of teachers' effective practice is their active inquiry and a determination to continually improve their teaching. Comprehensive performance management processes promote teacher reflection and development ...

> Teachers share decision-making with students and support student exploration in their learning. They are highly professional educators who work collaboratively together. Skilled support staff work closely with teachers in complementary ways to support student learning.

> [S]ignificant strengths of the school include ... cutting-edge professional learning, based on highly effective practices, that is clearly building teaching capacity.

> Overall, there is strong evidence of a student-centred philosophy that is implemented through strong school management systems. (Education Review Office, 2014, n.p.)

Leadership

The principal acts as a North-East leader at the whole-school level using whole-of-school data modelling and reinforcing the pedagogic approaches and the support systems so that team leaders in turn are able to use these approaches with their teams. The distribution of a North-East leadership model, where the principal is the head Leader of Learning, is replicated through the school at each level. Team leaders are supported to become Leaders of Learning for their staff who in turn support the teachers in their teams to become leaders of students' learning. This transformation of leadership practices from the traditional administrative role is fundamental to the success of this school. This means that teachers are no longer on their own. Nor are groups of teachers left on their own. Leaders take responsibility for the learning of the people in their team in this way, supporting the spread and implementation of the common code of pedagogic practice within the new institutions of the school.

The ERO reports for this school speak loudly about the importance of the principal taking a professional leadership role in developing excellent outcomes for the students in their schools. Their reports speak very highly of the personal and professional commitments of the principal, her ability to inspire others, and to make it possible for all others in the school to perform to their potential. It is interesting that she made a point of working with the existing staff of the school, in this way emphasising that the school was a whānau. Just as it is the task of the whānau to look after all of its children, it must also look after the adults. These staff were teachers who had aspirations to see improvements in learning outcomes for their children, but who were not being successful prior to the intervention led by the principal. In this way, the same people were enabled to make the tremendous difference to Māori and other marginalised students' learning outcomes once it had been made possible for them to do so. In other words, it is the principal who made it possible for others to do their job effectively. This is the mark of an effective North-East leader.

ERO reviewers identified that a distributed pattern of North-East leadership is well embedded at Sylvia Park School:

> The principal provides strong and professional leadership. She
> builds and distributes leadership effectively so that it operates at
> management, teaching and learning levels. The principal's effective
> interpersonal skills enable parents and community members to
> feel welcomed and comfortable in the school. She participates in

educational and national forums that benefit outcomes for students … Senior managers and teachers have worked effectively together to design a curriculum that promotes student progress and achievement … Effective leadership exists at governance, management, teaching and learning levels. … (Education Review Office, 2010)

Highly effective and committed professional leaders serve the school community well. They continue to promote teacher leadership and development to benefit student learning. (Education Review Office, 2014)

It is in the last line that the ERO reviewers identify that leadership is distributed throughout the school and is not just positioned within the senior ranks. They also identify that the function of this distributed leadership pattern is to promote teacher learning in ways that will benefit student learning. Perhaps we could encourage the ERO reviewers to make more of this circumstance in schools when they see it happening because it is crucial for teacher learning.

Spread: Including all staff and parents in the learning process

Including all staff in the transformation

Spreading the reform to include all teachers and leaders was an integral part of the means that the principal used to introduce the revitalisation of the literacy learning approach used in the school. In order to provide their children with a common and effective learning experience, it was vital that all staff took part in the professional learning opportunities provided either by outside experts or by school leaders. It was also important for the purpose of supporting all teachers to be successful and effective implementers of the literacy approach within the wider pedagogic framework that all leaders become supportive of teachers' learning. This meant that they, in turn, needed to be supported to be able to use the observation schedules and matrices that were developed to support teacher learning of the preferred approaches.

Including parents and community members

What is also notable about this school is the means they used to include parents into the decision making and problem solving of the school's literacy programme. Including parents became central to their making progress as a learning institution by their adding value to their children's learning. Barbara Ala'alatoa explained that, firstly, they needed to acknowledge that

> [o]ur accountability also went out to the parents and the community. This became an important part of our pedagogy. That is, it is hugely important to take into account their home background and recognise their home culture. Knowing that child. Knowing their whānau and building on what knowledge they bring to school as the base for their learning.

If teachers find this culturally responsive concept difficult to grasp, it is important that school leaders take the opportunity to demonstrate what this approach to learning entails. It can also be demonstrated to pre-service teachers in ITE institutions, by using an approach called Funds of Knowledge.[34] This programme was developed by Luis Moll and others in the southern US. It is based on a simple premise—people are competent and able to make sense of the world and develop knowledge in their own culturally determined ways. In other words, their life's experiences have given them knowledge. Children learn these funds of knowledge through their engaging in whānau, community, and cultural practices and events informally through participation and observation.

In the Funds of Knowledge programme, in-service and pre-service teachers are provided with an opportunity to spend some time with families of their children, especially so when they are from different cultural backgrounds to their children. This method has at least two major benefits. The first is that it counters the tendency among teachers from the majority culture to see minority culture students has having learning deficiencies in terms of their having inadequate understandings and knowledge upon which they can build further learning. The second is that, often, teachers from the majority culture misunderstand or do not know about the "funds" of knowledge that minority cultural groups actually have. They may not have the knowledge valued or understood by the members of the majority culture, but they will have

---

34 https://fundsofknowledge.org/the-funds-of-knowledge-approach/

knowledge nonetheless about how they make sense and understand the world. In this way, such understandings put the onus on professional educators to be responsive to the children, rather than is often the case where the children have to learn majority cultural ways of knowing before they can take part in learning alongside their peers from the majority culture.

It is important that teachers gain an in-depth understanding of what culturally responsive pedagogies actually entail so that they can develop a proficiency in implementing this approach. This pedagogic approach places the culture of the child—the ways they make sense of the world—within the conversation that is learning. It is not "child-centred" learning; rather, it is "relationship- and interaction-centred" learning where the child takes part in dialogue. These dialogic learning interactions include teachers drawing on students' prior knowledge, their providing and being provided with feedback and feed-forward, their engaging in co-construction activities, asking questions, and engaging in co-operative learning. It is the mode of conversation that brings their experiences and understandings to their new and emerging understandings.

A second focus on including parents then developed

Barbara Ala'alatoa explained that

> [w]hen it came to including parents, we used to talk to them as a whole hall or library full of people, and we talked to them about literacy and numeracy. Now we have a very tailored and targeted approach to the way in which we share data with each of our parents of our children in the junior school, so that they can go home that night and make a meaningful, authentic impact on their child's learning … It has grown their understanding about the sort of language we use at school. They know what assessments mean. So suddenly school's this very doable kind of place where we've got a shared language where they can participate and better support their children's learning at home.

The principal continued by explaining how they had worked to further improve engagement with the parents and families by including them in the deliberations about evidence of their child's literacy learning.

We run three-way conferences with parents, and we have informal discussions before and after school where possible. They come along and they hear the child talking a lot, and they hear the teachers talking a lot … and [instead of not being to participate as before], they are now able to take part.

She explained the reason for their participation in these conversations was two-fold. Firstly, it was because they understand the language of the school being used by the teachers and their children, such as "learning intentions" and "success criteria", and, secondly, the parents have become far more targeted in the questions they ask about their children's learning, about levels and expectations.

To ensure that these learning conversations are able to take place, sometimes it is necessary for the school's leaders and teachers to go out to the parents' workplaces or meet them at their homes or vary the school day so as to fit work patterns and timings. Also, as many of the families are Tongan, it is important that the parents have access to the learning conversations in Tongan as well as English, so, when necessary, a translator sits in as well. "If you are prepared to do these things … people will turn up."

The development of Mutukaroa

This process of including parents in the conversations about learning assessment data to further improve learning outcomes became the base for the development of a unique home–school partnership. This partnership was based on the sharing of assessment data in a comprehensive, methodical and formative way with whānau. This relationship grew into a programme called Mutukaroa. The focus of the programme was not on literacy and maths as such but rather on developing a shared language of assessment with families so as to improve outcomes in reading, writing, and maths.

Ariana Williams, Mutukaroa co-ordinator for Sylvia Park School, explained that

[w]hat we found prior to Mutukaroa was that we had a lot of kids on entry that were coming in [with] really low [literacy skill levels]. So we wanted to do something about that. We knew with great teaching and quality-based practice that we could get them to a certain point. What

we found by introducing Mutukaroa was that by the time that they were 6, they weren't just at the level ... lots of kids were also above. And that's what we wanted to see. That was something that we hadn't seen before.[35]

The implementation of the programme involves a co-ordinator, who is released from teaching duties to go out and meet with the parents as soon as the child starts school. The purpose of this early visit is to show the parents' their child's school entry assessment and what they will be learning and the next steps their child needs to work on. They also make visits at other times during the first 3 years at the school to re-set learning targets and to provide supportive resources for learning at home. Mutukaroa is focused on learning; the co-ordinator does not discuss behaviour in meetings. Questions about behaviour are directed to the children's classroom teacher, the co-ordinator being able to help with letters or emails to the classroom teacher.

The programme has been extended now to run in over 100 schools throughout New Zealand. It is funded externally and co-ordinators network to support one another.[36] Nevertheless, the initial success elements of the programme remain.

> Learners are assessed on school entry at 5 years old then again at 5 ½ years, 6, and 7 years, with the intention of tracking progress during their time at school.

> At each stage of the assessment process, the coordinator reviews the data, discusses any issues with the teacher, and agrees the next steps in the child's learning journey.

> Next steps complement and support what teachers are doing in the classroom. Whānau are invited to a 45 minute–1 hour meeting with the coordinator to discuss the assessment data and learning targets.

---

35 https://elearning.tki.org.nz/Snapshots-of-learning/Snapshots-of-Learning/Mutukaroa-A-home-school-learning-partnership

36 Problematically, this involves start-up funding, leaving schools to develop their own ways to fund the programme beyond the initial set-up period. This provision of "soft money" for the initiation of programmes has often proven to be problematic for schools as competing priorities for funding tend to leave what look like "core" business aside. It is only when the school's leaders are determined to sustain the programmes that funding is forthcoming. This, however, is not that common in New Zealand or internationally for that matter.

... Translators are provided if needed.

The coordinator utilises a learning framework and toolset to offer whānau structured and specific advice about how to support their child's learning.

Coordinators take a very tailored and targeted approach to sharing data with individual parents, so that they can make a meaningful, authentic impact on their child's learning. This supports parents to participate in three-way conferences and to support their child's learning at home.

...

Mutukaroa supports learning-focused relationships with parents. The emphasis is on the child and their learning, focusing on student achievement and fostering the active engagement of parents through a learning partnership.[37]

The Education Review Office reports clearly identify the benefits of inclusion:

Close relationships between the school and its community benefit students' learning. Transition into and through the school is highly effective. Mutukaroa, the school's partnership programme, begins at enrolment. Teachers work closely with families to develop and review personalised learning plans throughout students' time at the school. (Education Review Office, 2014, n.p.)

Evidence

The initial analysis of the problems facing the school also identified the lack of any evidence of student performance in relation to teaching practice for formative purposes. They were gathering evidence of student performance but is was mostly for summative purposes. The ERO reviewers noted that this process was well embedded when they visited in 2014.

School leaders monitor and evaluate students' progress and achievement very effectively. They analyse achievement information

---

37 https://elearning.tki.org.nz/Snapshots-of-learning/Snapshots-of-Learning/
Mutukaroa-A-home-school-learning-partnership

and know how well groups of students and individuals progress over time. Leaders and teachers are well informed by educational research and they work collaboratively to enhance student learning. (Education Review Office, 2014, n.p.)

However, the principal also wanted to gather evidence of teaching practices so that the schools' leaders and the teachers themselves could use evidence of student performance and progress in relation to teaching practices for decision making and problem solving about next teaching steps. To do so, she instituted classroom observation schedules to be used to gather evidence of teachers' activities so that these data could be used to support them to change their practices to be more effective. Then she developed these practices into an institutional means whereby this formative assessment process became an ongoing part of school life.

These formative assessment practices are used in team meetings to collectively interrogate what strengths and weaknesses are shown, and where teaching needs to go next. What is also important about this approach is that teachers are not left on their own to identify where they need to take their teaching to—they are supported by team leaders to support teachers with improving their teaching practices. ERO's reviewers were able to see clear evidence of this process in action; that is, of data being gathered and, most importantly, being used in association with evidence of student performance, and of leaders supporting teachers to improve their practice.

> Robust processes are established for making judgements about student achievement. Data analysis is timetabled during staff meetings to collectively interpret, analyse and to identify strengths and weaknesses and strategies for further improvement … All teachers participate in scheduled staff analyses of data, to identify strengths and next steps for teaching and learning. Professional development for teachers is provided to support any identified gaps in teaching practice or curriculum expertise. (Education Review Office, 2010, n.p.)

This formative process of using evidence of student achievement to build the capability of all members of the school whānau includes and extends beyond the classrooms to include parents and board of trustee members.

> Senior managers use achievement information to build the capability
> of students, staff and parents and have identified strategies to sustain
> improvement. Trustees receive high quality and frequent information
> about student achievement in reading, writing and numeracy. They
> use the information to identify appropriate priorities and review their
> strategic direction. (Education Review Office, 2010, n.p.)

That these formative processes have become institutionalised within Sylvia Park School is attested to by the ERO visit 4 years later. Indeed, there is evidence that the process of analysing evidence of student performance in relation to teaching and leadership practices has become even more sophisticated and inclusive. Now students have been included in learning how to take responsibility for their own progress. The final line of the next quote, where it states that students *are self-managing learners and highly engaged in learning,* is very exciting. It shows that the outcomes of the pedagogic approach used in this school has taken the children beyond being recipients of knowledge or simply being task orientated and included them in learning how to be self-managing learners. This means that, not only are these children learning how to read and write more effectively than others in their age group nationally, but they are also being inducted into the secrets of what it is to be a lifelong learner, which is precisely what the school states on its website as being its major goal for their children. Well done indeed!

> School leaders monitor and evaluate students' progress and
> achievement very effectively. They analyse achievement information
> and know how well groups of students and individuals progress
> over time ... Teachers use achievement information well to evaluate
> student progress. Students also closely and clearly monitor their
> own work, taking responsibility for their progresss ... They are self-
> managing learners and highly engaged in learning. (Education Review
> Office, 2014, n.p.)

As was identified earlier, achievement information is also used with other groups including whānau for formative purposes so that responsibility for learning is shared and value is added. One can only wonder the impact on our wider society if more schools were able to engage family members in this way, instead of leaving them out in the cold.

Useful achievement information underpins learning conferences with families and students. Whānau know how well their child is achieving and how they can help them achieve their learning goals. Sharing responsibility for student learning is an integral part of the school's kaupapa. (Education Review Office, 2014, n.p.)

Finally, student achievement data are used to inform their resourcing decision making so as to ensure that their focus on improving student learning outcomes is realised and done so readily. This is clear evidence that this school has taken ownership of the issues facing their students' learning and have oriented all their actions towards realising their goals of improving student learning and, more importantly, learning how to learn.

> Overall, trustees use student achievement information very effectively
> to inform planning and decision making. Challenging targets focus
> on promoting student learning and realising student potential. Other
> self-review information is also used well by trustees and leaders
> to review resourcing decisions and respond quickly to learners'
> requirements. (Education Review Office, 2014, n.p.)

Ownership

The final, and all-encompassing dimension of the GPILSEO model is the need for schools to take ownership of any problems their children have with learning and provide them with timely solutions. They do not look outside of the school and its community to find blame, but rather work with their whānau to promote outstanding outcomes. They take professional responsibility for improving their students' learning by transforming their practices. The process of looking in the mirror to see where the problems and the solutions lie is well embedded in this school.

It is not a deficit focus. Rather, self-review is a means of professionals addressing problems presented to them in ways that involve them taking responsibility for their actions. This is what we expect of any member of a profession. They do not blame people for their problems but rather work with them to address issues based on reference to a body of knowledge about how to go about realising these solutions.

Leading to the North-East: Ensuring the fidelity of relationship-based learning

The whole school whānau was involved in achieving these outcomes because they had been supported to take ownership of the problems as being their responsibility, not those of other people. The principal and other leaders had led the transformation of this school into an extended family-like context for learning and they supported all their teachers to replicate this context in their classrooms. This context is one where, above all, teachers address and reject negative stereotyping about Māori and Pacific students. Teachers at Sylvia Park School clearly care for their students as culturally and language-located individuals, building on the knowledge they bring to school as the base for their further learning. Teachers also have high expectations for their learning and know what they need to learn and how to ensure this happens. This context creates security for the children, assuring them that, at this school and with these teachers, they will become successful learners. They will feel good about themselves as learners and learn cognitive and affective domain skills—such as self-regulation and self-control—that will serve them well in their subsequent years at school and in later life. And above all, their children are able to maintain their own mana, ensuring cultural sustainability.

The creation of this context enabled teachers to interact effectively with students and also with parents in ways that addressed learning needs, accelerated learning where needed, and supported learners to become self-regulating and self-determining—in short, lifelong learners. The interactions that supported learning include teachers drawing upon students' prior knowledge and understandings so that different culturally generated ways of making sense of the world are given space to provide the base for further learning.

To realise their goals, the principal led the introduction of effective pedagogic interactions, restructured the school to provide teachers with supported learning opportunities, and institutionalised collective ways of interrogating evidence of student performance and teacher practice. They also institutionalised effective, supportive leadership practices; spread assessment practices use to include parents and families; prioritised evidence-based decision making and problem solving; and took ownership of the problem and the solutions by orienting (and funding) all the schools' and classrooms' activities of the school to address the central problem of literacy. This successful transformation process then enabled the staff to move onto other curriculum areas, ensuring success in these areas as well. Essentially, they gave away any notions that the children were at fault and insisted on teachers working together in supportive collectives to address the learning needs of their children.

Chapter 10
Te Kura Tuatahi o Papaioea – Central Normal School

Introduction

I am very grateful to Dr Jennie Watts for her help with this case study. She is a senior lecturer in Communication Studies at AUT in Auckland. However, more importantly for this story, she is also a very strong advocate for what has come to be called a "structured" literacy approach to literacy learning. Like many parents, including myself, one of her children had major difficulties learning to read with the traditional "balanced" literacy approach that remains the most commonly used early learning literacy strategy in New Zealand. In contrast, once her child was introduced to the "structured" literacy approach, his ability to read developed rapidly and any associated learning and behavioural issues also improved. Hence the understandable strength of her advocacy.

The "structured" literacy approach is one that is often confused with the old phonics teaching system, but while it maintains elements of this approach with its focus on the importance of phonological awareness, it is more complex, sophisticated, and systematic than the previous system somewhat derogatorily referred to as "drill and kill". In our conversations about the efficacy of this new approach, Dr Watts pointed me in the direction of the Lifting Literacy Aotearoa website[38] for more information. Here I found the story of Te Kura Tuatahi o Papaioea – Central Normal School, one school that has recently successfully implemented this approach to literacy learning.

The case study on Lifting Literacy Aotearoa's website tells about the school's new principal, Regan Orr, introducing a very effective literacy intervention and the difference it has made to Māori student achievement. What really grabbed my attention was that, after only a short period of time, Māori students were achieving at the same level as their non-Māori peers. This is very rare in New Zealand schools, and it is one of the reasons for choosing this school for inclusion in this book.

Te Kura Tuatahi o Papaioea – Central Normal School is a large decile 4, dual-medium primary school in Palmerston North. There are 470 children enrolled in Years 1 to 6, 50% of them identify as Māori. One of the school's responses to this group of students has been the development of an immersion and bilingual hub, Te Arawaru. This hub comprises six classes with Level 1 and Level 2 immersion education for students in Years 3 to 6 as many students across the team are first time learners of te reo Māori. *Te Marautanga o Aotearoa*, the Māori-medium curriculum, has recently been introduced for these classes in consultation with whānau. A second major response has been the introduction of a structured literacy approach to the whole school in order to address the literacy learning needs of Māori and other marginalised students.

Achievement patterns
Again, my primary interest in this school was how well Māori children and other marginalised students are achieving. This is my primary focus because I want to see that the school is meeting this basic requirement that Māori students are able to realise their learning potential. I also want to see if the school is able to ensure that this achievement is supportive of their parents' aspirations for cultural sustainability, and other children are also being supported by these developments. I was therefore delighted to be introduced to Te Kura Tuatahi o Papaioea – Central Normal School because of their outstanding picture of Māori student achievement.

---

38 https://www.liftingliteracyaotearoa.org.nz/support/case-studies

Goal 1. Māori achieving on par with non-Māori students within 2 years

When I spoke to Regan Orr, the principal of Te Kura Tuatahi o Papaioea – Central Normal School in 2022, he was quick to assure me that the achievement outcomes of their Māori and other often-marginalised students were now on par with their non-Māori peers. This had not been the case when he and the new leadership team had arrived at the school in 2018. He explained to me that, following the recent introduction of a "structured" literacy approach, Māori students' achievement rates had accelerated to now reach parity with their non-Māori peers. Overall, the implementation of the "structured" literacy programme had resulted in rapid improvements in the achievement of Māori students in the school to that which characterises North-East schools; parity in achievement for all students being based on teachers realising their potential, not membership of an ethnic group. He explained in mid-2022 that:

> [o]ver the past 12 months, our achievement data has also shown that we have reduced the disparity between Māori and New Zealand European, where Māori are achieving equitably with New Zealand European. Recent data shows that Māori are actually performing better than their European peers. This is the first time I have seen this success for Māori during my tenure as a principal.

That the means of realising these wonderful outcomes was already in place in 2019 was verified by their most recent ERO report.

> The school is working towards achieving equitable and excellent outcomes for all its students. There is a strategic focus to promote equity of outcomes. ... The school is strengthening its effectiveness in accelerating learning for those Māori and other students who are at risk of underachievement. The school identified specific cohorts and groups of children to accelerate learning in reading and mathematics in 2019. For those Māori students targeted in the school's 2019 annual plan, a large majority show acceleration in reading and mathematics. (Education Review Office, 2019a, n.p.)

That this process of transformation was implemented in such a short period of time is testimony to the urgency and effectiveness of the principal's response to what he found on his arrival at the school.

Goal 2. Māori succeeding as Māori

The second goal of North-East schools is to ensure that Māori students do not have to leave who they are—their identity—at the school gate when the go to school. North-East schools use culturally responsive means to build on what young people bring to school with them in ways that reinforce their cultural identities, thus ensuring cultural sustainability. The ERO reviewers saw this happening at Te Kura Tuatahi o Papaioea – Central Normal School.

> Learning partnerships provide further learning opportunities for
> students that positively support success for Māori as Māori …
> Students learn in settled environments that reflect respect for all.
> Teaching and learning experiences are managed effectively to promote
> participation and engagement in learning. Positive attitudes, increased
> engagement and ownership of learning is evident. Te ao Māori is
> woven into school life and fostered throughout classes. Te ao and
> tikanga Māori are authentically reflected through the students'
> participation in schoolwide practices. (Education Review Office,
> 2019a, n.p.)

Goal 3. Other marginalised students also benefit from the transformation of the school to be a North-East learning institution

The third goal of North-East schools is to support the learning of those groups of students who are currently most likely to be marginalised from the benefits that schooling has to offer them, by what they bring to school being seen as deficiencies rather than potentialities. The ERO reviewers were also able to identify evidence that the benefits of the school's transformation were being spread to other children as well.

> Outcomes for second language learners in reading show nearly all
> these students make accelerated progress … Children with additional
> and complex learning needs have learning plans linked to their
> very specific individual strengths and needs. Progress and strategies

for support are regularly reviewed. School provided data for 2019 shows progress for many and acceleration for some students in other targeted interventions. (Education Review Office, 2019a, n.p.)

So, overall, that wonderful pattern of achievement outcomes that we have come to expect of North-East schools is seen in this school. The question now is how did this school achieve these North-East outcomes? And perhaps more importantly, what support systems has the principal introduced so that these achievement gains will be sustained? When telling the story of Te Kura Tuatahi o Papaioea – Central Normal School, I will follow the GPILSEO sequence of goals, pedagogy, infrastructure, leadership, spread, evidence, and ownership to identify the process the principal has led the school through to ensure the sustainability of their North-East positioning. I will use relevant ERO evidence of the changes that the principal led so that they could realise the school's equity and cultural sustainability goals.

The need for goal setting—goal setting commences with an analysis of the current situation

When the new principal and deputy principal arrived in 2018, along with a number of other school leaders and teachers, they recognised that reading data were incredibly low. Indeed, they were lower than they had ever seen before, especially among Māori students. They also identified that, associated with these data, despite sufficient time being timetabled for literacy learning, there was great variability of teaching practice of literacy across the school. In the words of the principal, the pattern was of an "inconsistent pedagogic approach".

He explained to me that this was the time soon after the removal of the standards-based assessment approach that had resulted in "teachers teaching to the test" in the hope that this would raise student achievement. Unfortunately, the "standards-based" approach meant that assessment took precedence, to the extent that it was very difficult to focus on teaching that was responsive to the learning needs of the children. The principal saw, in contrast, that the removal of this approach was a great opportunity to re-engage with the New Zealand curriculum in ways that would better serve the needs of the school's learners.

This initial analysis of the situation in the school led the principal to lead a collaborative process of goal setting, which included the development of a strategic plan to realise the goals. The deliberations identified the need for the focus of the school to be squarely on improving student learning. The most recent ERO report identifies that "[t]he 2019 strategic plan gives priority to ongoing improvement for students in engagement, learning and wellbeing. Current goals and targets include a strategic focus on raising achievement for Māori and accelerating learning in reading and mathematics."

The ERO reviewers also noted that the 2019 strategic plan was developed collaboratively by the new leaders of the school seeking the aspirations and perspectives of the Central Normal School community, including specifically targeted sessions with Māori iwi representatives. These discussions were then collaboratively developed into the school vision, values, and learning dispositions. It was clear to the review team that the goals of the school clearly serve to orient all the activities of the school towards the realisation of the goals. These are also the targets against which the school holds itself accountable to the local community.

Pedagogy

As the principal had experience of the positive impact a structured literacy programme had had at his previous school, a literacy consultant was hired to provide a "cohesive, structured and research-based approach to the teaching of literacy over the next two years" (Lifting Literacy Aotearoa, 2021, p. 2). This was achieved by introducing a "structured" literacy learning programme in their school. A budget to support teachers to learn the processes was allocated; $75,000 on PLD and resources—around $57 per child per year for the next 3 years.

The literacy coach initially worked with Years 1 and 2 teachers, introducing a variety of models, coaching them, assisting with analysing data, and sharing the latest research. It was expanded to the whole school soon after. The programme was not limited to the English-medium classrooms, as two teachers from Te Arawaru—the Māori immersion unit—learnt alongside the English-medium teachers and then used the new learning to create an approach suitable for their area. Suitable resources in te reo Māori were also created and used.

All staff received the same professional development programme that emphasised the need for a systematic, consecutive, consistent way for teaching literacy. It was not just focused at new entrants; it was a whole-of-school approach. A number of assessment tools were introduced. These are formative in function and they provide very clear next steps of what to teach and learn. The process is not "lock-step"—although there is a lesson sequence commencing with phonological awareness, through decoding and encoding, to reading texts, teachers are expected to be diagnostic, delivering what is necessary for their students, irrespective of their year and age.

Teaching and learning are informed by ongoing daily informal monitoring of student progress along with formal assessment tools that range from a Phonological Awareness Screening tool, to Decoding Stages, Running Records, Progressive Achievement Tests, to Encoding Stages. The approach uses specially purchased texts that are readily decodable by early readers, such as the new Little Learners Love Literacy early readers series. Reading is enhanced by texts being used alongside the particular parts of the approach to reinforce the scope and sequence of learning, systematically building skills and knowledge in a cumulative manner. These texts are used because it is felt that the early texts of the traditional Ready to Read series, common in many schools using the "whole language" approach, are confusing to early readers. Assessments are also used for writing and spelling, the results of which are reported to parents every 6 months.

Specific to the programme, elements of a "structured" literacy approach are to be found in each literacy session: phonological awareness, alphabetical principles, fluency, vocabulary, and comprehension; the emphasis changing for each as the learners move from a "learning to read" to a "reading to learn" position. It must be emphasised that there is a high level of student–teacher interaction in this approach across the school which, in the words of one teacher, Lesley Blackmore, "the structured literacy environment allows prompt and corrective feedback for reading and writing". This, in turn, builds seamlessly into a wider "assessment for learning" approach where teachers respond to information generated by evidence of student performance (feedback from students) so as to inform their next teaching and learning steps.

Assessments are used to pinpoint gaps in learning and to inform teachers exactly what they need to teach. Marianne Brown, a tier 2 intervention teacher, describes the outcomes of the programme in comparison to the traditional means of teaching literacy in New Zealand. She explained that, when she used the whole language approach, she had had mixed results.

> The results totally speak for themselves. Not only are our children confident readers, but they are confident writers and spellers as well. I could never go back to teaching using Whole Language, knowing I was statistically failing 30–40% of my students … Teach is the keyword, no more exposing them to books and leaving the learning to chance.

A wider pedagogic context for learning is evident

The specific approach to literacy learning in the school is provided within a wider pedagogic framework. The 2019 ERO report identified that students were learning in settled, well-managed learning settings that reflect respectful relationships. To me, the context being created is that found in North-East Leaders of Learning classrooms. For example, teachers are supported to reject the use of deficit explanations about Māori children's potential to be successful learners. That they care for the learning of Māori students as Māori is seen in culturally responsive practices that ensure that the Māori world, te ao and tikanga Māori, is authentically woven into school life and fostered throughout classes along with the emerging relationships with local iwi. High expectations for learning are evident, as are positive attitudes to Māori learners' potential among teachers. It is also seen in Māori students' participation in schoolwide practices where they are accepted as part of the wider school whānau.

The students exhibit positive attitudes to learning, increased engagement, and ownership of learning; a reflection of teachers' positive, agentic approaches to Māori students as being capable learners, all of these being characteristic of teachers' abilities to create whānau, relational, learning contexts in their classrooms.

The creation of these caring and learning relationships has enabled teachers to use learning interactions that promote learning by providing teachers with evidence of how well the students are making sense of what is being taught.

The school has implemented a common code of pedagogic practice for literacy learning so that students' learning experiences are similar across the school and at different levels. From the outset, the principal was clear that "structured" literacy would provide a cohesive and consistent approach to literacy learning that would support all staff to provide an evidence-based pattern of teaching. He emphasised that it was important that all staff were involved to further support students' literacy learning as they advanced through the school, building on their previous successful learning.

The school has also ensured that teachers know what to teach and how to teach it in order to create a context wherein students are confident and competent learners. There is now a consistent pedagogic pattern across the school. All teachers use the same language, the same pedagogy, and are engaged in like-minded discussions about process, scope, and sequence.

Overall, the importance of reducing and eliminating the variability in teaching practice the principal found on his arrival at the school in 2018 is emphasised by the adoption of a common code of pedagogic practice that is aimed at improving learning experiences and student learning outcomes.

Is a structured literacy approach a means to an end or an end in itself?

One of the potential problems of a "structured" literacy approach was mentioned in Chapter 2. It was suggested that, as this approach to literacy learning needs to be taught in a direct, somewhat transactional manner using direct, overt methods, it is important that the learning process does not stop there. This is only the first three steps of the Hattie/Marzano model for example. If the teaching approach stops there, then it will not be successful because how does the teacher know the impact of their teaching if they do not engage with their learners in some form of formative assessment? That is, how can they support student learning beyond the initial stages if teachers do not have a means of receiving feedback about the impact of their initial teaching efforts on student learning? Nor will they get opportunities to provide feedback to their students in ways that we know enhance learning.

Perhaps of most concern is that if the Hattie/Marzano teaching process, or something like it, is not used, then students will not get multiple opportunities to apply their knowledge to solving problems in collaboration with others. Whatever model of teaching is used, it has been shown time and again the importance of repetition of application of new knowledge to building feelings of self-efficacy. These are feelings that the student gains through successfully applying new knowledge to new situations that engenders both the knowledge that the student can be a successful learner and to develop the willingness to go on learning. This means that learning, and learning how to learn, is far more complex than just learning the mechanics of reading. If a "structured" literacy approach were to be reduced to this level, then its true potential to radically improve Māori students' literacy learning, how to read and to move onto "reading for learning" will not be realised. In other words, if teaching is limited to just the expository, direct instruction, then it is less likely to be successful.

The principal of Te Kura Tuatahi o Papaioea – Central Normal School was very clear that, while direct instruction provides the foundation for learning the new skills and knowledge associated with their "structured" literacy approach, this is part of a wider pedagogy that ensures teachers learn how to move onto providing opportunities for feedback and feed-forward, for example. In this way, the learning pathway to self-efficacy, learners taking responsibility for their own learning and becoming lifelong learners is guaranteed. The principal was very clear that there was a seamless progression within the pedagogy from the initial transactional approach to an "assessment for learning" approach and this is the pattern across the whole school.

Infrastructure—a comprehensive process of institutional and programmatic transformation has also been implemented

At first, it might look as though it is the literacy strategy that has done the job of raising Māori student achievement in this school, and that all another school needs to do is to replicate the implementation of the same strategy with its teachers for similar results to occur. However, a more detailed examination of what has been happening in this school reveals that there is more to the success of this school than might appear. In addition to the literacy approach, this school's leaders have implemented a comprehensive process of institutional and programmatic transformation that is responsive to their and their communities' aspirations for an excellent education with equitable and culturally sustaining outcomes for their children.

What I mean by this is that the new "structured" literacy approach contained a means of ensuring implementation fidelity from the outset. The outside expert who was retained to provide the school with the new approach provided a professional development programme that emphasised the need for a systematic, consecutive, consistent way for teaching literacy. Clearly, it was important that the teachers implemented the new approach in the way designed and verified by the developers of the approach. There was no place for teachers to modify or use different reading books, for example. In other words, they needed to ensure that the approach was implemented as it was designed; that is, implemented with fidelity, so as to ensure the outcomes were as expected.

This in turn identifies why the principal then put in place the institutional and programmatic transformation that he did. The reason was to ensure the ongoing fidelity of the implementation of the literacy intervention and hence outcomes, once the initial support provided by the outside expert was no longer available to them. In this way, the school's leaders have made sure that the school is organised so that the potential for variability in teaching practice over time is eliminated. The harm done to students' literacy learning by this tendency for teaching practices to be implemented variably over time and has been addressed with urgency by the leaders of this school implementing a supportive infrastructural system to ensure ongoing fidelity of implementation.

How does this work at this school?

The school provides teachers with collaborative opportunities to promote their critically reflecting on their and their students' learning. These include coaching, modelling, and sharing of practice. The principal emphasised that their aim was to provide their staff with the best PLD they could find. The leaders' aim was to support their teachers to grow in their confidence and competence. He explained that they "valued their people", and saw it as their professional responsibility to do so and, in turn, this attitude has spread among the staff.

Teachers are supported by infrastructural developments in the school. In these support systems, team meetings use assessment for learning processes to provide them with opportunities to interrogate, with other teachers in learning teams, evidence of students' performance in relation to their teaching practices. In this way, they are able to decide how to modify their practices responsively and determine next teaching steps. This provision of a responsive infrastructure is implemented to ensure the ongoing implementation fidelity of the literacy approaches and approaches used in other curriculum areas.

The principal spoke of their school being a whānau, the use of this term emphasising that all members are to be included and supported to learn what they need. In this context, teachers know they are being supported by others, they are able to make and learn from their mistakes, and grow confidence and competence in a consistent setting. No one, student or staff, is to be rejected because of their supposed deficiencies or limited performance. Students are supported to learn the curriculum. Teachers are supported to learn how to implement the new "structured" literacy approach with fidelity.

Leaders are also supported to learn how to support teachers in their teams to learn the new pedagogic approaches in ways that will ensure implementation fidelity in the long term. They understand that it is no use making great gains initially, only to see these gains wither away over time because of the lack of a means of ensuring successful outcomes are maintained. The principal has dedicated one senior staff member to lead the transference of what the literacy learning approach entails from the outside expert into the skills and knowledge set of this leading staff member, in this way, ensuring the school takes ownership of the learning approach.

Also, the whole process of transformation is undertaken with a critical eye. This means that only those innovations that add value to the pedagogic focus of the school are included. More tools are constantly being introduced using specifically targeted PLD, such as including writing workshops and sound walls. However, nothing is introduced that does not enhance the purpose of embedding the "structured" literacy approach into the school. PLD is very strategically focused in this school.

In addition to and because of the provision of formal support systems in the school, the school's leaders have encouraged the deprivatising of classrooms so that there is a high level of informal support available to younger, less experienced teachers, for example. Less experienced teachers do not have to struggle with how they might respond to the learning needs of particular students but can readily call upon assistance from teachers in adjacent teaching spaces. Being able to seek assistance is becoming a powerful part of the school's culture.

The ERO report identifies that this is clearly happening. "Knowledge building and inquiry are promoted and supported at every level of the school." But they are not random. PLD opportunities are aligned to the strategic goals and are responsive to teacher development needs that focus on student outcomes. This formative approach to teacher learning mirrors that which is expected to be used with students in their classrooms, thus providing coherence and consistency across and within the school. This embedded approach also ensures that teachers are able to experience what it is like to be a learner so that there is coherence of approaches across the school.

Leadership

North-East leadership practices and systems include the promotion, strengthening, and sustaining of professional learning and collaboration to improve teaching and student outcomes in achievement and engagement. ERO reviewers noted that:

> Manawatū, the school leadership team, demonstrate an understanding that growing teacher capability is a key for improving all students' learning outcomes. Professional learning and development is aligned to the strategic goals and responsive to teacher development needs that focus on student outcomes. Leadership sets a clear direction for systematic and well-paced school development. Collaborative opportunities include coaching, modelling and sharing of practice. Knowledge building and inquiry are promoted and supported at every level of the school. (Education Review Office, 2019a, n.p.)

What is clear from talking with the principal is that he is the lead Leader of Learning. He is fully conversant with the whole scope and sequence of the "structured" literacy approach they are using in the school and the wider pedagogic framework this approach sits within. Leading the pedagogic intervention is his role and responsibility. He does not delegate that responsibility to others. There is a distributed pattern of leadership, and his role and responsibility is to ensure this is taking place effectively. There is a clear pattern of distributed responsibility of instructional leaders to support learning. One of the school's deputy principals, an assistant principal, and the school's intervention leader, with the principal, form the pedagogic leadership team whose task it is to ensure that all other team leaders and teachers are provided with necessary learning opportunities. Team leaders are then supported by this team to support the learning of teachers in their area. This internal leadership pattern is embedded in practice so that it will be sustained in the long term and there is no dilution of the impact of the pedagogic intervention.

Spread

The school's leaders have spent considerable time and energy strengthening relationships with Māori parents, families, and local iwi. The benefits of developing these relationships are to be seen in at least three levels of the school. The first is that Māori people are actively present at school events and in the daily activities thus emphasising that this is their school as much as it is anyone else's. Ownership of the school by its local community is a strong reflection of the seriousness that the school's leaders place upon these relationships. This is seen where "[w]hānau and community are actively encouraged and involved in the life and work of the school." (Education Review Office, 2019a, n.p.).

The second is the development of learning partnerships. The aim of learning partnerships is to add value to the children's learning by actively involving their parents. The process in this school is where "[c]hildren have deliberate opportunities to share their learning with parents and whānau … Ongoing communication, formally, informally and digitally continues to strengthen learning partnerships." (Education Review Office, 2019a, n.p.). It needs to be emphasised that sharing learning does not just mean the children engage in "show and tell" with their parents, but that their parents are actively engaged in deliberating about their children's performance on tasks and understanding of learning processes.

The third benefit of developing these relationships is that, in addition to the traditional content knowledge of schools, engagement with iwi through their participation and presence at the school promotes the development of learning partnerships that provide "further learning opportunities for students that positively support success for Māori, as Māori" (Education Review Office, 2019a, n.p.). In other words, Māori students are not having to sacrifice their language and culture to learn what are traditional benefits of schooling—reading, writing, mathematics, and so on—because their being Māori is supported by the participation of local iwi members.

The principal is very aware that developing a relationship with Rangitāne o Manawatū, the local iwi, is a long-term process of building trust and effectiveness. He knows that this relationship is in its infancy, but he was adamant that his aim is to build a purposeful relationship to add value to their students' learning. As such, it will necessarily take time.

A further feature of the spread of the school's goals is that all teachers are supported to be able to take an active, positive part in the preferred pedagogies of the school. And the same approach that is used for literacy is being successfully used for mathematics.

Evidence

Evidence of student performance and progress is available and used at a number of levels within the school in order to ensure that the "assessment for learning" approach is embedded in the school. This has been made possible by the purposeful selection of a student data management system that "enables analysis of relevant student data and information about teaching practices and is used effectively to evaluate and inform goal setting" (Education Review Office, 2019a, n.p.). It is the evaluation of the relationship between these two variables at a number of levels that enables this school to be effective. The data are used at least at three levels.

The first level that the evidence of student performance and teaching practices is used is by the senior leadership team. Here they use the data in aggregate form to inform their decision making about the sorts of support they need to provide at a school level to further support student learning.

The second level this evidence of student data and teaching practices is used is at the team level. Teachers are divided into teams according to the levels they are teaching at in the school—new entrants, junior learners, and senior learners. The team leaders lead the collaborative deliberations by the team members about what the data are telling them about student performance and progress in relation to current teaching practices. From these understandings, they are then able to identify next teaching steps they will need to implement in their classrooms.

The third level of data usage is by teachers in their own classrooms. Here they collaboratively deliberate with their students about the messages for their ongoing learning that are to be found in evidence of their performance and practice. In this way, teachers are moving learners towards their becoming able to undertake this evaluation on their own so they can identify where to take their learning to next. The aim is to move students to become self-regulating and determining learners.

Ownership

The first clear piece of evidence of the school principal taking ownership of the problems of inequitable outcomes in the school was, as a result of the initial analysis of the situation the principal found on his arrival at the school, his leading a collaborative goal-setting exercise. This goal-setting activity included the development of a strategic plan to orientate all of the school's actions to realise the goals.

The second piece of evidence of the principal having taken ownership of the problems of Māori student achievement was leading the allocation of funding from their own resources to initiate the introduction and implementation of the new literacy approach. This is an essential undertaking if change is to occur at the school level. The ERO reviewers also noticed that ownership was well exhibited by the board of trustees who were particular to ensure that resourcing in their control was also fairly distributed in order to "maximise student outcomes".

> The board draws on their expertise and networks to strengthen their organisational capacity and effectiveness. They have undertaken training and provide competent oversight of school operations. There

are sound systems and procedures to support students' safety and welfare. Trustees maintain a strong focus on equitable resourcing for the school to maximise student outcomes. (Education Review Office, 2019a, n.p.)

The principal was clear that the school did not rely upon outside funding for what they see as their core business and have reprioritised funding for this purpose. When it is identified that they need additional PLD, they use their own funds for this purpose. They find the best providers of PLD that suits their pedagogic approach and fund it themselves. Decisions about PLD content and provisions are based on the best research evidence available.

> Children with additional learning and behaviour needs are well
> supported within an inclusive environment. A robust pastoral system
> combines effective systems and processes with a range of innovative
> programmes to maximise wellbeing and learning outcomes.
> Appropriate planning for students with complex needs are inclusive of
> parent input and incorporate external agency support. Thoughtfully
> planned transitions in, across, and out of school enable cohesion for
> students and families. (Education Review Office, 2019a, n.p.)

A third piece of evidence that the school has taken ownership of the process of transformation is evident in their self-review processes. The processes included surveys and reviews of whānau members. Staff and student voice is collected and used formatively. All of the school's support systems are regularly evaluated for how well they are suiting their expected purpose. The overall purpose of the self-review process is to ensure that the school's primary purpose—promoting positive outcomes for students—is realised. The ERO review team identified that this process was made up of many parts.

> Internal evaluation contributes effectively to school improvement.
> Purposeful surveys and reviews are carried out and whānau and
> the community are regularly consulted. Staff and student voice is
> collected and used to determine future actions. Systems, processes
> and practices are subject to ongoing scrutiny and evaluation to
> promote positive outcomes for students. (Education Review Office,
> 2019a, n.p.)

Summary

This outstanding school is led by an experienced, outstanding principal. He has led the school's whānau taking ownership of the problems and solutions for Māori student achievement. This has been achieved through a process of goal setting and strategic planning so as to orientate all of the school's actions to realise these goals. They have also seen the need to allocate funding and other resources to ensure their goals are realised. Their taking professional responsibility for improving their students' learning by transforming their practices is enhanced by a process of self-review. They understand self-review to be a means whereby professionals take responsibility for addressing problems presented to them and not blaming others or expecting others to sort out problems for them. Outside support was used by this school's leaders to implement the new literacy approach, but it was within parameters set by the leadership. They owned the problems and how they would be addressed.

The principal and other leaders have led the transformation of this school into an extended family-like (whānau) context for learning and they support all their teachers to replicate this context in their classrooms. This context is one where, above all, teachers address and reject negative stereotyping about Māori and Pacific students. Teachers at Te Kura Tuatahi o Papaioea – Central Normal School clearly care for their students as culturally and language-located individuals, and build on the knowledge they and their community leaders bring to school as the base for their further learning. Teachers have high expectations for their learning and know what they need to learn and are supported by the school's leaders to ensure they gain and sustain this knowledge.

This context creates security for the children, assuring them that at this school and with these teachers, they will become successful learners. The achievement gains made so rapidly in this school have made the students feel good about themselves as learners "as Māori", and they are being supported to learn *how* to learn as much as *what* they learn.

Overall, to realise these goals, the principal led the introduction of a strategic plan to orientate all actions. He led the selection and introduction of an effective literacy approach within a wider pedagogic approach that supported students to become competent learners. The principal led the means of restructuring the school to provide teachers with supported learning opportunities and institutionalised collective ways of interrogating evidence of student performance and teacher practice. One of the school's deputy principals, an assistant principal, and the school's intervention leader—with the principal—form the pedagogic leadership team whose task it is to ensure that all other team leaders and teachers are provided with necessary learning opportunities. They have not delegated it to someone else. Pedagogy is the most important activity in this school for its leaders.

They spread institutionalised North-East leadership practices through the school so that all leaders play an integral part in realising the school's goals. They have moved to include parents and community leaders to support the learning processes in the school and understand that, while this may take time, indications are that progress is being made in this area. They have prioritised evidence-based decision making and problem solving and instituted a means of providing evidence for this purpose. This successful transformation process has enabled the staff to move onto other curriculum areas, ensuring success in these areas as well.

What is also wonderful is that this was all achieved in a very short period of time.

Chapter 11
Kerikeri High School

Introduction

Kerikeri High School is a large, decile 6,[39] Years 7 to 13, co-educational secondary school in Kerikeri, a rural town in Northland. It serves a large Pākehā population and a smaller Māori population. In 2022, the school had some 1,550 students and a staff of 140, 90 of whom are teaching staff. Thirty percent of the school population are Māori. Elizabeth Forgie has recently retired after being the principal for almost 30 years. She has recently been awarded an MNZM for her services to education.

---

39 The decile system, at the time of writing this, to be phased out, is a measure of the socioeconomic status of the families in the contributing area. Extra funding was allocated to schools based on their decile rating; however, as shown in the text, the decile rating was often not representative of the actual needs of a school. Kerikeri High School, for example, is decile 6, because it has students coming from decile 1 to decile 10 communities. The funding allocated to a "6" therefore did not match the needs of the students. The new system now funds on identified need and should prove to be more effective.

Achievement patterns

Goal 1. Māori students achieving on par with their non-Māori peers

Māori student achievement in terms of academic measures at Kerikeri High School prior to 2005 was lower than that of their non-Māori peers. The school's leaders were keen to do something about changing this situation, but, as the principal explained, they did not have "the way". They were aware that achievement levels were not as they should be and were also aware that, due to their not being able to intervene in any meaningful ways, these patterns tended to continue throughout the time the students were at the school.

At that time, 20% of their students were Māori and only approximately one in four (28%) of them were achieving level 2 qualifications, compared with 60% for the Pākehā students. This latter figure was also lower than expected due to low achievement levels among boys—another achievement level issue that was later rectified using the same means as was used to improve Māori student achievement. The school's leaders were not satisfied with Māori students' performance in external examinations. They determined to do something about it.

When Kerikeri High School was invited to become one of the 12 schools to take part in the third phase of the Te Kotahitanga project, the principal and the whole staff gladly accepted.[40] The principal had this to say in her recent sabbatical report:

> It was brave stuff, coining a language that included no deficit
> theorising or blame, 80% discursive teaching compared to talk from
> the front, agentic (know what I can do), know your Māori learner,
> power sharing, culture counts (don't have to leave your culture at the
> school gates), shadow coaching (not correction) and relationships,
> relationships, relationships. We had embarked on culturally
> responsive and relationships based pedagogy. (Forgie, 2021, p. 10)

---

40 The first two phases of the project had focused on changing classroom practice, but the third involved a whole-school approach because it became clear that, unless classroom teachers are supported appropriately by school leaders, the necessary reforms are unlikely to spread or remain very long.

As a result of the intervention, the school began to see dramatic changes taking place in their Māori students' achievement rates for NCEA level 2.[41] From the base of 28% in 2005, Māori student achievement more than doubled by 2007 to 60%, reaching parity with "all students" in the baseline. Then on to 70% in 2008, and 80% by 2010, by this time, reaching parity with their non-Māori peers of the same year level. By 2020, the pass rate was 90%; a full 60% more Māori students attaining level 2 NCEA qualifications than were doing so in the baseline year. They just didn't double the percentage, they increased it almost three-fold. And this change took very little time to achieve. Two years in fact was all that was needed to see the start of these changes in Māori student achievement. To put it another way, in 2005, if you were a Māori student at Kerikeri High School and you were entered for NCEA level 2 qualifications, you had approximately a one in four chance of gaining this qualification. Now you have a nine out of 10 chance of achieving the same qualification, and there is no significant difference between ethnic groups.

Kerikeri High School has also addressed a major concern that the Associate Minister of Education raised with her Cabinet colleagues in December of 2021. In her proposal for a new literacy and numeracy strategy, she identified that many students across the country were having difficulty in attaining the literacy and numeracy co-requisite requirements for awarding each NCEA level. She explained that this adjunct qualification is vital for students going on into further education, especially into tertiary-level institutions. At Kerikeri High School, the literacy and numeracy statistics for Māori students mirror their achievements in the overall qualifications, with some 90% of candidates achieving these literacy and numeracy co-requisites, so this potential barrier to further education or employment has also been removed by this school.

The most recent report from ERO about Kerikeri High School is very positive about these achievements. They state that:

---

41 I am using NCEA Level 2 as a proxy for other achievement levels because this is a crucial level for students to attain. The OECD has identified Level 2 qualifications as being the minimum entry-level qualification for someone entering the modern economy—a major "life chances" hurdle.

Student achievement in the National Certificates of Educational Achievement (NCEA) at levels 1, 2 and 3 show continual improvement each year. Level 1 literacy and numeracy results are consistently high with over 90% of students achieving these credits every year. Senior leaders consistently set school goals that reflect their high expectations for student achievement. (Education Review Office, 2015, n.p.)

Kerikeri High School is effective in achieving equitable and excellent outcomes for all students … Schoolwide achievement information indicates that some groups of students enter the school below expected curriculum levels in literacy and numeracy. Most of these students are making expected and/or accelerated progress and access meaningful pathways. Most Māori students have made accelerated progress in numeracy and literacy over time and this rate of progress has been sustained … Almost all Māori students leave achieving NCEA level 2. (Education Review Office, 2019b, n.p.)[42]

This means that for over 17 years (at the time of writing) the school has provided young Māori people with an opportunity denied many other Māori students in a number of secondary schools in New Zealand.[43] It is also important to note that these gains were not made by limiting the numbers of Māori students entering NCEA assessments. The total

---

42 The school's leaders have identified that one factor still impacts on Māori student achievement. It is the mobility of students. The leaders have identified that those students who enter the school in the senior years have more difficulty attaining outcomes similar to those who enter at Year 7. In fact, they tell their students, "stick with us and we will get you there". It is this sort of surety that attracts other Māori students to Kerikeri; however, their previous schooling experiences and levels of learning do have an impact. This pattern of student mobility with its negative impact on student outcomes is something that affects Māori people more than others in New Zealand. The reasons are various but mostly have to do with poverty, parental employment opportunities and "being sent off to Aunty" for a spell. In South Auckland, we noticed that Māori students had a sort of "round the schools" route, hoping to find a school where they could stay without having to leave again. This migratory pattern had serious detrimental impacts on their progress with learning.

43 I agree with authors such as Tā Mason Durie that this is not the only measure that matters to Māori people, but it is a good indication that things had changed. However, it is also clear that Māori students' identity and cultural pride are also improved by these means, and in this way, responding to Māori peoples' aspirations for their children to be successful Māori learners as Māori. To me, what is important is that young Māori people are provided with a choice, not a blank wall. NCEA level 2 is part of the pattern that provides this choice.

number of students at Kerikeri High School has actually increased over the years, and the percentage of Māori students has also grown from 20% in 2005 to now 30%. The percentage of Māori students entering external assessments has also grown in similar proportions. So it is good news all round.

Goal 2. Māori succeeding as Māori

The second goal of North-East schools is to ensure that Māori students do not have to leave who they are—their identity—at home when they go to school. North-East schools build on, rather than reject, what young people bring to school with them in ways that reinforce their cultural identities, ensuring cultural sustainability. Again, the ERO reviewers saw this happening at Kerikeri High School.

The latest ERO report for Kerikeri High School is also very positive about these gains in achievement.

> School leaders, staff, trustees and whānau have a relentless focus to achieve equitable outcomes for Māori. Strategic resourcing and an ongoing commitment for Māori success has enabled significant improvement in overall Māori student achievement. School leaders and trustees value the positive impact te reo and tikanga Māori has on student success. The school is successfully embedding bicultural and culturally responsive practices to increase student engagement and promote equitable outcomes for Māori students. These practices include authentic partnerships with hapū and iwi. ... Staff focus on students' wellbeing, confidence in their identity, language and culture, and engagement. (Education Review Office, 2019b, n.p.)

Goal 3. Other marginalised students also benefit from the transformation of the school to be a North-East learning institution

The third goal of North-East schools is to support the learning of those groups of students who are currently most likely to be marginalised from the benefits that schooling has to offer them by what they bring to school being seen as deficiencies rather than potentialities and the schools' means of responding to their students. That the benefits of the intervention that was initially focused on Māori was also beneficial to other students is seen in a number of groups of students.

The first impact was seen on the achievement levels of the non-Māori students, the majority being NZ Pākehā. It may seem strange to talk about children of the majority culture as being marginalised, but they were marginalised from realising their full potential by the pedagogy and the systems that were being used in the school prior to the introduction of Te Kotahitanga. Their achievement levels were not what they should have been. They were "good", until the principal determined that "good" outcomes were not "good" enough. They needed to be "great".

In fact, what had caused the lower achievement of the mostly Pākehā group, as the principal identified using differentiated data, was that the boys' achievement levels were much lower than the girls', their lower achievement levels thus lowering the overall average for the group. When the principal led an investigation into why this was occurring, using the same questions we had used earlier to identify the schooling experiences of Māori students, the boys told their interviewers that their teachers had lower expectations for their learning than they did for the girls in their classes. Their teachers did not seem to care if they were there or not, and they spoke about them as their having deficiencies, not caring about reading and learning, for example, and only being interested in sport and leisure activities.

As a result of the intervention that was introduced to improve the outcomes of Māori students, non-Māori students' achievement levels were able to be improved as well. Non-Māori achievement levels increased from the 60% at the baseline year of 2005 to 83% in 2010, and on then to 93% in 2020. The rise is not as dramatic as for Māori students, but non-Māori students, starting point was higher in the baseline. However, it still shows an additional 30% of non-Māori students achieving the NCEA Level 2 qualification compared with those in the baseline.

The ERO reviewers were also able to identify other groups that benefited from the Te Kotahitanga intervention that had originally been designed to improve Māori students' learning outcomes.

> The inclusive, student-centred culture and positive respectful relationships within the school support the board, school leaders and staff to continue the school's growth as a dynamic learning community.

The school is a signatory to the Code of Practice for the Pastoral Care of International Students (the Code) established under section 238F of the Education Act 1989. The school has attested that it complies with all aspects of the Code. ERO's investigations confirmed that the school's self-review process for international students is thorough … At the time of this review there were 46 international students attending the school. These students come from a range of European, Asian and Latin American nationalities. Students report that they feel fully included in school activities and programmes and have gained an appreciation for New Zealand's bicultural heritage.

International students are thoughtfully placed in programmes that enable them to achieve their goals. Their English language needs are very well supported. Ongoing monitoring helps to ensure that students are well integrated into the school and the community, and international students have increasing leadership opportunities. (Education Review Office, 2015, n.p)

Students with additional needs are well catered for and experience a responsive and individualised approach. (Education Review Office, 2019b, n.p)

This school has achieved what the Ministry of Education has set as one of its major goals for schools—an excellent education system with equitable achievement for Māori and other marginalised students. And they have sustained the practices that created the change for nearly 17 years. It does go to verify our contention that what is good for Māori is good for all. But what is good for everyone, which was the school's practice prior to the intervention, is not necessarily good for Māori.

Goal setting

Kerikeri High School's vision is to "empower students to achieve success across four areas; academic, sporting, cultural and leadership with service". The ERO reviewers were able to verify this vision was being realised in the school in their 2019 report. It states that, as well as academic achievement, "[s]tudents achieve very well in relation to other school valued outcomes. Students participate, experience and successfully achieve in the wider life of the school." The ERO reviewers explained that it was clear that:

[t]he value placed on developing students' strengths, talents and interests through the school's four cornerstones for learning are key drivers for student success. Kerikeri High School is an environment in which both adults and students demonstrate a strong sense of belonging and are empowered to be successful. School leaders, staff, trustees and whānau have a relentless focus to achieve equitable outcomes for Māori. (Education Review Office, 2019b, n.p)

The principal illustrates the power of goal setting by demonstrating how, as the lead Leader of Learning, she leads the collaborative setting of goals. Along with this process is her ensuring that the school's senior leadership team and team leaders are supported to set goals for their own areas of responsibility. They, in turn, set goals for their own learning, the learning of goal setting practices for the teachers in their teams, and so on throughout the school so that the school's actions are all oriented towards this "relentless pursuit" of equitable outcomes for Māori. In this way, goal setting is used to channel leaders', teachers', and students' energies and actions into finding ways in which the goals will be realised and actions prioritised in the face of multiple demands on their time and resources. This narrowing of focus, sense of purpose, and successful realisation of goals increases staff willingness to take on further challenges.

As will be described in detail in a later section, a significant feature of the school's growth and development over the past 20 years has been growing a working relationship between the school's leaders and the local hapū, Ngāti Rēhia. From initially institutionalising a means of promoting the school's accountability to the hapū, through to now when local hapū leaders are taking a far more proactive part in the setting of goals for the learning of Māori and other students at Kerikeri High School. In this way, the goal-setting horizon has moved from the near future to being intergenerational. The value of these relationships is seen in the support the principal and the school have among the local community in times of stress and celebration.

Pedagogy: Introducing the discursive classroom

The reason for the outstanding growth in Māori and other students' literacy and overall achievements is due to the school's leaders' insistence on the transformation of the school's pedagogic foundations and support infrastructure. This transformation consisted of a huge paradigm shift from the then dominant traditional transmission pedagogy to a relationships-based, culturally responsive, dialogically interactive pedagogic approach.

The leaders also understood that it was important that they and the teachers could explain why they were to use this new pedagogy. They knew that teachers understanding the fundamental purpose of the new pedagogy assisted with ensuring the fidelity of its implementation. Understanding the basic principles of the pedagogy also meant that they would be able to respond to new circumstances and problems in an interactive manner without reverting to the traditional transmission approach—a common problem when introducing a new pedagogic approach.

When asked recently if the teachers are able to articulate this pedagogy, the principal was adamant they were very clear that their practice needed to be 80% discursive and 20% transmission, and "they all know what this entails". This paradigm shift in pedagogic interactions was enabled by their teachers being supported to create caring and learning relational contexts for learning in their classrooms within which the interactive pedagogy was able to flourish. These dimensions—the creation of a caring and learning relational context that enabled teachers to use dialogic, interactive pedagogies—were the fundamental intervention elements of the Te Kotahitanga programmme.

The main purpose for moving away from traditional transmission teaching practices was that teachers' agendas and cultural ways of making sense of the world tended to dominate the modes of learning, the curriculum content, and the ways of making sense of this content. In the traditional classroom, the teacher is active (in transmission mode) and the students are passive (in receptive mode). The curriculum content is monoculturally defined and developed. The acceptable and official ways of making sense of the content are monocultural and assimilationist; the dominant discourse maintaining its hegemony by the use of the transmission pedagogy.

This is especially problematic when the teacher and children are from different cultural backgrounds because it is the culture of the teacher that dominates the learning, albeit often unwittingly, because of the choice of pedagogy. In this way, the pedagogy perpetuates the assimilationist project of cultural domination that commenced with the arrival of Western-orientated education. It means that teachers will be found in the "South-West" instead of the "North-East" where they will be demonstrating "low levels of relationships and low levels of learning interactions" instead of high levels of both relationships and interactions.

The main purpose of introducing an alternative interactive, dialogic pedagogy is to facilitate teachers moving to the North-East where there are "high levels of relationships and interactions". These North-East classrooms are called "discursive classrooms" because the pedagogy is based on the concept of discourse which acknowledges that there are always different perspectives; that is, different culturally generated way of making sense of any content or topic. Hence the need for power-sharing strategies that promote dialogue and interaction; that is, "learning conversations". These strategies include co-operative learning, narrative pedagogies, and student-led questions, among others. These strategies facilitate the use of learners' prior knowledge, the provision of feedback and feed-forward, and co-construction activities. These strategies allow a range of explanations and ways of making sense to be included and acceptable in learning conversations. These pedagogies thus mediate the potential for discursive dominance by traditional transmission pedagogies by enabling the use of various forms of interaction to take place within learning conversations. These include:

- discussion and debate
- collaborative decision making and problem solving
- co-operative deliberations on emerging understandings
- amalgamating and synthesising explanations and theorising
- negotiating, compromising, and reaching consensus
- responding to and accepting feedback and providing feedback
- practising collaborative investigations through teamwork.[44]

---

44 It is probably worth remembering that these skills are among those termed "21st century thinking skills" and are those most sought after by employers as opposed to passive, receptive skills. You do not see many job adverts asking for people with passive, receptive skills, yet students get plenty of practice with these in our current classrooms and not a lot with the skills that the modern world is asking for.

These interactions enable students to practise developing and revisiting new concepts in a variety of ways based on their culturally different ways of making sense of the world. In these classrooms, the teacher's role is to set guidelines and purposes for interaction and discussion to engage students in learning conversations. These promote learning by using skills of collaboration, communication, and co-construction of knowledge through interaction and dialogue.

When John Hattie completed his first synthesis of 134 meta-analyses of possible influences on achievement in 1992, it became clear to him that feedback was among the most powerful influences on achievement. Initially he thought that it was the amount of feedback teachers gave to students that mattered most. Later, however, he discovered that feedback was most powerful when it came from the student to the teacher. A further benefit of implementing a discursive classroom is the facilitation of this very powerful means of promoting learning.

Strategies that promote regular feedback from the student to the teacher about their progress with learning and understanding of new concepts and knowledge are not possible in the traditional transmission classroom. Here, teachers have no ready means of knowing if students are learning new concepts and actions until they implement a summative assessment after a period of "teaching" at the end of a topic, for example. And by then it is often too late to rectify matters. Or the student has to be involved in remediation strategies; in effect, being blamed for what is an inappropriate pedagogy.

In addition, the focus of traditional classrooms on behaviour tends to cloud learning difficulties, for behaviour modification strategies are mostly not focused on learning, but on improving behaviour. Ostensibly, they are implemented to improve learning, but more often than not, they become an end in themselves and do not necessarily lead to improved learning. There is a tenuous link at best between improvements in behaviour through implementing behaviour modification strategies and improvements in learning. The problem with this approach is that it positions the student as the sole source of the problem and it relies solely on the student to make changes in their behaviour, rather than both participants in the learning relationship between them and their teacher. The causes of inappropriate behaviour are blamed on the student, rather than on their probable frustration over their learning needs being ignored.

A further benefit of implementing discursive classrooms is that they enable cultural affirmation and sustainability because those skills that teachers develop as part of the pedagogy are those where the "culturally responsive teacher will … demonstrate cultural competence … to see themselves as learners alongside whānau and all decisions are made in partnership" (Teaching Council of Aotearoa New Zealand, 2019). These learning partnerships include competencies with the values that need to be present when engaging with Māori learners. They are:

- Wānanga: participating with learners and communities in robust dialogue for the benefit of Māori learners' achievement.

- Whanaungatanga: actively engaging in respectful working relationships with Māori learners, parents and whānau, hapū, iwi and the Māori community.

- Manaakitanga: showing integrity, sincerity and respect towards Māori beliefs, language and culture.

- Tangata Whenuatanga: affirming Māori learners as Māori. Providing contexts for learning where the language, identity and culture of Māori learners and their whānau is affirmed.

- Ako: taking responsibility for their own learning and that of Māori learners. (Teaching Council of Aotearoa New Zealand, 2019, p. 2).

An additional consequential benefit of this pedagogy is that it affirms the identity of Māori students in ways that have been sought after by their families for generations, but never realised. The caring and relationship-based context created by teachers in their classrooms has certainly had a major impact on the reduction of deficit explanations for Māori student performance, increased visible caring for Māori students as learners, and raised learning expectations. Further, within this context, the interactive, discursive pedagogy has enabled Māori students to learn as Māori, to be successful learners, to stand tall and be proud of their identity as Māori, and take their rightful place alongside the rest of the successful learners at Kerikeri High School. Explicit teaching of Māori values and identity does not appear to have this level of impact. On the other hand, discursive pedagogies are both culturally responsive, affirming and sustaining in ways that meet the Ministry of Education's goals for achieving excellence and equity.

As for evidence for this improvement in Māori students' feelings of belonging, of their identities being valued and strengthened, and their being able to succeed as Māori at Kerikeri High School, the best place to look is their latest ERO report. This report identifies that:

> [s]taff actively promote practices that ensure equitable opportunities for learning. They focus on students' wellbeing, confidence in their identity, language and culture, and engagement. The value placed on, and respect for students' cultural heritage, is clearly evident. (Education Review Office, 2019b, n.p.)

What is really interesting is that the reviewers were not able to find many things that needed remediation prior to the next review in 5 years time. All they could suggest was the school's leaders continue to strengthen acceleration strategies for students who need this and also to continue "to prioritise the school's focus on Māori students achieving equitable outcomes and enjoying and experiencing success as Māori" (Education Review Office, 2019a). In other words, keep up the good work!

Literacy across the curriculum

Although the school's leaders might not use this term, they are effectively implementing what is termed a "literacy across the curriculum" approach, the results of which are seen in their Māori students' achieving the co-requisite literacy requirements associated with each NCEA level alongside the overall qualification. A discursive approach means that teachers ensure all students are able to use the literacy of each subject so they are confident and competent learners. It is about teaching students subject-specific vocabulary within the subject teaching itself, so they are able to think about, discuss, interact with, and use texts in subject-specific ways. They will also be able to read subject-specific language and texts and understand and construct multi-modal texts themselves from each learning area so as to communicate new knowledge in the language of the area. The discursive classroom creates a dialogic interactive space where learners are immersed into the discourses of the subject. In science, for example, it is not about replicating science experiments set out by the teacher to demonstrate predetermined outcomes; instead, they become scientists. Instead of learning about art, they become artists and talk using artists' language. In this way, discursive classroom environments provide students with learning opportunities similar to the ways that "members of a particular knowledge community think, believe, speak, read and write (Gee, 2008)".

In order to achieve this goal, most learners will need some explicit instruction of the specific vocabularies of the texts used in new learning areas—to identify the new vocabulary for instance. With transmission pedagogies, that is often as far as learning goes. However, in order to become familiar with how the language works in action, within the discourse, learners also need repeated opportunities to immerse themselves in subject-appropriate activities. When practising writing a report or an essay, for example, a discursive approach using feedback and feed-forward provides learners with prompts before and feedback after a written statement so as to extend and revisit understandings. In this way, the learning is not static, but evolving, developing, and growing through interaction. This pedagogy enables learners to examine their thinking, reasoning, and explanations in an ongoing manner, reducing the static nature of learning common to the transmission model where knowledge is received, not negotiated or co-constructed. Such an approach is far closer to how scientists, for example, behave in the real world. Further, learners being able to explain their thinking is moving them towards understanding how learning works; the goal of their becoming self-regulating learners. It is also the means of teaching the John Hattie and Robert Marzano process described in Chapter 6 as being the most effective means of impacting on student learning.

A discursive classroom is also a place where students who come from different language and/or cultural groups, who may not have had background learning experiences of those literacy skills expected to meet the curriculum learning appropriate to their year level, are able to be included into learning conversations on their own terms. In this way, students' different knowledge and experiences can provide a resource base from which to explore how texts and learning resources can be seen from different perspectives. For example, in science, when examining the topic of astronomy, Pleaides for one culture is Matariki for another and Subaru for yet another. This means that the discursive classroom enables the differing meanings these different names have for the various cultural ways of making sense of the world can be "incorporated into class work on the languages, texts and literacy practices of a learning area" (Gee, 2008). Proportionality in maths can be learnt from students' experiences of catering at a marae, just as easily as it can from another cultural context. The task is to learn about proportions; the means of getting there can vary. Enabling students to draw upon their background experiences includes them in an authentic learning experience in a way that traditional classrooms are not able to do.

Literacy beyond early years

A further reason for implementing pedagogic reform is that literacy learning is more than learning at an ECE or as a new entrant into primary schools. There is also the drop off in literacy learning at Years 4 to 8 to consider. Nina Hood recently identified on "Nine to Noon", that, at Year 4, only 63% of students are reading at expected levels, and by Year 8, this figure has decreased to 56%. These statistics decrease again on entry to secondary school and then within secondary schools. This is because the expectations of teachers at these levels means that students are expected to be skilled in "reading to learn" on their arrival at secondary school. If they are not, they are left behind and deficit explanations are used again to explain and perpetuate the drop in performance.

How a secondary school can respond to these circumstances is shown at Kerikeri High School. For example, Maria Halliday, the Student Educational Needs Co-Ordinator at Kerikeri High School, had this to say in response to an inquiry about how the school responded to the learning needs of students arriving in Year 7 with literacy learning issues. She stated that the approach taken was one where:

Leading to the North-East: Ensuring the fidelity of relationship-based learning

Early identification followed by a systematic and sustained process of highly individualized, skilled teaching primarily focused on written language, with specialist support, is critical to enable learners to participate in the full range of social, academic, and other learning opportunities across all areas of the curriculum. Students attending Kerikeri High School have their learning needs recognised as soon as they start Year 7. Those demonstrating low to moderate learning needs (ave 40 students) are supported, with the KERI Reading programme and/or the Literacy Programme. Year 13 students volunteer and are trained as Tutors in the Pause, Prompt, Praise method of reading. They then work with a Year 7 one hour per week reading. We also apply for or provide assistive technology, including C-Pens to support curriculum access. Teachers are provided with Confidential Profiles outlining Specific Learning Difficulties, levels, and strategies to ensure adapted or differentiated tasks are provided.

Year 8 and Year 9 students are then recognised by their teachers and Dean and provided with support including attending a literacy programme or the CHOICE programme. CHOICE is a *Metacognitive Literacy* Group. This programme focuses on how to learn rather than remedial *literacy*. Students involved with the CHOICE Programme are encouraged to be actively involved with their learning by being participants and contributors not just recipients of knowledge. They are equipped with strategies for overcoming potential difficulties while also raising their sense of being a successful and able learner. (M. Halliday, personal communication, 25 August, 2022)

What is happening here is remediation within a wider pedagogic frame that positions learners within an agentic frame of potentiality, not deficiencies. In effect, here is a series of literacy learning practices that merge with the overall pedagogic principles implemented at Kerikeri High School. In practice, they use the Pause, Prompt, Praise approach within a tuakana–teina relationship and meta-cognitive learning within a "literacy across the curriculum approach" so that students who would otherwise struggle are supported to be able to participate successfully in the discursive classrooms in this school.

Leadership makes it happen

The implications for leaders of this movement from the traditional to the discursive classroom are also huge. This movement is a large paradigm shift undertaken within supportive learning environments for teachers. If the support is not there, there are dangers that teachers will revert to traditional methods, leaving behind the possibility of students from different cultures being able to participate on their own terms. Even worse, perhaps, is teachers approximating the approach, meaning that, on the surface, it looks like a discursive classroom, whereas, in reality, it remains one where the teacher's cultural ways of making meaning continue to dominate, with the potential to further alienate students from different cultures. Hence the need for leaders to lead the transformation of the school by instituting a structural reform that is responsive and supportive of the pedagogic innovation so that the new pedagogy is implemented with fidelity. The leaders at Kerikeri High School have undertaken such a transformation as will be detailed below, with consequent benefits for their Māori and other students.

What further enhances this approach to learning are relationships with the parents and communities of the students from different cultures, a process that Kerikeri High School has been involved with in an increasingly productive way since 2005. This relationship and the way it has enhanced student learning at Kerikeri High School will also be detailed below.

Infrastructure

The main means of transforming teaching practices were two-fold. These interventions were based on teachers firstly being inducted into the "discursive classroom" practices at an induction hui, a hui whakarewa. At these hui, stories of Māori students' schooling experiences, along with those of their whānau members, their teachers, and their school principals, were used to provide teachers with a vicarious experience of what it was like to be a Māori student in mainstream schools (Bishop & Berryman, 2006). As most of the stories described the learning relationships Māori students experienced as being toxic, many teachers found these stories to be very confronting and they determined to make a difference to the learning experiences of Māori students in their school. They were then introduced to the profile of what an effective teacher of Māori students looked like, and the means of their implementing this picture in their classrooms. At Kerikeri High School, these hui have been implemented annually for nearly 20 years now and have become an integral part of the school's annual events. At these hui, new teachers are inducted into the common code of practice and current staff are also included so that the importance of this common code of practice is continually reinforced. And, as the hui are usually held at a local marae, the haukainga of many of their Māori students, they are continually reinforcing their commitment and accountability to these families.

Kerikeri High School leaders have maintained this institution and, pre-COVID, had expanded on it with a Matariki evening where senior students are given certificates. There is a performance by the kapa haka group and the principal speaks to the local Māori community to describe the successes of their children and the school's commitment to Māori enjoying and experiencing success as Māori. The principal explained in her recent sabbatical report that these mid-year hui were important for reinforcing the message about the importance of the common code of practice, and providing another opportunity to learn from leaders, fellow teachers, students, and local whānau members about the preferred pedagogy in a group setting.

While the hui whakarewa was an essential part of the induction process for teachers and leaders, and despite teachers leaving the hui with very clear understandings about what they could do to raise Māori student achievement, no change occurred in student outcomes following these hui. The main reason is that talking about making changes at a hui does not enable change to occur. Rather, it makes it possible for it to occur. In effect, therefore, another action is needed.

What was necessary for changing teaching practices were in-class observation and coaching sessions. It was only through the institutionalising of this intensive coaching programme based on targeted classroom observations and feedback sessions that teachers began to understand how to move their practices towards that of the "effective teacher". The observation sessions were followed by intensive, one-on-one coaching. These interactions initially involved facilitators providing feedback based on the data gathered during the observation about teaching practices. Gradually, however, teachers became involved in co-constructing with the observers common collaborative understandings of what the data showed and what next teaching steps would be necessary for them to introduce and perfect the profile of an effective teacher.

The second institution introduced as part of the Te Kotahitanga programme was a collaborative decision-making and problem-solving meeting called a co-construction meeting. In these meetings, evidence of student progress was used to identify next teaching steps. These meetings were very valuable because they brought the power of collective decision making to support identified areas of need. The power of these meetings was also seen in teachers no longer being on their own in the search to improve their teaching practice. The meetings reinforced the understanding that the solutions lay in the implementation of the common code of practice; the profile of an effective teacher of Māori students.

In this way, these new institutions were aimed at addressing and removing problems caused by the prior variability in teaching practice by supporting the rigorous implementation of the common code of effective practice with fidelity. Teachers did not have to find the secret of improving Māori student achievement on their own, and neither did they have to find how best they could implement these secrets. They were provided with an evidence-based profile of what an effective teacher of Māori students actually did, and they were supported by their team leaders and colleagues to identify how best they could realise these practices.

As I have noted on a number of occasions in this book, John Hattie's meta-analyses have shown that probably the most important activity that teachers can engage in when seeking to improve student achievement is collaborative decision making and problem solving. This case study of Kerikeri High School certainly illustrates the value of this understanding for improving practice. The whole process took the mystery and confusion out of teaching, and it resulted in raising Māori student achievement. A win-win solution.

A further benefit of these institutional means of supporting teachers to change their practice was their learning about how formative assessment procedures work in their classrooms. At Kerikeri High School, this is no longer a problem because teachers were supported—albeit somewhat interrupted recently by COVID-19 restrictions—by a highly effective, in-class and student-evidence-related PLD process to learn about and use this very effective learning process. They do this by using evidence from observations of their own practice in relation to evidence of student performance and progress. Because they were using this process themselves to identify steps for their own next learning and practices, they are better able to use these practices with their students.

The ERO reviewers saw this happening as well:

> Expectations for high quality teacher professional practice are clearly articulated and well understood. Teachers participate in effective professional development aligned with the school vision, values, goals and targets. (Education Review Office, 2019b)

Leadership

Distributed leadership practices were introduced into the school as part of the Te Kotahitanga programme and subsequent formative assessment-based PLD initiatives. Initially, Te Kotahitanga identified the need to develop a number of in-school facilitators whose task it was to support the school's leaders to conduct the hui whakarewa, undertake the observations, associated feedback sessions, chair the co-construction meetings, and provide the follow-up associated shadow-coaching. They were initially funded externally by the Ministry of Education, but once the funding ceased, the school leaders took over the funding of these roles.

In addition, the focus of these roles has been modified over time in order to better suit the school's own hierarchy of expertise and responsibilities. The co-construction meetings now consist of curriculum subject department members, rather than collectives of classroom teachers. It was felt initially that this latter approach would foster a focus on learning rather than on specific teaching strategies for teaching a curriculum area. However, this class focus left many very useful people out of the deliberations and the concern that curriculum issues would overshadow the necessary focus on learning did not eventuate.

Now heads of curriculum areas are included in planning and running the co-construction meetings and they are also involved in follow-up shadow-coaching. Further modifications were made to the timing and frequency of co-construction meetings from once or twice a term to being conducted more often so as to be responsive to student learning needs in a more timely fashion.

Spread

Connectedness or whanaungatanga for Kerikeri High School is exemplified in their relationships and their responsiveness to their Māori community. How this has changed over time is also interesting. Initially, as part of the process of bringing more teachers into the Te Kotahitanga programme, the school would hold an induction hui at the commencement of each year. These hui would be held at a local marae, hosted by the local marae community. Most of the hui was given over to inducting new teachers into the discursive teaching approaches. On this occasion, the principal was able to make a statement of intent to the local people. In these statements, she would feed back to the local community about the achievements of their children over the past year. Then she would set out the teaching and learning intentions for the coming year. This form of accountability was very powerful because it brought the school and the Māori community closer together.

As time went on, the relationship began to change. This change was signalled to the local community by the school principal by the official appointment of a kuia for Kerikeri High School. This appointment connected the school even more closely with the Ngāti Rēhia.

The principal explains that "Ngāti Rēhia had always been the guardians of this rohe and were always going to be here." And it was strongly suggested that the strategy should be presented in such a way that it reflects the aspirations and cultural understandings of the local community, not just the schools. It "should be intergenerational in focus and speak to our most treasured values and aspirations". The leadership surveyed and invited feedback for the new strategic direction from the whole community.

Ngāti Rēhia kuia and kaumātua prepared a document that was to become foundational for the new strategy. It included the aspiration that all tamariki, both Māori and Pākehā, would be able to kōrero

Māori by Year 12 or when they left school. The school had previously made te reo Māori compulsory in Year 7 and voluntary from then on. In this way, the aspirations of the local community were ahead of the school's leaders who are working to address the disjunction. This relationship has since been further extended to bring the local iwi into developing a more localised curriculum with local stories, knowledge, and history that support students' feelings of belonging and identity by improving whānau engagement.

At Kerikeri High School there has been a concerted effort to include Māori parents and community representatives in the decision-making and problem-solving processes of the school. Central to these conversations has been the question of what works best for their children as Māori learners. As whanaungatanga is fundamental to the way this school runs, whānau perspectives are often sought by way of hui, informal gatherings, linkages with the local marae, and special events at the school such as the Māori students' excellence awards (Matariki) ceremony. Being equal partners with local parents and iwi in the education of their children is an important part of the school's values. Local iwi, Ngāti Rēhia, has a permanent representative on the school board, leads other representative groups and committees, and is able to inform school practices and is included in PLD for te reo and tikanga ā-iwi. For example, at the annual induction hui for new teachers, existing staff are also included. This means that mana whenua are able to provide all teachers with an immersion into the world of Ngāti Rēhiatanga. These opportunities are being increasingly valuable as the culturally responsive pedagogy is embedded in this school. In this way, the staff continue to grow their understanding of the different world views that Māori students will be bringing with them to the learning interactions they make possible in their discursive classrooms.

These strong school–community relationships have been building over the years, from the local iwi being recipients of what the school was planning to do, to now including and implementing community informed practices and curriculum content that establish strong whānau–school learning partnerships that support student learning.

What is clear from this case study is that it was the school's transformation into a North-East learning institution that created the conditions within which a reciprocal, respectful relationship could flourish. If schools do not make this move, Māori parents and community leaders will continue to "see" closed doors.

There is also an expectation that the staff will continue to improve their knowledge and proficiency of te reo Māori and how they are implementing tikanga in their classrooms—how they are basing their practice on whānau values of manaakitanga, wairuatanga, tiakitanga, in their practice by implementing a family-like context for learning.

The ERO review saw the benefits of this relationship adding value to the students' learning.

> Staff work collaboratively with whānau and implement effective strategies that meet students' specific learning needs … The school proactively draws on the local environment and community resources to enhance student learning opportunities, achievement and access to meaningful pathways. This collaboration supports the future direction of the school. (Education Review Office, 2019b, n.p.)

The spread of the relentless focus on improving Māori student achievement is that the leaders had initially instituted an approach that included all members of the staff into the Te Kotahitanga programme over a number of cohorts of teachers over a number of years. This continued until all staff had been inducted and were included in the regular cycle of observations and co-construction meetings. Annual hui whakarewa ensure new staff are inducted into the programme, and their readiness to participate in the programme is made a condition of their employment.

Another connection acknowledged by the leadership is their long-term learning relationship they have with external providers of professional development from the Te Kotahitanga team and, more latterly, the Poutama Pounamu team, both from the University of Waikato.

Evidence

It almost goes without saying that evidence forms an essential part of daily decision-making and problem-solving practices at Kerikeri High School. In 2012, when we undertook an in-depth look at what was happening at the school, we spoke to a number of teachers and leaders about the use they were making of evidence. We found that most teachers said that the importance of relationships was now so ingrained in their practice they no longer needed regular reminders; however:

> when it came to pedagogy it was still easy to slip back into an over-reliance on instruction and monitoring. Therefore, the majority of staff embraced the regular term by term Te Kotahitanga co-construction meetings which provided opportunities to discuss evidence of Māori student achievement and participation as a result of their teaching practices. Co-construction meetings provided teachers with a forum to share evidence from their own practice, be reminded of the benefits of discursive pedagogies, learn new strategies, share resources and when necessary, professionally challenge each other. (Bishop et al., 2012., p. 52)

In this way, the use of evidence within structured settings ensures the ongoing implementation fidelity of those effective practices needed to ensure that the high level of Māori student achievement at this and other schools will continue into the future. One teacher summed up the feelings of many including their emphasising the necessity for ongoing support systems within the school to ensure the ongoing fidelity of the pedagogy:

> I am a really experienced teacher but the problem with teaching is you're in a room, on your own, and you think you're doing ok but you really don't know if you're doing ok. The facilitation, observations and the feedback meetings, and the co-construction meetings are the most powerful part of the whole programme. To keep it going as a sustainability model, you just continually need that. Otherwise, you can get out of the habit. It's easy to go back to standing in front of the classroom. You don't forget the relationship stuff, that becomes part of your nature, I think; but you do forget some of the basic teaching strategies stuff very easily. (Teacher 9)

Ownership

The principal and other leaders at Kerikeri High School have taken over complete ownership of the initiative that was introduced from the University of Waikato. Through the process of self-review, they have adapted it and institutionalised it in ways that reflect their own circumstances and needs. They have strategically maintained the central institutions of hui whakarewa, observations and coaching, co-construction meetings and shadow-coaching, but modified them to suit their own purposes. For example, the central purpose of the hui whakarewa of the induction of new teachers into the preferred pedagogical practices of the school was maintained, but they were modified to add opportunities for staff to become students themselves, learn about the local area, their stories, te reo Māori, waiata, tauparapara, the significance of place names and events, the importance of whakapapa, and the meaning of the land to the local people. In other words, they used these hui to "cross the bridge" that Kelvin Davis identified at a recent principals' hui, where the traffic had been one way for too long and the teachers needed to get their feet onto that bridge to te ao Māori.

The goal of improving Māori students' achievement was addressed initially by implementing the Te Kotahitanga initiative, then other initiatives were added on, but only if they supported the school's goal of improving Māori students' achievement levels. If they didn't, they were discarded or not even introduced.

Funding was central. Initially, releasing some staff from their classroom teaching responsibilities to become in-school facilitators was funded by "soft money" provided by the Ministry of Education. As time went on and the initial "seeding" funding diminished, the principal took over the need to provide ongoing resourcing of the programme.

Kerikeri High School provides us with an outstanding example of the commitment and determination of its leaders and their ownership of the problems facing their Māori community by re-allocating resources to sustain the initial gains made in Māori student achievement. Again, the ERO team was very complimentary of this school's commitment to seeing Māori students' achievement remain at its current high levels.

> Strategic resourcing and an ongoing commitment for Māori success has enabled significant improvement in overall Māori student achievement. School leaders and trustees value the positive impact te reo and tikanga Māori has on student success. The school is successfully embedding bicultural and culturally responsive practices to increase student engagement and promote equitable outcomes for Māori students. These practices include authentic partnerships with hapū and iwi. (Education Review Office, 2019b, n.p.)

A further example of the school leaders taking ownership of the initiative and relentlessly pursuing the goals of the school are the buildings. Many buildings have been re-purposed during the past 20 years as new demands and responses have been identified. For example, the dean's centre became the student centre, then it was rebuilt as Te Puna Waiora (the source of wellbeing). It is probably normal in the life of a school to reprioritise the purpose of some of the buildings, but what is significant in this case is that the reprioritising has been guided by how it fits with the school's goals of improving Māori student engagement and learning. It has not been a random pattern of change, of ad hoc responses to shifting and competing demands—it has been a purposeful reprioritising of functions for an over-riding purpose. For example, over the years, older teaching blocks have been remodelled in ways that suited the new emphasis on de-privatising classrooms and collaborative effort. Lots of internal glass was used: no closed-in classrooms; no classrooms smaller than 80m^2 so as to enable collaborative and group activities; no fixed furniture.

Anyone who applies to this school for a position quickly becomes aware of the specific conditions placed upon those who take up teaching and/or leadership positions. It is a condition of employment that teachers will adhere to the discursive mode of teaching so as to maintain the common, and effective, code of practice across the school.

As I said above, constantly reviewing the means of transforming the school into a North-East learning institution has further strengthened this process. This approach to quality assurance is a fundamental part of how the leaders at Kerikeri High School have maintained their relentless focus on improving Māori student achievement as Māori, and the achievement of all other students as well. The careful, evidence-based deliberations over the effectiveness of their means of implementing the central pedagogy has meant it has been implemented with the fidelity necessary to realise the gains being made in student outcomes. Their ongoing evaluations of the suitability of the support systems for teachers has meant they have been adapted and strengthened in their usefulness for purpose. Developing the now reciprocal relationships with Ngāti Rēhia has been facilitated by their continually reviewing how they could improve the conditions within the school that made such a relationship possible. They did not go to the community before they had something to offer in the way of improved outcomes for their young people. They did not ask the community to provide them with the means of improving their children's learning outcomes. They knew who was initially responsible. In this way, Kerikeri High School's leaders developed a reciprocal, dialogic partnership, similar to that developed in their classrooms that has reinforced the identity, language, and culture of their Māori students.

Summary

The school leaders led the collaborative development of goals to drive and align their efforts, introduced effective pedagogic interactions within metaphoric, extended family-like contexts, restructured the school to provide teachers with supported learning opportunities, and institutionalised collective ways of interrogating evidence of student performance and teacher practice. They also institutionalised North-East leadership practices; spread assessment practices and use to include parents and families; prioritised evidence-based, decision making and problem solving; and took ownership of the problem and the solutions by orienting, funding, and reviewing all the school's and classrooms' activities to address the central problem of Māori student achievement including literacy learning. Essentially, they gave away any notions that the children were at fault and insisted on teachers working together in supportive collectives to address the learning needs of their children. In other words, they have done a great job.

Coda

Kerikeri High School was an inaugural winner of Atatu—the Prime Minister's Award for Excellence in Teaching and Learning. Many other Te Kotahitanga schools have since been awarded this prestigious award.

Chapter 12
The benefits of North-East schools

Introduction

The first question I always ask the principal of any school I visit is "How are the Māori students going?" I ask this question because I need to know what impact all the effort that goes into a school is having upon Māori students' learning outcomes. I have been to numerous schools here in New Zealand and overseas where the principals have told me that they are doing numerous things for their Indigenous students. These include positioning Indigenous peoples' images and stories in teaching texts, curriculum content, and around the school. They also mention structural changes such as providing a kapa haka group and building a marae. In short, anything but changing the pedagogy used in the school. Then, when I ask to see the achievement results that all students who attend public schools should be able to attain, I find gaps between them and their non-Indigenous peers. And these gaps clearly have more to do with their being Māori than to their potential. I say this because even the Māori students in the highest achieving levels are achieving at a lower rate than their non-Māori peers.

This is crazy in a country like ours that has made so much progress in many social areas, such as being the first country to provide votes for women in the 19th century; the welfare state in the early 20th century;

our refusal to be drawn into the nuclear debacle in the late 20th century. Yet we cannot seem to provide an education system that suits all of our citizens, let alone a group of Indigenous people who were guaranteed, in writing in Article 3 of the Treaty of Waitangi, that they would benefit from their participation in the new society established in 1840. It is ironic that the children of the settlers at the time and their descendants, although they were not guaranteed in writing that they would benefit from their participation in the new society, have obviously done so.

To put it simply, it is time for us as a country to address these ongoing achievement differences. And it is time that we did it rapidly before the downstream effects of these disparities overwhelm us all. It is time that Māori students were able to attend public, mainstream schools in the knowledge that their full potential will be realised.

Whatever the case, some schools do already. These are North-East schools, and they are able to address the learning needs of all their students with the urgency needed.

Many school principals, when asked this question about how well their Māori or Indigenous students are going, are often not able to give me details of the Indigenous students' progress because they are grouped in with the rest of the students. Or, if they have differentiated data, their answers often range from "not so well" to "quite well, but …". If it is either of these responses, with a further probe, they will most often reveal that, despite the best efforts of their staff, there remains a gap between the achievements of the Indigenous and their non-Indigenous peers.[45]

My next question is invariably, "How come?", and almost without fail I hear tales of woe, of how the Indigenous students do not really want to come to school and, if they do, they have limited knowledge on which the teachers can build new learning. I hear an acceptance that nothing can really be done about the disparities. "They come from impoverished homes, no books, no interest in reading, and their behaviour is often very challenging" are among common explanations.

---

45 I am using the term "Indigenous" because I have asked principals this question in New Zealand, Australia, USA, Canada, and Malaysia and this has revealed a common response as well as a common experience for Indigenous students in these countries, and one might suggest in others as well.

In Canada, I even heard of physical challenges the children exhibit that limited their being able to participate in school life; they suffer from depression, foetal-alcohol effects, passive-aggressive behaviour patterns, and so on. I hear less of these physical explanations in New Zealand. Here, it is more common to hear explanations related to their cultural characteristics that impact negatively on learning. Whatever the case, the blame for low performance is put on the children or their families. It is also interesting to note how sophisticated these excuses are becoming now that the issue of deficit theorising has been brought to the fore.

The benefits of North-East schools

How refreshing it is to talk with principals of North-East schools such as the three featured in this book. I hear them use the language of whanaungatanga, of relationships and responsibility. I hear nothing from them like the tales of woe I hear from others. I hear from these principals that Māori students' achievement levels are on a par with their non-Māori peers, or if this is not the case, they are able to explain the reason why in terms that do not involve their blaming the students, but rather involve some external factors such as family mobility, which they are addressing. This lack of blaming the victims is refreshing and is vital if anything is to be done about improving the educational outcomes for those who are actually not being well served by our education system.

I say this because our research in Te Kotahitanga[46] and Relationships First[47] clearly shows that once schools' leaders and teachers move away from deficit explanations that blame Māori students for lower levels of achievement, they are able to support these students to achieve the success that is the expected outcome of mainstream schooling. However, it is important to re-emphasise that they are *able* to do so. It does not mean that *they will*.

In North-East schools, like these three remarkable schools in this book, their leaders have determined that they will make the difference needed. They have refused to accept ethnic-based disparities. As

---

46 https://tekotahitanga.tki.org.nz/About

47 https://www.cognitioneducation.co.nz/relationships-first/

a result, Māori students' achievements in literacy, numeracy, and other similar measures are on par with their non-Māori peers. There is no differentiation because of Māori students being Māori, as has been the seemingly unchangeable pattern in mainstream schools for decades.

Nor do North-East schools have issues with attendance, engagement, and retention; problems that are increasingly proving troublesome to many, if not most, mainstream English-medium schools currently. Overall, the seemingly immutable outcome differentials based on group membership that plague modern mainstream education systems just don't exist. These differentials used to exist, some until only recently, but they don't any more. All students in North-East schools like these three are able to achieve to the best of their potential. And, in each case, it took less than 2 years to realise these gains. So, 2 years is my benchmark from now on.

This finding about the time needed for change to occur was supported by Michael Fullan (2001) when he studied the implementation of literacy innovations in the United Kingdom and Ontario, Canada. He identified that "substantial progress can be made in schools in two years, in districts in three and even in whole nations" (p. 1). And this involved studies of 20,000 schools in the United Kingdom and 5,000 in Ontario. So, my sample size has just gone up somewhat to 25,003.

All three New Zealand schools solved the literacy crisis in less than 2 years, and other North-East schools will have no problems reaching this goal either. What this means is that they have moved significant numbers of members of the "35%" cohort into the "65%" successful cohort. That is, they move the students out of the group who were heading for functional illiteracy, to join the group who have functional literacy with all the life chances and opportunities this encompasses. I know which group I want my mokopuna to be in.

Secondly, North-East schools are responsive to Māori people's aspirations that their children will be able to be successful learners "as Māori". They have all actioned the statements in their institutional documents about the need for their school to honour the Treaty of Waitangi. Specifically in this case, they have addressed the Article 2 guarantee that Māori people's treasures—in this case language, culture, and identity—would be protected. In North-East schools, Māori students do not have to leave who they are, and how they make sense of the world, at the school gate. They are able to do so because the relationship-based pedagogy used in their classrooms and across their schools is supported by the in-school support systems that have been instituted with fidelity, so as to ensure the ongoing embedding of this pedagogy with fidelity.

A third major achievement of North-East schools is that many students who are currently denied the benefits of participating in education by their membership of either an ethnic, refugee, migrant, or gender group, or belonging to what is increasingly being called the neurodiverse, are also able to realise their potential by their being in classrooms with North-East teachers in North-East schools.

The main reason for these developments: *leadership*. Primarily from the principal, but supported by all other leaders, including the teachers in the school. It is a pattern of leadership that is called "distributed" because the functions and tasks of leadership are spread throughout the school.

By this I mean that, in the introduction in Chapter 1, I put the onus on principals to lead the transformation of their schools into North-East learning institutions. I emphasised how important their role is and the opportunity they currently have to make a major difference to our country. However, I also need to emphasise that the part other school leaders and teachers play in this transformation is just as important. Many leaders are now talking about their school as being a whānau. This is a great term because it generates the idea of all working for the benefit of each other. However, it is important to emphasise that, while working within a whānau ascribes a number of rights, it also identifies a number of responsibilities for each member of the whānau. Hence the right to be a leader also contains the responsibilities of the position to ensure those you are responsible for are learning in ways that realise their potential. You, as a leader, cannot resort to deficit explanations for students' or teachers' performance. Their successful learning is your responsibility, as well as theirs of course. But above all, to use the term "whānau" in a metaphoric sense means that you take on the roles and responsibilities of an actual extended family; where each member is supported to fully realise their potential.

Finally, North-East leaders, led by North-East principals, are determined that these patterns of disparity can and will change. It is that simple. Any doubts about whether Māori are capable enough or "Do they really want to take part?" or "Will they take part?" need to be abandoned. This is part of the conceptual revolution we need in New Zealand schools.

And then they set about making it happen. How North-East leaders realise these goals has been the subject of this book. Based on an analysis of the current situation in their schools, they set goals to focus all involved onto solving problems. They then introduce a pedagogy that will realise the goals. The third action is to implement support systems that consist of a transformed infrastructure, re-oriented leadership, a means of including all teachers, parents, and community leaders, and the use of evidence, to ensure the pedagogy is implemented with fidelity, learning is enhanced, and decision making and problem solving are evidence-based. Lastly, they take ownership by planning, resourcing, and reviewing their actions to ensure the support systems work with the necessary fidelity.

What does it mean when North-East schools realise North-East goals?

1. Māori students achieve on par with their non-Māori peers

Equity is about acknowledging that not all learners start at the same place. In contrast, equality is about providing learners with the same opportunities as each other. However, all learners start from different places. This means that equality can only really be realised through an equity approach because adjustments and changes in focus need to be made to the school in order to rectify imbalances in outcomes. It does not mean a remediation approach to "rectify deficiencies". It requires of schools that they refocus their attentions onto those students whose learning is not being well served by an "equality" approach. Hence, North-East schools focus on Māori and other marginalised students by implementing a culturally responsive pedagogy to enable these students to bring who they are to the learning conversations so as to realise equality of outcomes.

However, equality of outcomes does not only mean that Māori students are able to achieve at test scores and external exams in traditional academic subjects. I am also concerned about how well Māori and other

Indigenous students are learning to become successful self-managing learners. We would be failing in our duty as teachers if we only focused on improving task- and content-level learning for Māori students. Don't get me wrong—this is very important. For example, "learning to read" is vital, so is "reading to learn", but "learning how to learn" and "learning how to be a life-long learner" is every bit as important. And all these skills need to be taught or included as part of a pedagogic process. The irony is that, if Māori students are only enabled to be successful in content learning, they would still not have the skills and knowledge necessary to participate on equal terms with non-Māori in the modern economy.

Currently, we are seeing many young Māori people taking their rightful place in many and varied professions such as the traditional ones of the law, medicine, and education. In addition, increasingly, we are seeing many entering the new opportunities being created in media, IT, communications, travel, tourism, and also returning to their iwi and hapū to play leading roles in the development of their people for the benefit of future generations.

However, I notice that a large proportion of these young people are Māori-medium graduates with their high qualification levels and fluency in both Māori and English opening many doors for them and their families. I suspect that Māori graduates from English-medium schooling are under-represented in these wonderful opportunities that are opening up to our young people.

The transformation of our mainstream, public schools into North-East learning institutions is a major means of our enabling young Māori people to take up these opportunities. This is made possible because higher levels of education and employment beyond schooling are increasingly requiring of participants that they not only have content knowledge, but also are competent in the means of attaining and processing new knowledge. These so-called "soft skills"—such as being able to work in teams, ask relevant questions, communicate effectively, provide and receive feedback, problem solve, and generally work with others—are not an adjunct to be picked up along the way, but are becoming essential parts of any modern workforce. Employers are actively soliciting candidates who have these "intangibles".

In a 2021 review of more than 80 million job postings across 22 industry sectors, education non-profit *America Succeeds* found that *almost two-thirds of positions listed soft skills among their qualifications.* And across all the job postings, of the 10 most in-demand skills, seven were "soft", including communication, problem solving, and planning. The same report showed certain types of positions "prioritise soft skills even more: they were the most desired qualifications for 91% of management jobs, 86% of business-operations jobs and 81% of engineering jobs—a fact that may be surprising, since it's a field generally considered highly technically focused".[48]

It is important to realise that Māori students are not going to get these skills in traditional transmission classrooms, nor is anyone else for that matter. What they all need are those discursive classrooms seen in North-East schools where these skills and knowledge are practised on a daily basis. In these classrooms, young people are actively engaged in dialogue, negotiation, evidence-based decision making and problem solving, providing and receiving feedback, and generating questions among other such skills. And their teachers monitor how well they are learning these skills and knowledge so that they can continually improve their and their students' learning of both "hard" and "soft" skills. All of these actions are undertaken within the language of the subjects, hence creating a "literacy across the curriculum approach" that supports the disciplinary literacy required in curriculum areas.

2. North-East schools enable young Māori people to be successful "as Māori"

A further outcome of North-East schools is that they are realising another of Māori people's goals for their children as represented in the Ministry of Education's Ka Hikitea policy. Ka Hikitia is defined as "to step up, to lift up or to lengthen one's stride" and challenges educators with, "stepping up how the education system performs to ensure Māori students are enjoying and achieving education success as Māori" (Ministry of Education, 2013). The Ministry of Education document spells out that, when this vision is realised, all Māori students will:

---

48 https://www.bbc.com/worklife/
    article/20220727-soft-skills-the-intangible-qualities-companies-crave

- have their identity, language and culture valued and included in teaching and learning, in ways that support them to engage and achieve success;

- know their potential and feel supported to set goals and take action to achieve success;

- experience teaching and learning that is relevant, engaging, rewarding and positive, and;

- have gained the skills, knowledge and qualifications they need to achieve success in te ao (the world) Māori, New Zealand and the wider world. (Ministry of Education, 2013, p. 13)[49]

I remember when I was looking into what had happened to my mother's family after New Zealand's civil war of the 1860s. Her father had travelled to the South Island to look after his recently widowed sister. He remained in the South and gradually lost contact with the northern part of the family. However, he did leave clues in my mother's names which were to lead me back to Ngāti Pūkeko and Ngāti Awa, ki Whakatane, then onto Tainui ki Taupiri. When I eventually met the family members living there, they told me of their parents who had been competent in both the Pākehā and Māori worlds. They had been fluent in both languages, customs, and protocols. They were kaumātua on their marae with all the expertise necessary for these roles. Some were also members of town councils, not as adjuncts, but as fully participating members, able to engage with "Robert's Rules" and suchlike. They, however, were the last generation of my family to have this dual level of cultural competency. Most of the children of their generation lived either as Māori or Pākehā; bicultural competence no longer being an option because of the dominance of the monocultural discourse and

---

49   This is variously termed a "culturally responsive approach" (the term used in this book), or a "culturally competent approach" and also a "culturally sustaining approach". Whatever the case, the main issue is that young Māori learners are able to bring who they are and how they make sense of the world into the learning conversations that characterise this type of dialogic, interactive approach to teaching. These approaches stand in contrast to traditional, transmission approaches where the skills and knowledge from the dominant culture are "transmitted" from an active teacher to passive students. The former approaches have proven to be far more effective for improving learning outcomes for children of cultures different from those of the teacher.

educational practices of the time. That is, until our generation, where we are struggling to regain what our family had once attained readily. We are now expecting that schools will provide us and our tamariki mokopuna with these opportunities. Just as with the older members of our family, our current family want access to both cultures, but we also understand that one will not necessarily lead to the other. Both have to be learnt.

In North-East schools, like the three featured in this book, Māori students do not have to leave their culture at the school gate like my mother's family did over many generations. In these schools, Māori students' identities are enhanced because the culturally responsive pedagogy used in these schools enables students to bring who they are and how they make sense of the world into the classroom, into the learning conversations, providing a cultural base for further learning. They are not passive recipients of knowledge from the dominant culture, but rather are active participants in the processes of learning, including learning how to learn. Further, the pedagogic processes include teachers exhibiting high expectations of their learning which supports them to realise their full potential through individual and group evidence-based goal setting, knowledge of how to go about learning, taking leadership roles, learning with others, and taking effective, evidence-based actions to achieve success. In this way, North-East schools provide Māori students with opportunities that ensure they learn the skills and knowledge necessary for their successfully participating in te ao Māori, New Zealand, and the wider world.

The relationship-based pedagogy that is central to the transformation of schools into North-East learning institutions means that Māori students can learn in culturally safe environments where their identities are enhanced, sustained, and they can then achieve at te reo me ona tikanga alongside traditional academic assessments. In this way, they will have the base from which they can participate effectively in all the worlds that will become open to them.

As was seen in Chapter 11 on Kerikeri High School, one main feature of a relationship-based pedagogy are discursive interactions. This idea is based on the concept of discourse which acknowledges that there are always different perspectives; that is, different culturally generated ways of making sense of any content or topic. Hence the need for a pedagogic approach that promotes the use of power-sharing strategies to enable dialogue and interaction, that is, "learning conversations", rather than one-way transmissions of knowledge to occur. Such strategies facilitate the use of learners' prior knowledge, the provision of feedback and feed-forward, and co-construction activities. These strategies allow a range of explanations and ways of making sense to be included and acceptable in learning conversations.

These 21st century thinking skills enable students to practise developing and revisit new concepts in a variety of ways based on their culturally different ways of making sense of the world. In these classrooms, the teacher's role is to set guidelines and purposes for interaction and discussion to engage students in learning conversations. These promote learning by using skills of collaboration, communication, and co-construction of knowledge through interaction and dialogue.

While there is some evidence that participating in kapa haka activities in high schools will improve Māori students' learning by promoting their cultural wellbeing, when schools are transformed into North-East learning institutions we see even greater gains being made. As we saw at Okaihau College, when Māori students became successful learners, they explained that "it is good to be Māori at this school". What happened then was that young Māori people sought out those opportunities that have been provided for them earlier, but which many had previously avoided. These opportunities had not been taken up prior to the school's transformation because, being Māori at that time, and engaging in Māori activities was seen in negative terms. As a result, they had shied away from opportunities to learn their own cultural practices and language. Once the school had been transformed into a North-East learning institution, however, and used culturally responsive pedagogies in ways that ensured Māori students were as successful as their non-Māori peers, Māori students flocked to te reo classes, kapa haka, and marae activities.

As we found at Kerikeri High School also, the provision of Māori activities, prior to their being successful members of the school's learning community, mostly fell on fallow ground. However, once Māori students became successful learners, the impact of the growth in their pride of being Māori was such that the whole school began to be further transformed by their aspirations to become biculturally competent. What also impacts upon these young people's decisions is the implementation of support systems in the school that improve relationships between the school and their local iwi. In this way, being Māori has been further enhanced and valued, reinforcing the choices young Māori people are making to engage with te reo me te ao Māori.

3. What is good for Māori is good for all

Our experiences in Te Kotahitanga and Relationship First schools shows us that addressing the learning needs of Indigenous students means that other marginalised students are also able to be supported effectively; and, further, no one else misses out. Research by Gail Gillon and Angus Macfarlane (Gillon et al., 2019) confirmed this observation that "what is good for Māori, is good for all". This means that, once a school has transformed itself to better serve the learning needs of its Indigenous students, it also finds it is better able to support the learning of other groups of students once marginalised by who they were or what they brought to the classroom. With this transformation, mainstreaming of children previously compartmentalised away from the rest of the school population starts to make sense because it is not forced upon traditional transmission classrooms, but rather included in discursive, dialogic, interactive classrooms where students can participate on their own terms.

Children of migrant and refugee families can similarly be included in the transformed classrooms in ways similar to how Indigenous students are made welcome. Children with different gender preferences, physical disabilities, and the neurodiverse are similarly better served when included in these classrooms. In short, children from diverse backgrounds find themselves accepted and included on their own terms in those classrooms and schools that have been transformed to better support Māori students' learning.

The messages from this book

I want to finish with some messages that come from my writing this book.

The first thing is that if you want to see these outcomes, you need to become a North-East principal. This means that you will need to lead the transformation of your school into a North-East learning institution. The emphasis here is on the principal leading and owning the transformation. As Elizabeth Forgie (2021), a very successful North-East principal, said to me recently, "If this does not happen, then don't bother. It won't work." However, please also remember that it takes the whole school to realise North-East goals. The rest of the school's whānau need to be engaged in the transformation as well and you need to provide the spaces wherein they can do so.

The second thing I want to say is that the pattern I have described in this book, while complex, is achievable.

- North-East schools are where Māori and other marginalised students are enabled to realise their true potential as learners. They are supported to achieve on par with their non-Māori peers, are able to do so "as Māori", and see others benefit from the North-East schooling practices that have supported their learning.

- It is the implementation of North-East relationship-based pedagogy, that is culturally responsive and sustaining, dialogically interactive, and formative-focused that ensures Māori and other marginalised students are able to become successful learners on their own terms.

- In order for this pedagogy to be embedded and sustained in teachers' practice, so that they can become and remain North-East teachers, North-East leaders, working within North-East schools' infrastructural institutions, support teachers to learn about how to implement the North-East relationship-based pedagogy in their learning spaces with fidelity in the long term.

- These infrastructural institutions are enhanced by the inclusion of parents, families, and community members and leaders into learning partnerships; that is into formative deliberations about the impact of teaching practices on their children's performance.

- Also vital is the development of evidence systems for use across the school by all involved for formative purposes.

- The final piece of the puzzle is principals leading the collaborative setting of goals, strategically planning ways to realise these goals and ensuring all actions within the school are focused on realising these goals, discarding those actions that don't contribute to these outcomes. Critical to this is happening is school leaders taking ownership of the problems by planning, resourcing strategically, and implementing a process of self-review that measures where the school is up to in their process of transformation, where they need to go and how to get there.

So, you will see that single solutions like getting rid of streaming, smaller class sizes, restructuring the board of trustees system, and so on, while probably important parts of the process of transforming schools into North-East learning institutions, will not do the job on their own. They might well be part of the picture, but schools are complex places so why should solutions be simple.

The final message is that here is a model for change that has been trialled and proven in a number, size, and type of schools, over a range of locations and over a long period of time. Those schools that have used this model, or one similar of their own making, have seen remarkable changes in the attendance, engagement, retention, and achievement of Māori students in ways that enable them to be successful learners "as Māori".

In this way, North-East schools honour their commitments to the Treaty of Waitangi. The first is their honouring Article 3's guarantee that Māori people will benefit from being citizens of the new society. The second is their honouring Article 2's guarantee to Māori that their inclusion would not be at the expense of those treasures, such as their language, culture, and identity, they valued. Thirdly, they are honouring Article 1's guarantee of partnership in decision making through the use of a relationship-based pedagogy in classrooms and with parents and local iwi leaders to further enhance the learning of young Māori people so that they can take their rightful place in te ao Māori, New Zealand society, and the wider world.

So, all things considered, what is a North-East leader?

In my early days as a teacher at Mana College in Porirua, I was invited by the principal to come back to school one evening to meet with the parents of the new Year 9 students. I was to be there as an example of a classroom teacher. It felt like one of those invitations that had been offered to a few other people but everyone else had managed to find a sick grandmother, another urgent meeting, or had a university assignment they just had to finish. Anyway, I went along and found the hall to be nearly full of eager parents, all keen to hear what the school was going to offer them and their children. I was invited to join the group up the front where there was quite a line-up of the school's leaders. The principal was central of course, the deputy principal was there, the guidance counsellor, and a number of heads of curriculum departments. I don't think the bursar was there, but you get the idea. There were a lot of talking heads to go through. And go through they did when it came time for the speeches to begin. The principal started and told the parents about the wonderful experiences their children were to have in the coming years. The deputy principal muttered something along the lines of "10% of students cause me 90% of my work" indicating that he did not want their children to be in that 10%. The guidance counsellor explained the intricacies of the pastoral care system that had been recently introduced to the school now that caning had been abolished. Then each curriculum department leader went on at length detailing the splendiferous machinations of their subject and how it was going to take their children to the stars and back.

Then it was my turn. What could I say after that line-up. I could see many furtive glances at watches and rolling of eyes. Things had gone way past what any person could reasonably be expected to endure when sitting on a wooden bench made of delaminating plywood that tended to catch any stray part of the body or clothing if you moved slightly in the direction of the door.

So, as I was expected to do, I stood up and greeted the assembled multitude. I said, "Thank goodness you have finally got to hear from me, because I am the most important person in this line-up."

There was a palpable silence.

I then explained that it was the likes of me who would be relating to and interacting with their children on a daily basis. Therefore I, and my fellow teachers were the most important people in their children's schooling lives. I then turned to the line-up of worthies to my left, thanked them for their support and explained to the audience that they had just heard from my "support team". There was a moment of reflection among the group at the front, but I believe that the message got through.

I must admit that I was interested in leaders assisting me to become a better teacher. I was always grateful for the casual conversations I had with my curriculum head that assisted me with developing my skills and knowledge of teaching and learning approaches current at the time. However, most of the support I received in those days about teaching and learning came from conversations with my peer group of young teachers. We spent many hours on this topic, albeit in very informal settings. I was unaware of the potential benefits of these conversations being formalised within team meetings for that purpose. But I knew there had to be a better way of inducting teachers into the profession.

I was actually unaware at the time that I was, in fact, challenging the then current notion of leadership which tended to see leaders as being the ones out front themselves "leading the way" for others to follow. Essentially, the traditional role was administrative. They were "clearing the way" for me to be able to become a teacher. However, what I needed was a different mode of leadership, one that assisted me more specifically to become an effective teacher.

To understand this transformation, the term "rangatira" is helpful, for "ranga" literally meaning "to weave", the "tira", a group of people gathered together for a common purpose. The *Te Aka* dictionary talks about a rangatira being the kairanga, the weaver of people. In the Māori world, rangatira use their leadership skills to ensure their people thrive and benefit. Their role is one of mana and prestige, but, more importantly, is one of responsibility *for the wellbeing of their people*. Indeed, it is by their actions of responding to and supporting their people that a rangatira is measured. In this context, the rangatira is responsive to and supportive of the learning needs of the people in their whānau.

In modern schooling settings, traditionally, principals have been seen as managers, a tendency exacerbated by the move to the self-managing schools' structures associated with the reforms known as Tomorrow's Schools. However, there are now significant moves taking place in this role to more closely approximate that of the rangatira concept of drawing the school's community together as a whānau so as to serve their collective goals. It is not a call for principals to neglect their management functions; rather, it is to shift from management first, to prioritise supporting the learning of all whānau members.

References

Alton-Lee, A. (2015). *Ka Hikitia: A demonstration report: Effectiveness of Te Kotahitanga phase 5, 2010–2012*. Ministry of Education.

Bishop, R., (2017). Relationships are fundamental to learning. *Principal Connections, 20*(3) 2–17.

Bishop, R. (2019). *Teaching to the north-east*. NZCER Press.

Bishop, R., & Berryman, M. (2006). *Culture speaks: Cultural relationships and classroom learning*. Huia Publishers.

Bishop, R., Berryman, M., Wearmouth, J., & Peter, M. (2012). Developing an effective education reform model for indigenous and other minoritized students. *School Effectiveness and School Improvement, 23*(1), 49–70. https://doi.org/10.1080/09243453.2011.647921

Bishop, R., & Glynn, T., (1999). *Culture counts: Changing power relations in education*. Dunmore Press.

Bishop, R., & O'Sullivan, D. (2005). *Effective leadership for educational reform*. Ngā Pae o Te Māramatanga. https://www.maramatanga.ac.nz/project/effective-leadership-educational-reform

Bishop, R., O'Sullivan, D., & Berryman, M. (2010). *Scaling up educational reform: Addressing the politics of disparity*. NZCER Press.

Bolman, L. G., & Deal, T. E. (2006). *The wizard and the warrior: Leading with passion and power*. Jossey-Bass.

Bruner, J. (1996). *The culture of education*. Harvard University Press.

Chapman, J. W., Arrow, A. W., Braid, C., Greaney, K. T., & Tunmer, W. E. (2018). *Early literacy project: Final report*. Massey University. https://www.educationcounts.govt.nz/__data/assets/pdf_file/0006/194532/Early-Literacy-Research-Project.pdf

Education Review Office. (2010). *Sylvia Park School ERO report 2010*. https://ero.govt.nz/institution/1522/sylvia-park-school

Education Review Office. (2014). *Sylvia Park School ERO report 2014*. https://ero.govt.nz/institution/1522/sylvia-park-school

Education Review Office. (2015). *Kerikeri High School ERO report 2015*. https://ero.govt.nz/institution/5/kerikeri-high-school

Education Review Office. (2018). *Building genuine learning partnerships with parents*. https://ero.govt.nz/our-research/building-genuine-learning-partnerships-with-parents

Education Review Office. (2019a). *Te Kura Tuatahi o Papaioea – Central Normal School ERO report 2019.* https://ero.govt.nz/institution/2418/central-normal-school

Education Review Office. (2019b). *Kerikeri High School ERO report 2019.* https://ero.govt.nz/institution/5/kerikeri-high-school

Elmore, R. F. (2004). Hard questions about practice (school organizational and instructional practices). *Educational Leadership, 59*(8), 22–25.

Elmore, R., Peterson, P., & McCarthey, S. (1996). *Restructuring in the classroom: Teaching, learning and school organization.* Jossey-Bass.

Forgie, E. (2021). *Te rerenga kotuku; Sabbatical report.* Kerikeri High School.

Fullan, M. (2001). *Whole school reform: Problems and promises.* Paper commissioned for the Chicago Community Trust, Toronto. Ontario Institute for Studies in Education.

Gay, G. (1999). *Culturally responsive teaching: Theory, research and practice.* Teachers College Press.

Gee, J. (2008). *Social linguistics and literacies: Ideology in discourses* (3rd ed.). Routledge, Taylor and Francis Group.

Gillon, G., McNeill, B., Scott, A., Denston, A., Wilson, L., Carson, K., & Macfarlane, A. H. (2019). A better start to literacy learning: Findings from a teacher-implemented intervention in children's first year at school. *Reading and Writing, 32*, 1989–2012. https://doi.org/10.1007/s11145-018-9933-7

Graham. S, Liu, X., Aitken, A., Ng, N, Bartlett, B., Harris, K., & Holzapfel, J. (2017) Effectiveness of literacy programs balancing reading and writing instruction: A meta-analysis. *Reading Research Quarterly*, 53(3). https://doi.org/10.3102/0034654317746927

Hamilton, A., Reeves, D., Clinton, J., & Hattie, J. (2022). *Building to impact: The 5D implementation playbook for education.* Corwin.

Hattie, J. (2009). *Visible learning: A synthesis of over 800 meta-analyses related to achievement.* Routledge.

Hattie, J. (2012). *Visible learning for teachers: Maximizing impact on learning.* Routledge.

Hughson, T. & Hood, N. (2022). *What's happening with literacy in Aotearoa New Zealand.* The Education Hub. https://theeducationhub.org.nz/wp-content/uploads/2022/03/Ed-Hub_Long-literacy-report_v2.pdf

Lifting Literacy Aotearoa. (2021). *Structured literacy case studies series. Central Normal School Te Kura Tuatahi o Papaioea.* https://www.liftingliteracyaotearoa.org.nz/support/case-studies

McNaughton, S. (2020). *The literacy landscape in Aotearoa New Zealand*. Office of the Prime Minister's Chief Science Advisor. https://www.dpmc.govt.nz/sites/default/files/2022-04/PMCSA-20-16_The-Literacy-Landscape-in-Aotearoa-New-Zealand-At-a-glance-final.pdf

Ministry of Education. (2013). *Ka Hikitia accelerating success 2013–2017*. https://www.education.govt.nz/assets/Documents/Ministry/Strategies-and-policies/Ka-Hikitia/KaHikitiaAcceleratingSuccessEnglish.pdf

Rātima, M., Smith, J., Macfarlane, A., & Macfarlane, S. (2020). *The Hikairo Schema for Primary: Culturally responsive teaching and learning*. NZCER Press.

Robinson, V. (2011). *Student-centred leadership*. Jossey-Bass.

Robinson, V., Hohepa, M., & Lloyd, D. (2009). *School leadership and student outcomes: Best evidence synthesis*. Ministry of Education.

Teaching Council of Aotearoa New Zealand. (2019). *Tātaiako—Cultural competencies for teachers of Māori learners*. https://teachingcouncil.nz/resource-centre/tataiako-cultural-competencies-for-teachers-of-maori-learners/

Timperley, H., Wilson, A., Barrar, H., & Fung, I. (2007). *Teacher professional learning and development: Best evidence synthesis iteration (BES)*. Ministry of Education. https://www.educationcounts.govt.nz/publications/series/2515/15341

Index

21st century thinking skills 206, 234

accountability 69, 168, 204, 214, 217
achievement
    see also Māori students' achievement
    and ethnicity xviii, xxii, 16, 25, 26,
    29, 45, 69, 71, 72, 86, 133, 156, 180,
    199, 227, 228
    marginalised students 57, 90
    patterns of achievement and
    progress 36
    teaching and curriculum
    expectations 24, 28, 31, 62, 91, 99,
    103, 176, 185, 195, 200, 202, 208,
    211, 233
AERA measures (attendance,
    engagement, retention, and
    achievement) 62, 64, 71, 101
agentic positioning
    leaders 85–86
    teachers 86
ako 208
akoako 91
Ala'alatoa, Barbara 26, 152–53, 156,
    160, 161–62, 166–67, 168, 169–70
assessment for learning approach 38,
    120, 184, 187, 189, 192
Atatu—the Prime Minister's Award
    for Excellence in Teaching and
    Learning 223

"balanced" approach to literacy
    learning 1, 2, 27–28, 34, 42, 43, 88,
    153, 178
    variability of teaching practices 5–6,
    21–22, 47
behaviour modification 10–11, 24–25,
    35, 62, 97, 139, 207

Better Start Literacy Approach
    (BSLA) 32–34, 44, 72
    funding 39, 40–42
Blackmore, Lesley 184
Brown, Marianne 184–85
Bruner, Jerome 24

Canterbury University 32, 39, 41
CHOICE programme 212
co-construction of learning 7, 31, 35,
    38, 83, 95, 96, 100, 104, 120, 122,
    125, 234
    see also North-East meetings
    Kerikeri High School 206, 207, 215,
    220
    Sylvia Park School 169
Code of Practice for the Pastoral Care of
    International Students 203
Cognition Education, Relationships First
    programme 54, 66, 93, 99, 115, 235
collaboration 50, 132, 133, 154
    decision making and problem
    solving 6, 36, 87, 88, 91, 97, 101,
    111, 118, 119, 133, 206, 215
    Kerikeri High School 206, 207, 215,
    222
    monitoring of student outcomes 12,
    36, 96–98
    Sylvia Park School 163–65
    Te Kura Tuatahi o Papaioea 182–83,
    188–89, 190, 193
collective efficacy of school staff, parents
    and community 15, 48, 53–54, 55,
    58, 59, 60, 101, 102, 105, 107–08,
    131, 137–39, 147, 236
    see also spreading the reform
    Kerikeri High School 201, 204,
    217–19
    responsive to expectations and
    aspirations 20, 30, 31, 57, 68–69, 74
    Sylvia Park School 167–72

Te Kura Tuatahi o Papaioea 179, 183, 184, 191–92, 196

teachers 29

colonisation 25, 206

community engagement with schools 53, 55, 57, 58, 59, 60, 79, 105, 107, 128, 131, 133, 137–39, 146, 147, 149, 155, 236

see also iwi

expectations, aspirations, and concerns 20, 30, 31, 68–69, 74

Kerikeri High School 201, 204, 213, 214, 217–19, 221, 222–23

as Leaders of Learning 141

part of support system xxi, 15, 45, 68, 69, 109, 148

Sylvia Park School 160, 166, 167, 168, 172

Te Kura Tuatahi o Papaioea 183, 191–92, 194, 196

co-operative learning 118, 206

COVID-19 216

"Critical Literacy" 37

cultural capital 27–28, 34

cultural competency 90–91, 124, 208, 232

cultural responsiveness 20, 28–29, 30–31, 33, 35, 36, 45, 54, 63, 73, 81, 82, 83, 88, 99, 229, 232

Kerikeri High School 198, 201, 204, 205, 209, 215, 217, 218, 221

Sylvia Park School 26, 167–72

Te Kura Tuatahi o Papaioea (Central Normal School) 181, 185

cultural sustainability 5, 11, 31, 36, 42, 43, 45, 46, 54, 55, 69, 71, 78, 81, 82, 83, 145, 147, 151, 232

Kerikeri High School 208

Sylvia Park School 176

Te Kura Tuatahi o Papaioea (Central Normal School) 179

data management systems 36, 57, 58, 64, 71, 143–44, 164, 173, 192–93

Davis, Kelvin 221

de Silva, Zac 77–78

decile system 197

de-cluttering 78–79

deficit explanations by teachers 3, 5, 20, 29, 36, 43, 44, 49, 71–72, 85–87, 88, 91, 99, 103, 112, 211, 225–26, 228

addressing by using narratives of students' and teachers' experiences 76

inappropriate behaviour 207–08

Māori student performance 7, 11, 22–27, 28, 30, 62, 65, 71, 74, 76, 86, 185, 208, 226

dialogic interactions 34–36, 45, 55, 81, 82–83, 92–96, 97, 99, 105, 124, 129, 143, 235

Kerikeri High School 205, 206, 209–10, 234

Sylvia Park School 169

discovery learning 116

discursive classrooms 205, 206–13, 217, 222, 231, 233–34, 235

Education Hub 121, 142

Education Review Office (ERO) 137, 139, 148, 154, 157–58, 160

Kerikeri High School reports 200, 201, 202–04, 209, 219

Sylvia Park School reports 157–59, 163, 165, 166–67, 172–74

Te Kura Tuatahi o Papaioea (Central Normal School) reports 180, 181–82, 183, 185, 190, 191, 192, 193–94

Elmore, Richard 13–14, 108

ELP (Effective Literacy Practice) 162

equity 36, 42, 43, 45, 46, 50, 55, 73, 145, 147, 151, 159, 200, 201, 209, 229

equity funding system 41

ethnicity, and achievement xviii, xxi, 16, 25, 26, 29, 45, 69, 71, 72, 86, 133, 156, 180, 199, 227, 228

evidence 101, 105, 108, 142–43, 236
  evidence-based decision-making and problem solving 15, 45, 55, 56, 87, 101, 109, 143, 146, 148, 196
  Kerikeri High School 219–20
  of school ownership of transformation 146–49
  student performance in targeted skills and knowledge 11–12
  student performance on task assessments 11, 12
  Sylvia Park School 172–75
  Te Kura Tuatahi o Papaioea 192–93, 196

expert assistance with school transformation 84, 87, 89, 125, 128–33, 134, 149, 150, 155
  Kerikeri High School 216
  Sylvia Park School 165
  Te Kura Tuatahi o Papaioea 183, 188, 195

families (whānau) 15, 25, 30, 31, 48, 54, 58, 59, 60, 68–69, 86, 97, 105, 131, 137–39, 147, 149, 155, 236
  see also parents; whānau relationships in schools
  engagement with Better Start Literacy Approach 33
  ERO study of school–family relationships 137–38, 139–41
  Kerikeri High School 208, 213–14, 217–19
  migrant families 90
  Sylvia Park School 69–72, 161–62
  Te Kura Tuatahi o Papaioea 191–92, 194, 196

feedback 12, 14, 31, 35, 37–38, 93–94, 96, 98, 100, 104, 113, 117, 120, 122, 127, 187, 206, 207

process feedback 94, 97
for self-regulation 94
task feedback 94, 97

feed-forward 38, 94–95, 96, 98, 100, 104, 122, 127, 187, 206

Forgie, Elizabeth xx, 15–16, 78, 152–53, 197, 236

formative approaches 12, 14, 15, 26, 37, 38, 45, 53, 55, 60, 80, 82, 96, 137, 139, 142, 190, 236

formative assessment 7, 14, 31, 35–36, 37, 83, 93–95, 100, 104, 105, 116, 126, 130–31, 142, 186
  Kerikeri High School 216
  Sylvia Park School 165, 173
  Te Kura Tuatahi o Papaioea 184

Fullan, Michael 227

Funds of Knowledge programme 168

Gillon, Gail 32, 40, 41

goals and goal setting 42, 84, 86, 101, 104, 145, 146, 153, 154, 155, 236
  BSLA approach 44
  generating acceptance for new approach 75–77
  GPILSEO model 54, 55–56, 57, 58, 59, 61–81
  identifying current relationships and interactions 63–67
  including Māori parents, families, and communities 15, 68–69, 151
  Kerikeri High School 203–04, 221–22
  main purposes 79–81
  monitoring 131, 143, 147–48, 149
  North-East leaders 15–17, 31, 36, 40, 43, 45–46, 50, 78–79, 80, 98, 144, 150, 229
  realisation of goals 229–35
  SMART analysis of North-East goals 70–74
  strategic planning 77–78, 80, 146

Sylvia Park School 160–61

Te Kura Tuatahi o Papaioea 182–83, 193, 195

teachers 12, 29, 45, 49, 67–68, 98, 127, 131, 143

GPILSEO model 50, 51, 54–57, 72, 101, 104–05, 120, 122, 126–27, 128, 144, 148, 149–51

see also evidence; goals; infrastructure; North-East leaders; ownership of school transformation; pedagogy; relationship-based learning; spreading the reform

in the case study schools 153–55 (*see also under* Kerikeri High School; Sylvia Park School; Te Kura Tuatahi o Papaioea)

sequence of the implementation of the dimensions 57–58

using for quality assurance purposes 58–60

graphemes 2

Halliday, Maria 211–12

Hamilton, Arran 78

Hattie, John 2, 6, 12, 53, 60, 78, 85, 93, 102–05, 112, 114, 115–16, 133, 207

Hattie/Marzano Teaching Practices model 116–21, 154, 186, 187, 210

use for inducting team leaders and principals 120–22

Hikairo Schema Primary (Rātima et al, 2020) 33

Hood, Nina 22, 35, 142, 211

Hughson, Taylor 22

hui xix, 21, 76, 150

induction hui 213–14, 217, 219, 221

Matariki hui 214

illiteracy impacts 18–19

implementation fidelity 42–46, 47, 79

see also GPILSEO model; North-East leaders; pedagogy; school transformation into North-East learning institutions; support systems; variability of teaching practices

fundamental to North-East leadership xix, 36, 40

impact of lack of fidelity 5–6, 19–22, 34, 41–42, 47

meaning xix–xx, 21

Te Kotahitanga project 4, 5, 39

Indigenous students 85, 224, 225, 230, 235

infrastructure 54, 55, 56, 57, 107, 108, 109, 111–15, 133, 142–43, 148, 155, 236

Kerikeri High School 213–16

structural reform 13–14, 49, 56, 73, 89, 108, 114–15, 154–55, 213

Sylvia Park School 163–65

Te Kura Tuatahi o Papaioea 187–90

Initial Teacher Education (ITE) institutions 42, 168

institutions, *North-East Leaders of Learning Profile* 101, 104

interactions

see also dialogic interactions; learning partnerships; relationship-based learning

different means of establishing 84

meaning 7

measures 63–67

teachers' skills 7–9, 11, 12, 13, 34–35, 36, 83, 99, 101, 104, 110

international students 203

"intra-actions" 12

iwi and hapū connections 48, 183, 191, 192, 201, 204, 217–18, 221, 222–23, 237

Ka Hikitia policy 231–32

Kāhui Ako model xxi, 124, 134

kapa haka 138, 214, 224, 234

KERI Reading programme 212

Kerikeri High School 79, 152, 153, 197, 223, 233–35

  achievement patterns 198–203

  Atatu—the Prime Minister's Award for Excellence in Teaching and Learning 223

  GPILSEO dimensions 203–23

  hui 213–14, 216, 217, 219, 221

  kuia 217

  re-purposing of buildings to achieve goals 222

Killian, Shaun 115–16

koha 150

kōtahitanga 158

language 99

  Māori students 90, 139, 183, 201

  migrant students 90

  and power 37

Leaders of Learning xxi, 26, 55, 57, 62, 80, 83, 105, 110, 116, 117, 127, 132, 137

  see also learning partnerships; North-East leaders; *North-East Leaders of Learning Profile;* teachers; team leaders

  Hattie/Marzano model for inducting team leaders and principals 120–22

  Kerikeri High School 204

  monitoring for sustainability 96–98, 101

  parents, families and community leaders 141

  profile of an effective leader 13

  Sylvia Park School 166

  Te Kura Tuatahi o Papaioea 185, 190–91

leadership *see* North-East leaders; *North-East Leaders of Learning Profile;*

principals; team leaders

Leading to the North-East model xx–xxi, 11–12

learning conversations 12, 30, 35, 93, 128, 169–70, 206, 207, 210–11, 229, 232, 233, 234

learning partnerships 54, 58, 102, 107, 112, 137–41, 147, 237

  Kerikeri High School 201, 208, 217–19

  Sylvia Park School 170–72

  Te Kura Tuatahi o Papaioea (Central Normal School) 181, 191–92

Lifting Literacy Aotearoa 179

literacy across the curriculum 209–11

literacy learning

  see also "balanced" approach to literacy learning; "structured" approaches to literacy learning

  beyond early years 211–12

  foundational literacy skill learning 32–34

  fundamental to subject learning 138

  Kerikeri High School 199, 200, 204–05, 209–12

  school success in solving the crisis 227

  students arriving in Year 7 with literacy learning issues 211–12

  Sylvia Park School 164

  Te Kura Tuatahi o Papaioea 183–85, 186, 189

lottery effect 41, 42–46

Macfarlane, Angus 32

"magpie effect" 89

mana motuhake 31

manaakitanga 30, 75, 90, 91, 124, 158, 208, 219

Māori students

  see also deficit explanations by teachers

  bilingual education 158, 159

effective teachers 8–9, 14, 34–35, 102–05, 176, 214–15

effectiveness of school systems and pedagogy 16, 21, 22, 26, 102–05, 109, 110, 124–25, 150, 151, 154, 163, 232

goals for Māori students 15 , 64, 66–67, 68–69, 151, 229–35

identity 11, 19, 30, 31, 63, 71, 90, 91, 138, 139, 158, 159, 181, 200, 208–09, 217, 223, 232, 233, 234–35

literacy learning xvii, 2–3, 7, 18–19, 20, 22, 25, 30, 32–34, 41, 42, 66–67, 179, 182, 199, 209

mobility 200, 226

negative schooling experiences 14, 27, 62, 66, 76, 123, 124–25, 213–14

relationships and interactions 23, 24–25, 64–67, 83, 149

self-regulating and self-determining learners 31, 35, 176

self-worth 11

"smoking" story 66

Māori students' achievement 2–3, 4, 16, 29, 31, 33, 39, 51, 52, 54, 55–56, 57, 63, 70–71, 220–21

deficit explanations by teachers 7, 11, 22–27, 28, 30, 62, 65, 71, 74, 76, 86, 185, 208, 226

graduates from English-medium schooling 230

Ngā Taiatea Māori-medium wharekura 75–76

parity with non-Māori students xxi, 77, 78–79, 90, 153, 156, 158–59, 179, 180–81, 198, 199, 224–25, 226–27, 229–31, 236

and self-respect 139

Māori students' success "as Māori" xxi, 30, 31, 43, 52, 57, 59, 66, 70, 73, 89–90, 109, 145, 153, 154, 156, 200, 227–28, 231–35, 236, 237

Kerikeri High School 201, 208, 209

Sylvia Park School 158–59

Te Kura Tuatahi o Papaioea (Central Normal School) 181, 185, 192, 195

Māori-medium wharekura 75, 86, 90

marginalised students

see also Indigenous students; Pacific students

achievement 57, 90, 180

benefits of school transformation xviii, xx, xxi, 27, 55, 57, 70, 71, 74, 145, 153, 154, 156, 159, 181–82, 201–03, 235, 236

deficit explanations by teachers 25, 64

effectiveness of school systems and pedagogy xix, 16, 22, 109, 110, 150, 151, 154

goals for marginalised students 46, 64

harmful teaching practices 4, 14

literacy learning 41, 42, 179

Marzano, Robert 115–16

Hattie/Marzano Teaching Practices model 116–21, 154, 186, 187, 210

McNaughton, Stuart 20, 22, 27–28, 29, 35

meetings *see* North-East meetings

meta-cognitive learning 212

Ministry of Education xxi, 4, 32, 38, 39, 40, 41, 52, 73, 78, 89, 216

Best Evidence Syntheses 162

Ka Hikitia policy 231–32

Strategy for Literacy and Mathematics & Statistics, and for Te Reo Matatini and Pāngarau (2022) 48–49

monitoring of learners' progress 11, 12, 13, 35, 83, 96–98, 101, 104–05, 231

see also formative assessment; North-East meetings; teachers' practice in relation to students' progress

Sylvia Park School 163, 172–75

Te Kura Tuatahi o Papaioea 184

monocultural focus 4, 5, 22, 25, 27–31, 35, 43, 45, 49, 90, 205–06 and "structured" literacy approaches 32–34, 37

Mutukaroa programme 170–72

NCEA 52, 75, 209
level 2 19, 78–79, 199, 200, 202
levels 1 and 3 52, 200

new entrants *see* school entry

Ngā Taiatea Māori-medium wharekura 75, 86

Ngāti Rēhia 204, 217–18, 222–23

North-East leaders 11–12, 36, 51, 52, 55, 56, 97, 98, 101, 104, 148, 238–40
see also Leaders of Learning; ownership of school transformation; school transformation into North-East learning institutions
building skills and knowledge 131–33
delegation of administrative responsibilities 59, 131, 147, 166
engagement with teachers 83, 86–87, 108–10, 120–21
expectations for teachers' learning and development 87–88, 92, 96, 104, 108–09
Kerikeri High School 204–05, 213, 216–17, 220–23
key role in implementation fidelity 108, 109–10, 113, 228–29, 237
knowledge of learners' needs and learning approaches 88–89, 91, 99, 103
senior and middle-level leaders xxi, 50, 53, 57, 60, 83–84, 105, 146, 149, 204 (*see also* team leaders)
Sylvia Park School 165–66
Te Kura Tuatahi o Papaioea 190–91, 194–95

North-East Leaders of Learning Profile 31, 57, 59, 82–84, 105–06, 112, 114, 115, 116, 123–24, 126, 127, 128
implementation using the Hattie/Marzano Teaching practices model 120
implementing the profile 84–98, 109, 110, 120–21, 130, 133–34, 136
verification of dimensions 102–05
the whole profile 98–101

North-East meetings 14, 95–96, 97, 111–14, 115, 122, 125–26, 128, 129, 130–31, 146, 148
Kerikeri High School 215, 216–17, 220
Sylvia Park School 165, 173
Te Kura Tuatahi o Papaioea 189

North-East teachers xvii–xx, xxi, 6–7, 8, 9, 10, 14–15, 29, 31, 34, 35, 36, 67–68, 83, 87, 120–21, 206, 228, 236
see also Teaching to the North-East model

North-West teachers 7, 8, 9, 10, 87

Okaihau College 139, 234

Orr, Regan 38, 152, 153, 179, 180

ownership of learning 97, 101, 105, 121, 127

ownership of school transformation 6, 15–16, 40, 42, 46, 52–53, 55, 56–57, 58, 59, 60, 78, 93, 144, 145–46, 148, 149–51, 155, 229, 237
see also North-East leaders
evidence of school ownership 74, 146–49
Kerikeri High School 220–23
resourcing 39–40, 41, 44, 52
role of community leaders 15
Sylvia Park School 175–77
Te Kotahitanga project 5
Te Kura Tuatahi o Papaioea 189, 193–94

Pacific students 157, 159, 163, 170, 176, 195

parents 15, 20, 53, 54, 57, 58, 59, 60, 97, 105, 107, 131, 137–39, 147, 149, 155, 236

   aspirations 27, 31, 59, 68–69, 74, 80, 200, 227–28

   engagement with Better Start Literacy Approach 33

   ERO study of school–family relationships 137–38, 139–41

   Kerikeri High School 213, 217–19

   of Māori students 23, 25, 30, 57, 59, 68–69, 80, 200, 227–28

   Sylvia Park School 167–72, 176

   Te Kura Tuatahi o Papaioea (Central Normal School) 179, 184, 191–92, 196

Pause, Prompt, Praise method of reading 212

pedagogy 15–17, 30, 43, 45, 56, 58, 73, 101, 104, 138, 145, 146, 153, 236

   common code throughout school 84, 87, 105, 106, 135–37, 143, 148, 162–63, 186, 214, 215, 222

   definition 82

   Kerikeri High School 204–12

   Sylvia Park School 26, 161–63, 165–66

   Te Kura Tuatahi o Papaioea 183–87, 191, 196

pedagogy of relations *see* relationship-based learning

phonemes 2

Poutama Pounamu programme 219

power relationships 64, 67

power-sharing strategies 7, 31, 35, 83, 95, 96, 100, 104, 206, 234

Prime Minister's Award for Excellence in Teaching and Learning 54

principals

   see also Leaders of Learning; North-East leaders; ownership of school transformation; school transformation into North-East

learning institutions

   assistance from outside experts 129–31

   attributes 16

   awareness of happenings in team meetings 36

   de-cluttering of school 78–79

   delegation of administrative responsibilities 59, 131, 239–40

   goal setting and strategic planning 55–56, 57, 58, 77–78, 80, 146

   Hattie/Marzano model for inducting as Leaders of Learning 120–22

   interventions 45–46

   interviews about Māori students' learning 22, 23, 25–26, 225

   Kerikeri High School 198, 204, 214, 217, 220–13, 226

   monitoring of team leaders 94, 95–96, 98

   parental and community relationships 68–69, 97

   role xx–xxii, 228, 229, 236, 237

   Sylvia Park School 165–67, 226

   Te Kura Tuatahi o Papaioea 179, 180, 182, 183, 186, 188, 189, 190–91, 192, 193–94, 195, 226

prior knowledge and learning 4, 27, 28, 29, 31, 35, 83, 96, 99, 100, 104, 116, 169, 206

   see also school entry

   Hattie/Marzano Teaching Practices model 117, 118, 120

   teachers, team leaders and principals 92–93, 95, 124

professional learning and development (PLD) 56, 87–88, 92, 104, 108–10, 123–27, 132, 148, 155, 194

   funding 40

   Kerikeri High School 216, 218, 219

   Sylvia Park School 167

   Te Kura Tuatahi o Papaioea 183–84, 188–89, 190

qualifications, importance of literacy 19, 199

racism 25, 123

rangatira 239, 240

Rangitāne o Manawatū 192

reading xvii, 27, 28, 32, 161, 162, 164, 178, 182, 183, 184, 211, 212

guided 1

independent 1

for pleasure 5

shared 1

relationship-based learning 6–11, 7, 12, 31, 45, 46, 54, 55, 56, 81, 83, 85, 104, 105, 139, 233, 236

see also interactions; learning partnerships; whānau relationships in schools

caring and learning relationships 7, 8, 12, 24, 25, 30, 35, 63, 67–68, 83, 91, 92, 103, 126–27, 129, 136, 185, 205, 208

Kerikeri High School 205, 206, 208, 220, 233–34

measures 63–67

teachers' skills 5, 8, 10, 13, 34, 35, 37, 126–27 (*see also* North-East teachers)

Relationships First programme (Cognition Education) 54, 66, 93, 99, 115, 235

research-based approaches 15

Resource Teachers: Learning and Behaviour (RTLBs) 132

Robinson, Viviane 106, 108, 110

School Advisory Services 132

school entry 28, 31, 32–34, 35, 72, 211

see also prior knowledge and learning

Mutukaroa programme 170–72

school transformation into North-East learning institutions 50–57, 152–53

see also expert assistance with school transformation; GPILSEO model; Kerikeri High School; *North-East Leaders of Learning Profile;* Sylvia Park School; Te Kura Tuatahi o Papaioea

acceptance of need for a new approach 75–77

benefits 226–29, 236–37

building North-East skills and knowledge 131–33

de-cluttering of schools 78–79

funding and staffing 5, 38–42, 44, 46, 50, 51, 52, 54, 58, 80, 146–47, 193–94, 195, 216, 221

involvement of all staff 111, 135–36, 167

objectives and strategic plan 77–78, 80, 146, 161, 183, 193, 195

problems to be addressed by North-East schools 44–46

structural reform 13–14, 49, 56, 73, 89, 108, 114–15, 154–55, 213

sustainability 96–98, 114, 133, 155, 220

teaching process 115–22

screen use 5

self-efficacy 118, 119, 120, 122, 126, 142, 187

self-esteem and wellbeing 137–39

self-managing and self-determining learners 11, 12, 31, 35, 55, 60, 105, 118, 120, 122, 127, 128, 163, 174, 176, 193, 230

self-review 46, 58, 146, 147–49, 154, 155, 175, 194, 195, 203, 220, 237

Senior Leadership Team (SLT) 130

SMART goals 55, 57, 70, 80, 146

social media 5

social promotion policy 34

socio-economic status (SES) 4, 22, 27, 29, 32

and "structured" literacy approaches 32–34

soft skills 230–31

South-East teachers 7, 8, 9, 10, 14, 34–35, 110, 139

South-West teachers 7, 8, 9, 10, 35, 110, 139, 206

spreading the reform 55, 58, 101, 105, 135–41, 147, 148, 155

   see also collective efficacy of school staff, parents and community; learning partnerships

   Kerikeri High School 201, 204, 217–19

   Sylvia Park School 167–72

   Te Kura Tuatahi o Papaioea 179, 183, 184, 191–92, 196

stereotyping 62, 63, 64, 85, 86, 102, 123, 176, 195

streaming 114

"structured" approaches to literacy learning 1, 2, 21, 32–34, 43, 88, 153

   becoming an end in themselves 37–38, 186–87

   Te Kura Tuatahi o Papaioea (Central Normal School) 178–79, 180, 183–85, 186–87, 188, 191

student outcomes 12

   see also achievement

   differences based on ethnicity, group membership or beliefs xvii, xxi, 16, 25, 26, 29, 45, 69, 71, 72, 86, 133, 156, 180, 199, 227, 228

   effectiveness of school systems and pedagogy 16, 21, 26

   impact of student mobility 200

   and implementation fidelity 21, 22

   teaching and curriculum expectations 24, 28, 31, 62, 91, 99, 103, 176, 185, 195, 200, 202, 208, 211, 233

"student voice" conversations 64, 66, 93, 123, 194, 213–14

summative approaches and

assessment 101, 116, 130, 142, 160, 172, 207

support systems xvii, xix, xx, 13–17, 26–27, 30, 45, 47, 48, 49–50, 56, 59, 73, 89, 107, 146, 147, 148, 153, 154–55, 236

   see also infrastructure

   community roles xxi, 15, 45, 68, 69, 109, 148

   dimensions 107–08, 154

   Hattie/Marzano Teaching Practices model 120–27

   Kerikeri High School 205, 214–15, 222

   limited nature or lack of support to teachers 29, 43, 44

   resourcing problems 38–40, 41, 42

   Sylvia Park School 164–66, 173

   Te Kotahitanga project 4–5, 6, 14, 22, 38, 51

   Te Kura Tuatahi o Papaioea 188–90, 194

Sylvia Park School 21, 26, 152, 153, 156

   achievement patterns 157–59

   GPILSEO dimensions 160–77

Tafa, Laurayne 156

tangata whenuatanga 208

targeted skills and knowledge 12

task assessments, student performance 11, 12

tautoko ki ngā tamariki 30, 91

te ao Māori xvii, 63, 76, 80, 181, 185, 221, 237

Te Kotahitanga project 2–4, 9, 11, 14, 15, 22, 27, 28, 29, 35, 43, 50–51, 52, 64–65, 71, 79, 113, 124, 132, 139, 235

   funding 4–5, 14, 22, 38–39, 51, 52, 53–54, 232

   Kerikeri High School 198–99, 202, 205, 216, 219, 220, 221

support systems 4–5, 6, 14, 22, 38, 51

Te Kura Tuatahi o Papaioea (Central Normal School) 38, 143, 152, 153, 178–79, 195–96

achievement patterns 179–82

GPILSEO dimensions 182–94

Te Arawaru immersion and bilingual hub 179, 183

Te Marautanga o Aotearoa 179

Te Puna Waiora 159

te reo Māori 90, 139, 179, 183, 201, 218, 219, 221, 227, 232, 233, 234, 235

teachers

see also deficit explanations by teachers; dialogic interactions; learning partnerships; professional learning and development (PLD); *Teaching to the North-East* model; variability of teaching practices

agency 86, 152, 185

beliefs and assumptions about learners 24

coaching and observation 39, 53, 122, 125, 127–28, 130–31, 132, 149, 164, 183, 188, 190, 198, 214–15, 216, 217, 221

differences from students' families and homes 27, 28–29

effective teachers of Māori students 8–9, 14, 34–35, 102–05, 176, 214–15

expectations of children entering school 28, 31

expectations of student achievement 24, 28, 31, 62, 91, 99, 103, 176, 185, 195, 200, 202, 208, 211, 233

induction hui 213–14, 217, 219, 221

interviews about Māori students' learning and achievement 22, 23, 24, 67–68

monitoring of performance 57, 96–98, 101, 106, 122, 143

multicultural teaching workforce 27

North-East teachers xvii–xx, xxi, 6–7, 8, 9, 10, 14–15, 29, 31, 34, 35, 36, 67–68, 83, 87, 120–21, 206, 228, 236

North-West teachers 7, 8, 9, 10, 87

responsiveness to student diversity 28–29, 37–38, 50

South-East teachers 7, 8, 9, 10, 14, 34–35, 110, 139

South-West teachers 7, 8, 9, 10, 35, 110, 139, 206

teaching process in North-East schools 115–22

teachers' practice related to student progress 14, 45, 50, 55, 58, 59, 142–43

see also data management systems; North-East meetings

case study schools 155

collaborative assessment 36, 53, 57, 96, 97, 112–13, 125–26, 142–43

feedback 38

Kerikeri High School 216, 219–20

monitoring by team leaders 88–89, 96, 98, 142

self-review 148, 149

student voice 93

Sylvia Park School 164–65, 172–75

Te Kura Tuatahi o Papaioea 192–93

Teaching to the North-East model xvii–xx, 11, 12, 13, 14–15, 31, 66, 84, 105, 125

team leaders xxi, 15, 42

see also North-East meetings

delegation of administrative responsibilities 59, 131, 147, 166

expository and responsive coaching teaching 127–28

goal setting 61

Kerikeri High School 204

Leaders of Learning 83–84, 92, 96,

97, 120–22

learning 87–88, 95–96, 132

monitoring and support of teachers xix, 49, 53, 58, 86, 87, 88–89, 94–95, 96–98, 101, 136, 137, 166

and outside experts 84, 128–29

performance, evidence and feedback 60, 62, 93, 94, 95–96, 98, 143

prior knowledge 92–93

support systems for learning and development 123–27

Sylvia Park School 166

Te Kura Tuatahi o Papaioea 191, 193

tiakitanga 30, 90, 219

tikanga Māori xix–xx, 21, 30, 47, 50, 150, 158, 181, 185, 201, 219, 221

time frames for goals 74

Timperley, Helen 69, 130

tino rangatiratanga 31

transmission mode of teaching 4, 5, 22, 25, 27–31, 34, 35, 43, 45, 90, 205–06, 207, 210, 231, 232

and "structured" literacy approaches 32–34, 37

Treaty of Waitangi 225, 227, 237

trustees 157, 159, 173, 174, 175, 193, 194, 201, 204, 221, 237

tuakana–teina relationship 212

values, Māori 30, 91, 138, 208–09, 219

variability of teaching practices 5–6, 18, 19–22, 36, 41, 49, 51, 73, 84, 88, 89, 147

function of infrastructure 111–14

Kerikeri High School 215

spreading the reform to all concerned 136–37

Sylvia Park School 160

Te Kura Tuatahi o Papaioea 182, 186, 188

wairuatanga 30, 219

wānanga 208

Watts, Jennie 178–79

whakawhanaungatanga 91, 158

whānau *see* families (whānau)

whānau relationships in schools xvii, xix, 7, 9, 30–31, 64, 73, 84, 85–91, 105, 138

BSLA approach 34

characteristics 120

common pedagogic code 55

Hattie/Marzano Teaching Practices model 120, 122, 124

Kerikeri High School 219, 223

parents' views 63

role of North-East leaders 13, 35, 45, 69, 82, 92, 97, 99–100, 103–04, 110, 136, 228

role of outside experts 129

Sylvia Park School 163, 166

Te Kura Tuatahi o Papaioea 185, 195

whanaungatanga 7, 90, 91, 208, 217, 218

Wiliam, Dylan 78

Williams, Ariana 170–71

writing 27, 32

Milton Keynes UK
Ingram Content Group UK Ltd.
UKHW052326230124
436540UK00036B/581